MEN AND CITIZENS IN THE
INTERNATIONAL RELATIO

Men and Citizens in the Theory of International Relations deals with the tension between the obligations of citizenship and the obligations of humanity in modern theories of the state and international relations. It contains an historical overview of the way in which the relationship between citizenship and humanity has been conceived in political theory since the seventeenth century. Drawing upon the German idea of freedom developed in the writings of Kant, Hegel and Marx, *Men and Citizens* argues for the primacy of obligations to the human race.

A postscript to this new edition provides a commentary on the writings of Habermas and Foucault. The line of argument developed in the first edition is reconsidered in the light of the current debate between critical theorists and anti-foundationalists. The case for a critical sociology of moral boundaries in international relations is presented in the final sections of the book.

Reviews of the first edition

'The earlier sections of the book, involving the initial presentation of the problem of international ethical theory and the critical discussion of the form it takes in the natural law tradition from Pufendorf to Kant, go right to the heart of the problem and challenge us to think clearly about the issues ourselves. Linklater's book is to be recommended to all those interested in the subject, not least because it is a serious work in a thinly populated field.' – John Charvet, *Millennium*

'[The book] suggests a whole range of criteria by which action may be judged, and it deserves to read for this reason as well as for the significant contribution it makes to international political theory.' – P. A. Reynolds, *International Affairs*

Andrew Linklater is Senior Lecturer in Politics at Monash University, Australia. He is the author of *Beyond Realism and Marxism: Critical Theory and International Relations* and editor (with G. Goodwin) of *New Dimensions in World Politics*.

Books published by Macmillan in association with the London School of Economics

Michael R. Bonavia
THE NATIONALISATION OF BRITISH TRANSPORT

H. M. Drucker
THE POLITICAL USES OF IDEOLOGY

George Feaver and Frederick Rosen (*editors*)
LIVES, LIBERTIES AND THE PUBLIC GOOD

Graeme J. Gill
PEASANTS AND GOVERNMENT IN THE RUSSIAN REVOLUTION

Tony Hayter
THE ARMY AND THE CROWD IN MID-GEORGIAN ENGLAND

Angus Hawkins
PARLIAMENT, PARTY AND THE ART OF POLITICS IN BRITAIN, 1855–59

Marian Kent
OIL AND EMPIRE: BRITISH POLICY AND MESOPOTAMIAN OIL, 1900–1920

L. H. Leigh (*editor*)
ECONOMIC CRIME IN EUROPE

Andrew Linklater
BEYOND REALISM AND MARXISM
MEN AND CITIZENS IN THE THEORY OF INTERNATIONAL RELATIONS

Michael Malet
NESTOR MAKHNO IN THE RUSSIAN CIVIL WAR

C. A. W. Manning
THE NATURE OF INTERNATIONAL SOCIETY

Terence H. Qualter
GRAHAM WALLAS AND THE GREAT SOCIETY
OPINION CONTROL IN THE DEMOCRACIES

David Seckler
THORSTEIN VEBLEN AND THE INSTITUTIONALISTS

Leonard Schapiro
THE ORIGIN OF THE COMMUNIST AUTOCRACY

Nicholas A. Sims
THE DIPLOMACY OF BIOLOGICAL DISARMAMENT

W. von Leyden
ARISTOTLE ON EQUALITY AND JUSTICE
HOBBES AND LOCKE

Men and Citizens in the Theory of International Relations

Andrew Linklater

Senior Lecturer in Politics,
Monash University, Australia

Second Edition

MACMILLAN

in association with
THE LONDON SCHOOL OF
ECONOMICS AND POLITICAL
SCIENCE

First edition 1982
Second edition 1990

Published by
THE MACMILLAN PRESS LTD
Houndmills, Basingstoke, Hampshire RG21 2XS
and London
Companies and representatives
throughout the world

Printed in Hong Kong

British Library Cataloguing in Publication Data
Linklater, Andrew
Men and citizens in the theory of international relations. — 2nd ed.
1. Foreign relations. Theories
I. Title II. London School of Economics and Political Science
327.1'01

ISBN 0–333–52435–7 (hardcover)
ISBN 0–333–52436–5 (paperback)

Contents

Acknowledgements

This book began as a doctoral thesis submitted to the University of London in 1978. In the course of writing my thesis, and subsequently redrafting it for publication, I have incurred many obligations. Firstly, I would like to record my gratitude to the Trustees of the Noel Buxton Studentship in International Relations at the London School of Economics for provision of financial support between 1974 and 1976. While a student in the Department of International Relations I had the privilege of being supervised by Michael Donelan whose encouragement, advice and example were invaluable. I would also like to thank Paul Taylor and Geoffrey Goodwin, the former for his supervision in the last few months of 1975, the latter for his interest and encouragement throughout.

My thanks are due to the Publications Committee at the London School of Economics, and its secretary, Patrick Davis, for their assistance in publishing this volume. To the University of Tasmania, which allowed me to spend six months in Britain to complete this book, I am most grateful, as I am towards the University of Keele which provided me with an ideal environment in which to write. Christopher Brewin and John Vincent of the Department of International Relations at Keele gave me considerable encouragement and advice, while Hidemi Suganami's exceptional generosity with time and advice was invaluable.

An earlier version of chapter two appeared in the *British Journal of International Studies* (published by the Longmans Group) in April 1981, and a previous draft of chapter four appeared in *Millennium: Journal of International Studies* of the London School of Economics, in Autumn 1981. I would like to thank the editors of these journals for their kindness in granting permission to draw upon this material in the present work.

Finally, throughout the period in which this book was researched and written I have been the recipient of my wife's unselfish support. I dedicate this book to Jane in gratitude.

A. L.

September 1980
Hobart, Tasmania

Preface to the Second Edition

A new postscript to this edition reconsiders the argument of *Men and Citizens* in the light of more recent developments associated with the writings of Habermas and Foucault. An earlier version was delivered at John Vincent's Research Seminar in International Relations at Oxford. I cannot recall taking part in a more rewarding discussion. I am also grateful to members of the study group on 'Modernity and International Relations', which was held at the London School of Economics, and to my colleagues, Michael Janover and Peter Lawler, for their comments on an earlier version of the argument.

The language of men and citizens reflects the terms employed in much of the historical material surveyed in the book. But it has its drawbacks and the postscript no longer uses the terms *man* and *men* when the intention is to refer to the whole human race.

Preface to the First Edition

The claims advanced in the following pages form an effort to overcome the limitations inherent in those traditions of political thought which have concentrated almost exclusively upon providing a philosophical account of the state in abstraction from a speculative theory of the international states-system; they arise also from a discontent, frequently sounded recently, with the serious absence of theoretical explorations of a more classical and synoptic kind within the analysis of international relations. My purpose here is to extend some of the themes which have been discussed in a small but growing body of literature which testifies clearly to the resurgence of international political theory in Britain in recent years;[1] it is, in short, to seek to establish a basic framework upon which to build a general theory of relations between political communities.

Hegel stated that philosophy must confront its own development through a search for the reason immanent within its history.[2] Accordingly, a philosophy of relations between political associations should not be advanced in abstraction from a search for the rationality inherent within the history of that philosophy. It will be argued below, in opposition to one of the prevalent themes in the literature mentioned above, that a very significant part of the history of modern international thought has centred upon what may be termed the problem of the relationship between men and citizens.[3] We may characterise this problem in different ways: as the issue of the proper relationship between the obligations which men may be said to acquire *qua* men and the obligations to which they are subject as citizens of particular associations; or, as the question of reconciling the actual or potential universality of human nature with the diversity and division of political community. The posing and answering of these problems is central to the further development of the theory of international relations; as we shall see later, they also lead to the establishment of important connections between a consolidated political theory of international relations and that remarkable tradition of political thought, beginning essentially with Rousseau, which is concerned with the enhancement of human freedom.

In the opening sections of this argument, I aim to establish some elementary principles of international political theory in connection with the theme that a tension between two concepts of obligation, two modes of moral experience, is firmly embedded within the theory and practice of the modern state. Thereafter, the argument will give an account of the way this tension was inherent within rationalist international thought of the seventeenth and eighteenth centuries. My purpose is to reveal that at least two exponents of rationalist thinking failed to give a satisfactory statement of the relationship between the idea of humanity, with its suggestion of a moral community more inclusive than the independent state, and the individually contracted rights and duties of citzenship. It will be argued that Kant is the sole representative of the rationalist *genre* to approach that coherent vision of world political organisation which had eluded his most immediate and prominent predecessors, Pufendorf and Vattel.

A philosophical and historical inquiry into the problem of men and citizens must confront two crucially important extensions of the romantic rejection of rationalism: historicism and universal, or philosophical, history. The immediate impetus for doing so arises from the observation that the moral foundations of Kant's international theory are especially vulnerable to the historicist critique of rationalism. Indeed the historicist assault upon the notion of an immutable, universal human reason subverted the traditional foundations, both medieval and modern, of international relations thought. Clearly, in the earlier ideas of Meinecke, and in the philosophy of Treitschke, the rejection of rationalism had as its aim the dissolution of that realm of humanity, or human obligation, which seemed to earlier thinkers to compete with the ethical dictates of the sovereign state. If the present work may be said to have any fundamental theoretical purpose, it is to seek a non-rationalist foundation for the traditional belief in obligations to humanity, and for the recovery of the critique of the international states-system. While the present work accepts the substance of the historicist critique of rationalism, it is unsympathetic with the bases of that criticism.

Undoubtedly, the rejection of theoretical persuasions should lead the theorist in a determinate direction; in this case it leads towards an alternative framework with which to defend the internationalist element within rationalist thought. In this work the failures of rationalism and historicism as philosophical doctrines point to the conclusion that the principles of a universal history can recover many important elements of an earlier tradition exemplified in, but not completed by, the Kantian theory of international society. It is within theories which sought to comprehend the nature of man as an historical subject, as a self-developing and self-transforming being realising the conditions of his freedom, that I locate the foundations of a modern theory of international relations. Various themes follow from this perspective. Among them is the argument that the division between citizenship and humanity is integral to the historical movement from attempting to realise autonomy within states to aiming to advance autonomy in relations between them. Further, it will be claimed that the existence of a moral community more inclusive than the sovereign state can be defended only on the basis of man's unique capacity for self-determination.

In the final stages of the argument, I employ one of the most valuable legacies of the philosophy of history: the attempt to mobilise principles of historical periodisation in order to place different social formations upon a scale of ascending types in accordance with the extent to which each approximates the conditions of realised human freedom. Through this development of the resources of philosophical history, the possibility arises of placing a variety of types of international relations upon 'a scale of forms' which expresses each one's distance from, or proximity to, a more adequate realisation and expression of the notion of self-determination.[4] Underlying this application is the urge to establish connections between the historical development of human capacities and the evolution of international life. In particular, the development of the capacity to overcome various forms of intersocietal estrangement, and to exercise control over the totality of social and political relations, will be reflected in the construction of a theory of ascending types. Our scale of intersocietal forms will trace the development of the freedom of human subjects in the area of their international relations. Beginning with their membership of tribal groups, estranged from one another, it proceeds to discuss their incorporation as independent and equal citizens within states; and it will consider the evolution of relations between political communities, including relations which take place within an evolving international states-system, towards the condition in which the species is united to form, in Kantian terms, 'a universal kingdom of ends'.[5] This theory, it will be argued, not only overcomes several deficiencies associated with alternative forms of international political theory; it is to be regarded as a more adequate fulfilment of the aspirations present in all philosophies of politics, especially the search for a rational and intelligible form of life.

Part One

Foundations of International Political Theory

1 The Case for International Political Theory

A theory of the state must be, from one angle, a philosophy of international law. (Laski)

The central purpose of the political theory of international relations is the presentation of a philosophical account of the experience of living in and among a world of separate, sovereign states. This identifying objective parallels the traditional concern of orthodox political theory with the provision of a theoretical representation of the experience of living within the state. Philosophies of politics aim to uncover the meaning and rationality of political existence without perpetuating the commonplace assumptions of everyday life or introducing their own undefended presuppositions. Typically, if it confronts a form of social life whose rationality seems less than fully realised or complete, the theory of politics becomes concerned with articulating the principles of a more perfect political order. The initial case for the political theory of international relations is derived from the need to undertake certain philosophical tasks which are often omitted from the scope of orthodox, more state-centred, social and political theories. No special method distinguishes it from that parallel enterprise which constitutes the history of political thought as it is conventionally understood – only the desire to consider the reasons which may exist for those structures which were not consciously determined for their own sake but shaped in accordance with the conflicts and compromises of earlier times. The international political theorist casts a Cartesian eye over that realm of politics, the international system of states, whose basic necessity or acceptability is too readily pre-judged by our more important traditions of political thought. In particular, two postulates of modern political life fall immediately under its scrutiny: firstly, the near universal belief that a person's most fundamental political obligations are interconnected with the form of social life of which he is part, and which his political structures are obliged to protect; and, secondly, the virtually universal presumption of the acceptability of that order or framework within which all social and political interaction occurs, and upon which the maintenance of all other social orders depends, the international order itself.

To transform our brief claim for the importance of international political theory into a body of concrete theoretical principles, we must first confront certain obstacles allegedly unique to the enterprise. Here we can do no better than refer to Martin Wight's famous argument that international theory as 'a tradition of speculation about the society of states, or the family of nations, or the international community . . . does not, at first sight, exist'.[1] The reason is that 'the belief in the sovereign state as the consummation of political experience and activity which has marked Western political thought since the Renaissance . . . has absorbed almost all the intellectual energy devoted to political study'.[2] The 'intellectual prejudice imposed by the sovereign state' explains the fact that political theorists 'have not been attracted by the possibility of maximising the field of political theory' by reflecting, for example, upon alternative foundations of world political organisation.[3] Furthermore, Wight argues, consideration needs to be given to the insurmountable fact that 'what for political theory is the extreme case [as revolution, or civil war] is for international theory the regular case'.[4] The international states-system is 'the realm of recurrence and repetition; it is the field in which political action is most regularly necessitous' and least 'susceptible of a progressivist interpretation'.[5] The distinctive kind of political conduct associated with the states-system means that international relations cannot be theorised 'in the language of political theory and law', a language 'appropriate to man's control of his social life'. While political theory can be 'the theory of the good life', international theory is limited to 'the theory of survival'.[6] The world of international politics, unlike its domestic counterpart, does not make available a body of ideas or actions from which a theory of classic dimensions may develop and flourish.

To many writing in a more contemporary idiom, Wight's position may be thought to reflect a misleading and indeed outdated appraisal of the dominant forces at work within the modern international system; to others it bears witness to what is permanent in the states-system, to what ultimately must be recorded in our experience of it.[7] Nevertheless, the argument that increased economic and social interdependence, and even integration of formerly discrete parts of the states-system, provides the basis for the development of a political theory of international relations must deserve serious consideration. This line of argument is particularly evident within Mitrany's writings and that tradition of functionalist thought inspired by them. Mitrany makes this important observation:

> If one were to visualise a map of the world showing economic and social activities, it would appear as an intricate web of interests and relations crossing and recrossing political divisions – not a fighting map of states and frontiers, but a map pulsating with the realities of everyday life.[8]

These developments may give added force to the proposition that

> the architectonic role Aristotle attributed to the science of politics might well belong today to international relations, for these have become in the twentieth century the very condition of our daily life. To philosophise about the ideal state in isolation, or to theorise about political systems in the abstract, has become almost meaningless.[9]

Observations about patterns of structural change in the international system lead in several directions: for example, to the notion of 'breaking away from a concept and practice which since the end of the Middle Ages has been inculcated as an ideal, the near worship of the national-territorial state';[10] or to the idea of establishing a multiplicity of 'international regimes' for the management of complex interdependencies.[11] More fundamentally, perhaps the transformation of the international system in the direction of a politics resembling those of domestic systems provides the international theorist with the opportunity for establishing a new focus of study.

It is unsurprising that in the study of international politics as elsewhere periods of flux and upheaval provoke partial or total reconsideration of the categories from which traditional theories are composed. Developments of an economic and technological nature within the contemporary world-system have prompted the observation that men are not only members of insulated sovereign states but much more, namely participants within a web of economic and social practices which spill over and even dissolve the boundaries between states. The citizen's diminished immunity from the power of events which have their origins beyond the national frontier has not only occasioned the development of more intricate systems of explanation and prediction; it has led to a new form of advocacy for a mode of political reasoning able to balance the 'introspective' character of that tradition of thought which enclosed 'the state in the circle of its own ideas',[12] a mode of reasoning whose impetus was formerly derived almost solely and only intermittently from confronting issues of peace and war.

Important though these developments are, considerable problems stand in the way of depicting international political theory as a theory of interdependence. Not only is the universality of interdependence uneven and in some accounts suspect;[13] its status as the most novel and profound change affecting Western industrialised societies, and as a force which can resist the potentially dislocating actions of national governments, is hardly secure. Any international political theory which specifies interdependence as the key to its development generates very substantial limitations; for it would be a regional theory and perhaps even an ephemeral one. This remark is not tantamount to an argument that the problems of an interdependent or world-system lie outside the proper jurisdiction of a political theory of international relations; rather that normative statements about the just or competent management of an interdependent world ought to be located within a framework resting upon somewhat different accounts of our experience of international relations.

Furthermore, it will be argued below, the categories which this theory should adopt ought not to echo those associated with that empirical discourse formed in response to international interdependence or economic and political integration. Too often that body of social–scientific thought concerned with modern developments in world politics positively encourages or uncritically conveys some version of scepticism about ethics hostile to the construction of a theory of international relations along classical lines and proportions; or, theorists have formulated their prescriptions in the absence of any explicit defence of the liberal-utilitarianism which underlies them. That considerable body of literature provoked, for example, by the neo-functionalist objective of proceeding 'beyond the nation-state' is created without the active and conscious involvement of political philosophy. Neo-functionalist thought approaches international cooperation 'without any utopian assumptions' on the grounds that empirical knowledge reveals that 'personal political loyalties are the result of satisfaction with the performance of critical functions by an agency of government'.[14] Assuming but not defending that philosophy of man which stresses the utilitarian composition of his nature and behaviour, and the exclusively instrumental purpose of his social and political institutions, neo-functionalism states that 'cooperation among groups' is unalterably 'the result of convergences of separate perceptions of interest and not a spontaneous surrender to the myth of the common good'.[15] This most radical of challenges to the sovereign state (in the shape of an argument for the severance of territory and authority) is ultimately inadequate. While it observes that the emergence of social and economic interdependence creates conditions which may facilitate the reconstruction of international relations, it fails either to give an acceptable account of social institutions and their history or to construct a system of categories adequate to the task of prescribing for human conduct. For various insurmountable problems accompany any theory reliant upon the concept of human interests. Of these the most important is the impossibility of providing any explanation of human interests in the predominantly individualistic terms in which these are so often cast. It cannot be claimed that interests are inherent in individuals as such.

Since individuation is, as Marx observed, a product of history, individuals are necessarily culturally located, just as their ends and interests are socially constituted.[16] The cultural location and varying content of human interests means that an appeal to interests cannot provide adequate foundations for a theory of international politics. To presume otherwise is to presuppose the validity of the socio-political framework which lends interests their determinacy, a validity which political philosophy must regard as at issue.

On what other basis might we construct a political theory of international relations, one whose categories refrain from narrowly concentrating upon immediate pragmatic concerns associated with interdependence or from claiming suprahistorical validity for culturally limited conceptions of social behaviour and political institutions? An answer to this question cannot be proposed in isolation from the recognition that the theory of international relations has a history; and it cannot be advanced without responding to the fact that this history has consisted to a significant degree of the erosion of the classical foundations of thinking about the structure of international society. This second observation will assume considerable importance at a later stage in the analysis when the argument seeks to develop an adequate system of philosophical categories through a critical investigation of the presuppositions of earlier theories of international relations. But we must begin first of all with the proposition that despite Wight's claims the theory of international relations has deep and familiar historical roots; and we must establish what these imply for the attempt to defend the enterprise of international political theory.

It may be claimed that the issues which comprised medieval or early modern international political theory were the necessary extensions or apposite reformulations of the traditional preoccupations of Western political thought given the acceptance of one or other version of the theory of natural law.[17] Consider, by way of example, the problem of the justification of obligations to the state and the determination of the state's legitimate area of jurisdiction over its citizens: modified to conform with the distinctive structure of the international states-system, these questions were extended in an earlier tradition to consider whether or not there were obligations between the members of different societies, and to consider to what extent, if at all, the government of one state might exercise legitimate power over other communities. The analysis of each of these issues is at the centre of that important history of reflection, upon the morality of force in relations between communities, which issued from the natural law tradition. As exponents of just war doctrines well knew, no adequate theory of the morality of force in international relations could be constructed in the absence of an effort at defending the institution of the separate political association or the decentralised world political environment of which it was part.

Clearly, an implicit conservatism would pervade any theory which considered the morality of warfare in abstraction from the prior questions which must be asked of the separate state and the institution of the states-system itself. We should have to defend the practice of belonging to a separate, sovereign community before engaging that more familiar set of questions concerned with either the principles upon which its internal political relations ought to be conducted or the form which its external relations should take. An adequate account of the problems of power and obligation in a world of states involves attempting to ascertain what it is that each member of mankind might reasonably claim from other men, and how their respective rights and duties are to be expressed in the structure of international society. This kind of discussion would absorb into the body of political theory the central issue of the acceptability or unacceptability of a world divided into separate and, in the main, self-regarding states.

A concern with the rationality of the practices of international society is evident within writings of the seventeenth and eighteenth centuries, and it is not entirely absent from later developments of those traditions. But it remains the case that most modern political philosophers have not embarked upon the quest for a philosophical interpretation of man's division between separate, sovereign states. One can argue, as Wight suggests, that these political philosophers have echoed those commonly accepted cultural assumptions which endow the state with an almost unqualified level of legitimacy. If this is so, the conclusion to draw is that political theory need only be relieved of its modern cultural limitations in order to begin addressing the broader dimensions of moral and political experience, those which accompany man's division into different sovereign states.

We noted earlier that Wight imputed responsibility for the non-existence of international theory to certain peculiarly Western cultural presumptions or prejudices – the belief that the sovereign state was the adequate forum in which to satisfy essential human needs, and the understanding that progress was confined to the internal structure of political associations where men had the capacity to exercise a greater degree of control over the conditions of their existence.[18] But the international political theorist must do more than simply protest against the cultural inhibitions which stand in the way of a more self-conscious form of reasoning than one whose supposedly illicit and undefended parameters have limited theory to a narrow preoccupation with the internal problems of the modern state. For the system of categories which made international political theory both necessary and possible (categories which were determined within the theory of natural law) became problematical in theories of the nineteenth and twentieth centuries. Indeed, as we shall argue later, the erosion of universalistic ethical reasoning has its origins within the rationalist theories of natural law of the seventeenth and eighteenth centuries. The international political theorist cannot rest his case with the sanguine observation that he brings a higher level of awareness to matters of political life than theorists elsewhere. He must be able to support the claim that there is a categorical framework which can support a philosophical theory of international relations, because it is the uncertainties attached to the earlier foundations of international theory, rather than any cultural limitations peculiar to modern political philosophy, which obstruct its development.

The case for international political theory rests not upon questioning the cultural inhibitions of mainstream political thought but upon defending or reconstructing the assumptions associated with much international theory in the past. We may explore this theme further through posing the Kantian question 'what makes international political theory possible?'. It may be said of any social and political theory that one of the conditions of its existence is man's consciousness of his capacity to understand and modify the social environment in which he lives. Social theory generally is the product of an easily overlooked but crucial development of human powers. For Hegel, who explored this theme with greater insight than any of his predecessors, the development of social and political thought in Greece reflected the evolution of the human spirit beyond that unreflective form of consciousness, principally Oriental, which assumed that the social world was fixed and unalterable.[19] Social and political thought was an important expression of the growth of man's self-knowledge, of his capacity to intervene in the social world to realise consciously constructed human projects. Theoretical activity was to be understood in the context of the evolution of human freedom towards a condition in which men attained rational and conscious control of their social relations.

An initial response to our Kantian question is that both domestic and international political theory must possess at least one postulate in common. If it is to resemble other types of social theory, international political theory must contain some awareness of the possibility of human intervention in the social world in order to modify its nature. We shall not confront here the argument, present in the writings of Wight, that relations between states are incapable of being fundamentally modified or reconstructed. That argument will be challenged in the next chapter. At this stage, it is important to note that the distinct theoretical concerns and the separate historical evolution of international political theory suggest that it is a form of theoretical activity which depends upon distinct postulates. Historical evidence reveals that domestic political thought emerged before its international counterpart. While the former's history is more or less continuous over a long period of time, the latter's evolution is short, sporadic and fragmented. Not surprisingly, early political theories were directed at the nature of immediate political experience, the *polis* for instance, and they sought to comprehend what may be termed relations of familiarity – relations which comprised a relatively cohesive form of political organisation which citizens uncritically accepted. The international political theorist, on the other hand, as the theory of the morality of warfare reveals, confronted not harmonious social relations but modes of international conflict or relations of intersocietal estrangement. What is important is not the fact that the theorist contended that these relations could be modified, but the foundations from which this orientation was derived. Where a theory urges the modification of the international system, a modification which should be collectively determined through reasoned consensus rather than unilaterally induced by one of the system's more powerful members, there is a clear expression of a postulate which need not accompany the political theory of relations of familiarity. To defend the belief in the possibility of overcoming relations of intersocietal estrangement, the international political theorist must justify the use of categories which depict what it is that unifies, whether actually or potentially, insiders and outsiders. The very possibility of his enterprise depends upon his ability to give an account of the existence of shared moral capacities or of the nature of a universal natural law, or some substitute phenomenon, to which all individuals are subject irrespective of their particular membership of distinct social systems.

It is impossible then for a society to generate an international political theory, a general theory of relations between societies which does not simply reflect its own perspective or interests, in the absence of a justified discourse which connotes the existence of characteristics or capacities shared by insiders and outsiders alike.[20] The distinctive nature of international theory is expressed when either one of two conditions is satisfied: when the theorist seeks to establish whether or not relations of familiarity might exist between insiders and outsiders, or when he aims to construct systematically a theory of what these shared characteristics imply for the structure of political life. The availability of such a language is by no means a universal and unsurprising aspect of social experience; it is the outcome of a complex process of social development whose origins and subsequent history deserve a prominent place in the sociology of intersocietal life. Moreover, a society which produces ideas of community or affinity with outsiders can no longer give a coherent account of its moral and political experience through conceptual frameworks which reflect simply the importance of citizenship or membership. To give that coherent and exhaustive statement, it must incorporate within its theory those categories which represent what unifies insiders and outsiders. It must provide that more expansive account of moral and political experience which the existence of universalist categories requires.

One of the most substantial traditions of international thought contends that both domestic and international politics might be regulated in accordance with the dictates of universal and immutable principles of natural law. Indeed, both the theory and practice of the modern state bear the imprint of that complex form of moral experience which incorporates universalistic ethical categories and dispositions. As human beings, it is argued within a famous Western tradition, men owe horizontal moral obligations to one another, obligations which survive and are as profound as their separation into sovereign states. As citizens, however, they acquire more specific obligations which they share with fellow-members of their political association alone. Indeed, insofar as there has been an impetus for the development of international political theory in the West, it has stemmed from the existence of this dichotomy. Theorists have confronted not a world whose 'recurrence and repetition' is alien to a discourse concerned with order and, more importantly, progress, but a world of moral tensions, and their first preoccupation has been to discover a means of understanding and resolving them.

Not all political theorists or theories have responded adequately to their sense of a distinction between obligations to the state and a belief in obligations and responsibilities to the remainder of humanity. They did not realise that a conflict between a person's status as a man and as a citizen complicated their attempt to give an account of political experience. An astute and decisive criticism of social contract theory reveals the depth of the problem. Without pre-empting the conclusions of a later discussion of certain representatives of that tradition, it is useful here to consider Filmer's identification of an inconsistency within contract thought. Central to that genre, of course, is the fiction of a state of nature composed of individuals free from a system of political rights and obligations. Because of their natural freedom, legitimate political power could not be exercised in the absence of explicit individual consent to submit to political authority. In the case of Locke (the position is more complicated in the theories of Pufendorf and Vattel, as we shall see later) an account of the formation and perpetuation of legitimate political authority is submitted without an analysis of the processes whereby men might arrange themselves into separate, sovereign communities.[21] It is against this shortcoming that Filmer's critique is directed. For, according to Filmer, the division of men into separate states would itself appear to require the consent of the whole of mankind. Of the contract theorists, he writes:

> If they understand that the entire multitude or whole people have originally by nature power to choose a King, they must remember that by their own principles and rules, by nature all mankind in the world makes but one people, who they suppose to be born alike to an equal freedom from subjection; and where such freedom is, there all things must of necessity be common: and therefore without a joint consent of the whole people of the world, no one thing can be made proper to any one man, but it will be an injury, and a usurpation upon the common right of others. From whence it follows that natural freedom being once granted, there cannot be any one man chosen a King without the universal consent of all the people of the world at one instant, nemine contradicente.[22]

This argument's implication that the whole of mankind would have to consent to the movement from the natural condition of undivided humanity to the formation of separate, sovereign states (prior to any individual act of consent to submit to a particular government) points to a devastating critique of contractarianism. If human relations can be conducted fairly only when they conform with the mutual consent of actors, then the rationality of all political relations, whether domestic or international, must be determined by a unified set of criteria. Regarded against the background of a system of universalist ethical categories, based for example upon the necessity of establishing consensual social relations, the international states-system and many of its dominant practices are immediately problematical.

Filmer's criticism is decisive against any universalist doctrine which fails to incorporate an analysis of the normatively preferred structure of international society within its comprehension of political experience. Under such circumstances, the very narrowness of political theory must be conceived as an endorsement, however implicit, of the sovereign state and as a devaluation of the moral and political problems which arise in the conduct of its external relations. But this criticism is without force in the company of those doctrines which deny the validity of universalistic ethical categories and renounce the distinction between obligations to fellow-citizens and responsibilities to fellow-men, to those in particular with whom we are not associated. The case for international political theory must then rest not upon correcting the limitations of universalistic doctrines which lack a theory of international society, but upon a claim either to be able to defend the traditional grounds for the belief in the existence of obligations to humanity, or to have the capacity to recover that belief, or some equivalent, upon new and incontrovertible foundations.

The fact that a dichotomy between a sense of obligation to the state and a belief in obligations to humanity persists within Western theory and practice is sufficient justification for the present analysis. An account of our experience of the modern state and our relations with outsiders would be defective if it did not probe that moral dualism or conflict embedded within the state's theoretical traditions and practical behaviour. These two concepts of obligation create an important problem or tension within the state which we may characterise as the problem of reconciling our existence as men with the acquired status of citizenship; we may characterise it also as a division within the lives of modern citizens, a sense of being pulled in competing directions by antagonistic ethical demands, manifest most clearly in both theoretical and practical attempts to produce a conclusive statement of the relationship between private and public morality. If the dominant traditions of Western political thought are guilty of omitting the consideration of forms of international life from their enterprise, it is because they have not given the problem of men and citizens the prominence it deserves. It is the tension between different concepts of obligation, and neither the need to confront the undeniably important and recurrent problems of survival nor the practical need to respond to interdependence and integration, which provides the international political theorist with some purchase on the world of international relations and which determines his immediate task, that of effecting a convincing philosophical reconciliation of the components of an apparently bifurcated moral and political experience.

This identification of the tasks confronting the international political theorist does not presume that the notion of obligations to humanity has credence; it may indeed be the case that it is an untenable belief and that we are without a strong argument for engaging in the normative theory of international relations. But if this were to be our conclusion we would have gained a greater certainty of why we must belong to states and what must be the basis of their interaction. This in itself would amount to a more complete account of our political experience since it confronts directly rather than obliquely the present historical norm, man's division into a multiplicity of politically organised communities. If, on the other hand, it is possible to find some basis for the idea of obligations to humanity the consequences for theoretical representations of political life would be considerable. Political theory could not remain content with the antinomy between the theory of the good life and the theory of survival, or concentrate exclusively upon the qualities of the good citizen or the good society conceived as a separate unit. A concern for determining the structure of a rational form of political life would have to extend as far as consideration of the proper organisation of the species as a whole rather than conclude with an analysis of the structure of its constituent parts. At the end of our investigation, therefore, we should possess a clearer understanding of either the reasons for states or the foundations of a theoretical system which would be more than a theory of the state, namely a wider and more fundamental conceptual system concerned with the affairs of the species in its entirety.

2 Men and Citizens in International Relations

> . . . it is possible to be a good citizen without possessing the excellence which is the virtue of the good man. (Aristotle)

> The patriotic spirit is an exclusive one, which makes us regard all men other than our co-citizens as strangers, almost as enemies. Such was the spirit of Sparta and Rome. The Spirit of Christianity, by contrast, makes us regard all men as our brothers . . . does not allow us to make odious distinctions between compatriots and strangers; . . . its ardent zeal embraces all the human race without distinction. (Rousseau)

In the previous chapter we referred to the juxtaposition of two concepts of obligation within the theory and practice of the modern state. The present chapter begins by referring to the problem of men and citizens within those modern theories of politics concerned with the re-creation of community in a society shaped by the presence of individualism and universalism. We shall attempt to show that the problem of man and citizen within these theories of domestic political community is connected with parallel concerns in the history of international thought as well as being the instigator of one of its most important traditions.

It is useful to contrast this tradition with more familiar, mechanistic theories of international relations which identify competition for power as the predominant and distinctive feature of any states-system. The exponents of this perspective claim that necessitous relations are inherent in the condition of international anarchy; they advance a mechanistic reading of the international system which denies that necessity can be removed from a world of separate, sovereign states. That tradition of international thought developed around the problem of men and citizens maintains, on the other hand, that necessitous relations are a consequence of the particularistic associations into which men are currently divided. Moreover, because modern citizens are more than mere members of their communities, since they are responsive to universalistic moral claims, it is within their power to transform international relations in a direction which realises their capacity to lead free lives. The division between men and citizens becomes the basis of a radical theory of international relations, a critical rather than mechanistic theory which is desirous of overcoming those particularistic associations which inhibit the growth of more free and universal relations. We shall claim that this theory not only overcomes the limitations of our more familiar international relations theories, but fulfils the aspirations present within those theories which regarded the division between men and citizens as a barrier to the enjoyment of an integrated political community.

Since Rousseau political theorists have had frequent recourse to a contrast between the fragmented nature of modern political life and the allegedly more communitarian character of the Greek *polis*. At the heart of this opposition was the belief that the *polis* represented a condition of unsurpassable harmony in which citizens identified freely and spontaneously with their public institutions. Unlike their ancient counterparts, modern citizens exhibited less identification with their public world than resolution to advance their separate individual interests and pursue their private conceptions of the good. Nevertheless, the disintegration of the *polis* was not depicted in the language of unqualified loss. History had not been an unmitigated fall, because the individual's claim to scrutinise the law of the *polis* on rational grounds involved a significant advance of man's self-consciousness. The positive aspect of its decline was man's transcendence of a parochial culture in which neither the right of individual freedom nor the principle of human equality had been recognised. If the modern world had lost the spontaneous form of community enjoyed by the ancients, it had surpassed that world in its understanding and expression of freedom.[1]

In the writings of Hegel much is made of the necessity of integrating the ancient ideal of community with the modern principles of individuality and universality. Indeed, for Rousseau, Hegel and the early Marx the modern political problem is how to make good citizens out of modern men, men who are no longer spontaneously citizens.[2] This problematic relationship between men and citizens combines with an equally important if less discussed political problem: how should men relate the obligations they have as men and the obligations they acquire as citizens? Again, Hegel's account of the experience of the Greek *polis* is important. Within the *polis* only citizens lived properly human lives; neither slaves nor the citizens of other states were thought to possess equal worth. Moreover, the citizen's integration into the life of the *polis* involved an unquestioning acceptance of the social roles and responsibilities of membership. This immediate identification dissolved on account of the individual's claim to criticise the life of the *polis* in accordance with the principles of human reason. A new type of moral consciousness challenged both the exclusiveness of the *polis* and the supremacy of its civic obligations. Later it made possible the claim to belong to two societies: the natural society of birth and the universal society embracing all men by virtue of their reason.[3] The distinction between men and citizens created an important problem for political theories and political structures: the problem of how to reconcile the actual diversity and division of political community with the newly developed belief in the universality of human nature.

A brief analysis of certain elements in the development of universalism in the Graeco-Roman world is worth undertaking here for two reasons: it helps both to highlight certain distinctive ingredients of the ethical background of the modern states-system, and to determine how the experience of this states-system may be best represented within the parameters of an international political theory. Against this background, we shall be better able to determine the relative merits of mechanistic and radical theories of international relations.

We may begin by recalling that it is often remarked that

citizens of the Greek city-state understood that the highest concept of morality was exhibited in the excellent performance of allotted social roles or functions, a vision of moral life which was clearly central to the Platonic theory of justice. Aristotle, too, regarded goodness in terms of the performance of civic virtue. Nevertheless, within the writings of Plato and Aristotle the idea of a more inclusive social morality, one involving Greeks as such, is clearly present. Plato has Socrates say:

> Then when Greeks and barbarians fight, we shall say that they are natural enemies, warring against one another, and this enmity is to be called war; but, when Greeks fight with Greeks, we shall declare that naturally they are friends, and that when anything of this kind occurs, Greece is sick and affected by sedition, and this kind of enmity is to be called sedition.[4]

Socrates maintains that 'a difference with Greeks is to be a difference with kinsmen'.[5] Similarly, Aristotle suggests that there are criteria for distinguishing between honourable and dishonourable conduct in international relations:

> Yet it cannot, perhaps, but appear very strange, to a mind which is ready to reflect, that a statesman should be expected to be able to lay his plans for ruling and dominating border states without any regard for their feelings. How can a thing which is not even lawful be proper for a statesman or lawmaker? And how can it ever be lawful to rule without regard to the right or wrong of what you are doing?[6]

The Greeks cherished the view that as Greeks there were certain standards which they ought to respect in their relations with one another. This belief was no more evident than in the common antipathy to subjecting another Greek to the indignity of slavery.

Although there was a sense of identification with the common stock as well as with the *polis*, the former was never sufficiently powerful to provide a basis for the complete transformation of Greek political life. As Phillipson maintained: 'The Greeks as Greeks cherished aspirations for unity, but as citizens their constant aim was decentralisation; and the claims of citizenship invariably triumphed over those of kinship.'[7] The Greeks appear to have been unprepared to disregard the values of liberty and equality, the principal concerns of citizens, in the conduct of their external relations; consequently, they could not avoid that experience of moral and political tension which Bozeman has described as their difficulty 'in finding a working relationship between the principles of equality and security as long as they professed to retain the political system of multiple independent states'.[8]

Undoubtedly the view that the *polis* was the highest association in which humans could develop their capacities, or that citizenship was the most prized human possession, accounts for the Greeks' inability to establish long-lasting international associations or seriously reconsider their division into separate city-states. These ideas, moreover, account for the poverty of international relations theory in the ancient world, just as the primacy of the sovereign state hinders the development of international theory in the modern world. Nevertheless, there was a sensitivity to the tension between moral value and diplomacy which indicated that at least the Athenians 'were more interested in preserving the integrity of their ideals by admitting that they had failed to live up to them, than in saving their egos by compromising on these ideals'.[9]

Modern Western orientations towards international relations are clearly influenced by those developments within the Stoic–Christian tradition which extended the idea of a more embracing human community. Hellenism itself, prior to the emergence of Stoicism, came to be conceived as 'a thing of the spirit and not dependent on the race to which a man belonged or the place he was born'.[10] As Isocrates writes in his *Panegyricus*:

> And so far has our city distanced the rest of the world in thought and in speech that her pupils have become the teachers of the rest of the world; and she has brought it about that the cause 'Hellenes' suggests no longer a race but an intelligence, and that the title 'Hellenes' is applied rather

> to those who share our culture than to those who share a common blood.[11]

This was a remarkable change whereby Hellenism became not an attribute of birth but an individual achievement; it was no longer the exclusive possession of a group but a set of acquired human capacities which a man might develop by his own effort. There was within this development the makings of that imaginative breakthrough which could not be contained within the narrow preserves of the city-state. Later, Stoic thought would emphasise the primacy of individual and intellectual virtues above civic ones. Convinced that all men possessed reason, Stoic thinkers believed less in the exclusiveness of their city-states, more in the whole inhabited world (*oecumene*) and their loyalty to the society of mankind. The expansion of political vision led to the dualistic loyalties of Stoic philosophy:

> There are for every man two laws, the laws of his city and the law of the world-city, the law of custom and the law of reason. Of the two the second must have the greater authority and must provide a norm to which the statutes and customs of cities should conform. Customs are various but reason is one, and behind variety of custom there ought to be some unity of purpose. Stoicism tended to conceive of a world-wide system of law having endless local branches. Localities might differ according to circumstances without being unreasonable, while the reasonableness of the whole system tended to keep the variation from becoming opposition.[12]

There was an expansion of community through the breaking down of the more exclusive loyalties of the city-states. Citizenship of the *polis* was no longer the highest status, owned exclusively by one section of its membership. Transformations of political consciousness were accompanied, moreover, by practical political experiments which sought to reconstruct the foundations of organised social life. Ultimately, their outcome was the extension of citizenship to non-Roman inhabitants of the Empire.[13] Ancient forms of political exclusiveness gave way to the more inclusive form of social life which prevailed within the Empire and later characterised Christian Europe.

Early modern accounts of international relations, both theoretical and practical, were deeply influenced by that tradition of universalist thought which reached its culmination with the Stoic–Christian belief in the unity of mankind; and, of course, they recognised that modern culture not only continued the universalism of earlier periods but recovered the classical belief in the value of the separate political community and the importance of civic virtues. Each recognised that an adequate account of modern international relations should respond to the fact that the modern state and the international states-system evolved out of that larger but disintegrating medieval religious and political framework expressive of the universalism of the Stoic–Christian tradition. What was unique about the modern structure of international society was its superimposition of the universalist ideal upon a recovered commitment to political separateness and a revived acceptance of citizenship. It was the particular historical location of the modern states-system, the very fact that it existed at a point of intersection between particularistic and universalistic ideas, which explained why the tension between men and citizens came to be felt most deeply within it. The problem of reconciling men and citizens was the point then at which the uppermost concerns of an important tradition of domestic political theory overlapped with the recurrent issues of a central strand of international thought. It is not too great an over-simplification to state that while the former emphasised the need to make good citizens out of modern men, the latter aimed to make good men out of modern citizens, citizens who felt the attraction of both universalistic beliefs associated with their humanity and the particularism which accompanied their membership of separate, sovereign states.

This conflict between men and citizens is fundamental to the experience of the modern states-system. Its importance is evident in those earliest systematic writings on the international states-system which attempted to provide an account of international relations which clearly integrated the idea of humanity. As human beings, it was argued, men have obligations to one another which are prior to the formation of sovereign states; but as members of these states they must recognise specific political obligations owed to fellow-citizens alone. Since political obligations are superimposed upon primordial moral ones, the individual has to determine their precise relationship and respective claims upon him. For the classic writers of the modern states-system 'the services of humanity' ought to survive the establishment of any 'special bond to some particular society';[14] they claimed that 'no convention or special agreement can release [men] from the obligation . . . to fulfil the duties of humanity towards outsiders', a responsibility now assumed by the state and its rulers.[15] The classic writings assumed the possibility of men being able to balance the obligations they incurred as human beings and the obligations acquired as members of separate states.

A later stage in the history of international thought highlighted an endemic weakness in this proposed solution to the problem of relating two types of moral experience. Classic theory itself conceded that the processes of establishing special bonds within states were concluded without contractors conforming with their natural duties.[16] Rousseau and Kant made the more fundamental claim that since competition was inherent in a world of separate, sovereign states the performance of wider ethical obligations was necessarily compromised. Man's condition was transformed totally by the experience of living in and among states. It was now necessary for individuals to behave not as citizens and men, but merely as citizens. Thus, for Rousseau,

> each one of us being in the civil state as regards our fellow-citizens, but in the state of nature as regards the rest of the world, we have taken all kinds of precautions against private wars only to kindle national wars a thousand times more terrible; and . . . in joining a particular group of men, we have really declared ourselves the enemies of the whole race.[17]

The states of Europe exhibited 'glaring contradictions' between 'our fair speeches and our abominable acts, the boundless humanity of our maxims and the boundless cruelty of our deeds'.[18] Extending this theme, Kant wrote that 'the same unsociableness which forced men [into a Commonwealth] becomes again the cause of each Commonwealth assuming the attitude of uncontrolled freedom in its external relations';[19] citizenship provides men with security with the result that a kingdom of ends may emerge within states, but it threatens the possibility of a kingdom of ends between them. Thus, the contradiction between men and citizens came to be regarded as the critical problem of international relations.

Although their individual responses vary considerably, Rousseau and Kant confronted a common political problem within a relatively similar understanding of the purposes of international relations theory, one which was harshly critical of the dominant practices of the international states-system. Common to each writer was the belief that our experience of living in and among sovereign states cannot avoid a sense of moral division and political estrangement. As an exclusive moral community, the sovereign state emphasised its liberty to promote its interests without recognising any fundamental obligations for the welfare of outsiders; the willingness of states to promote their one-sided interests was in addition a source of their perpetual conflict and the inevitable competition which existed among them. While men remained estranged from one another through their membership of particularistic communities they could lead neither morally unified lives nor enjoy a social and political world subject to their control or responsive to their capacity for individual and collective self-determination. What characterised these writings was a sense of the divided and estranged nature of our experience of international relations, a sense without precedent and subsequently unequalled. On the one hand, they confronted the expressions of the growth of moral self-consciousness; on the other, they exhibited both anguish and disenchantment with the structure of political relations.

Rousseau's international thought is renowned for its pessimism, for its inability to decipher a solution to the above problem.[20] But, in the writings of Kant and, later, Green an awareness of the historical development of moral life made it possible, it was claimed, for modern men to systematically transform their international relations so creating a world in which they were associated with other men as their equals. Both Kant and Green concentrated on the fact that the modern world possessed unique political possibilities given its access to those higher forms of moral self-consciousness which had facilitated the movement from particularism to universalism in the ancient world. Since modern men were more than simply members of states, more than mere identifiers with their immediate political institutions, they had the capacity to express their freedom, their unique human capacity, in the fundamental reorganisation of their international relations. Their historical experience was not that of being unchanging and unchangeable insiders condemned to live within particularistic social systems, but of being self-developing and self-directing beings with the possibility of transforming existing relations of intersocietal estrangement into relations of familiarity, so completing a process which had begun in the ancient world. An unprecedented political project was made possible by the historically developed notion of the rights and duties inherent in humans themselves, a concept which produced the possibility of fundamentally extending the boundaries of moral and political community.

A distinctive type of international political theory accompanied the identification of the cultural and historical context of the modern international states-system. In the beginning, it recognised that states are not quasi-physical entities whose external relations may only be manipulated in order to fabricate some system *ex nihilo*. The state and the states-system were regarded as being at least partially constituted by our ideas about them, by our suppositions about the most desirable system of social relations. Far then from confronting a natural world the component parts of which might be repositioned but whose ultimate constitution defied modification, men faced a world which was their own historical product; and they did so as agents capable of transforming the conditions of their social and political existence. This analysis warned against issuing ahistorical, mechanistic explanations of the necessary composition of international life. It was claimed that to depict the states-system with recourse to the language of necessity would not be to conclude our account of the experience of international relations but to determine the foundations of one. The conclusion to draw from the awareness of necessity in the international system was that political processes contradict the nature of human agents as potentially free, self-developing beings. Our experience of living in and among sovereign states could not simply be that of participating within a necessitous system of relations, but of confronting a social world in contradiction with our humanity. As such, social necessity demanded supersession, and required the eventual provision of a progressivist account.

Few of our contemporary theories of international relations have provided other than ahistorical and mechanistic readings of the international system. Most have been content with locating the source of multiple phenomena arising from relations between states in the anarchic structure of international society itself, in its tendency to revolve around relations of power-competition and conflict.[21] This characteristic is largely a function of that sharp distinction between domestic and international politics which was observed in the writings of Wight. In a very important passage, Wight states that

> If Sir Thomas More or Henry IV, let us say, were to return to England and France in 1960, it is not beyond plausibility that they would admit that their countries had moved domestically towards goals and along paths which they could approve. But if they contemplated the international scene, it is more likely that they would be struck by resemblances to what they remembered.[22]

If Wight's tendency to characterise international politics in the language of 'recurrence and repetition' is insufficiently precise to convey a sense of the variegated nature of international relations, it also fails to do justice to the complexities of international thought. The statement that political theorists have 'not been attracted by the possibility of maximising the field of political thought through establishing a world state' remains particularly insensitive to the existence of radical and internationalist aspirations within the history of international thought. Because they brought an awareness of both the extension of community in international history and the modern tension between particularism and universalism to their analysis, various theorists, of whom Kant and Green are the most sophisticated, criticised and condemned the sovereign state and the states-system as fetters upon the further development of a properly human community. To overlook this literature is to give a distorted representation of the development of international thought; it is also to fail to perceive what is at issue between critical and more modern and mechanistic descriptions of our experience of international relations. To discuss this theme further it is useful to consider one of the most important mechanistic understandings of international relations, that offered by Kenneth Waltz's *Man, the State and War*.

This work seeks not to give an explanation of the causal antecedents of any particular war, but to identify at a more systematic and general level the source of the practice of warfare itself; to comprehend what Waltz defines as war's 'permissive cause'.[23] The core of Waltz's argument is that in principle the source of war can be located either in man's corrupted nature or in the ways in which belligerent states are domestically constituted, or in the anarchy of the international states-system itself, in the absence of a common international government. The last mode of analysis is held to be the most adequate because it situates conflict within that more general competition for power which states must undertake in order to solve or mitigate their respective 'security-dilemmas'.[24] This analysis leads to clear and unambiguous prescriptive conclusions. Sound prescription recommends constraints which will make it difficult for states to pursue their ends through force without incurring a hostile counteractive response from others. In short, it involves legitimating the international balance of power.

What is limited about this perspective is not its belief that the fundamental problem of international relations – the problem of war – can be overcome only by adjusting the external relations of states, but the supposition that this transformation might be effected while the ethical basis of the state remained uncriticised and unchallenged. Within Waltz's analysis there is no need to undertake a reconsideration of the way in which citizens organise their obligations to the state and to the remainder of humanity; the rights and duties of the citizen and the state are not understood to enter into the permissive causes of war. But this is to overlook Kant and Green's claim that disputes, conflicts and war are inseparable from the state as a limited moral community. It is to overlook the argument that war can be presumed to be an aspect of the division of mankind into separate, sovereign states, not because of the anarchical condition of international society but, more profoundly, because of the particularistic character of its component parts.[25]

If Kant and Green are right, then Waltz's approach may be criticised in two further respects. Firstly, while it considers the nature of man, the organisation of the state, and the nature of the international environment in which it is placed, at no stage does it consider the particularity of the state itself. As a result, Waltz's analytical framework is not logically exhaustive and its prescriptive value is less than it might otherwise have been.[26] Secondly, if the nature of the state may be regarded as a permissive cause of war, it is illegitimate to disregard philosophical approaches to the state or to deny the relevance of moral philosophy when analysing the source of, and solution to, international conflict. The management of relations between states becomes as much a matter of adjusting their respective rights and duties, and those of their citizens, as balancing their power.

There appear to be two reasons for Waltz's tendency to overlook the role of moral and political philosophy in the construction of prescriptive international relations theory. Since political authority is understood to be the principal instrument of social control, there is a tendency to underestimate the place of moral ideas in the maintenance of social bonds among citizens. Closely related to this observation is Waltz's agreement with Kelsen that justice is not a rational idea:

> The important point, however, is not that there is in the state a way of making and enforcing correct decisions but that some decision be made and followed. Thus Hans Kelsen has argued that 'justice is an irrational ideal. However indispensable it may be for volition and action of men, it is not subject to cognition. Regarded from the point of view of rational cognition, there are only interests, and hence conflicts of interest'. One set of interests can be satisfied at the expense of another, or they can be compromised. But one cannot say that one of these ways of dealing with conflict is just, the other unjust.[27]

It is not the lack of a strong sense of moral constraint but the absence of actual physical constraint which accounts for the ever-present possibility of war. Consequently, prescriptive international relations theory can ignore the realm of normative discourse. We shall attempt to show that, on the contrary, analyses of, and prescriptions for, the international system cannot be divorced from an understanding of the way in which the world of politics is structured by our moral ideas. Moreover, to the extent that the idea of obligations to humanity can be defended, the appeals of a critical theory of international relations become irresistible. The alternative view that it is unnecessary to represent our experience of international relations in the language of moral conflict and political estrangement, or to posit a differently organised, more rational system of relations, becomes deficient.

A more complete theory of international relations, more complete in the sense of recognising moral development and its political consequences, may be discerned in the writings of T. H. Green. Some elements of Green's thinking seem vulnerable to Waltz's criticisms of the second image of international conflict (the view that conflict is a function of the imperfect organisation of the state). Green does state that with the disappearance of a 'privileged class', which denies civil rights to a 'suffering class', the source of war could be removed.[28] This proposition appears barely convincing given Waltz's claim that even perfectly organised political systems may come into conflict because that perfection itself is not a guarantee against external conflicts of interest.

What is important, however, is the meaning to be attached to the notion of perfectly constituted states. Within Green's writings there is another, more forceful argument which renders his claim that there is no such thing as an inevitability of conflict between states quite tenable. Green recognised in history the stages of moral progress. In the very earliest of societies, rights and duties were attached to persons only as members. A common good was recognised within such societies 'while beyond the particular community the range of obligation [was] not understood to extend'.[29] The essence of man's development was revealed in his latent capacity to recognise an ever-widening conception 'of the range of persons to whom the common good is common'.[30] The culmination of this development, which Green associated with the growth of freedom, was the universal understanding that fundamental moral obligations were not to be recognised simply in relations between citizens, or confined to relations between sovereigns and their subjects, but ought to permeate all relations between men *qua* men. Higher stages in the historical development of moral self-consciousness entailed an explicit commitment to the common good of a universal society co-extensive with mankind itself.[31]

In the course of their historical development, Green argued, men come to regard a certain right as worthy of recognition in human personality itself rather than associated with those with whom they share a particular tribe or political society. Green refers to this right as a right to 'a free life', the individual's natural right to life and liberty.[32] For Green, a state could not generate this concept of rights without recognising the necessity of establishing moral rather than physical constraints upon its external relations. Under these circumstances, there could be

> no ground for holding that a state is justified in doing whatever its interests seem to require, irrespectively of effects on other men. If those effects are bad, as involving either a direct violation of personal rights or obstruction to the moral development of society anywhere in the world, then there is no ultimate justification for the political action that gives rise to them.[33]

Therefore, to be a perfectly constituted state is to have first generated and then extended the realm of application of the concept of a natural right to liberty and equality. It involves the adoption of a critical posture towards the predominantly self-regarding practices of states, so supplying grounds for the belief that 'the dream of an international court with authority resting on the consent of independent states may come to be realised.'[34] For Green, war is inherent in the system of states only to the extent that states are imperfectly constituted, to the degree that they are organised around incomplete notions of rights and human personality. When in the course of human history these rights are properly understood and the possibility of including the whole species within a universal civil society finally arises, the problem of war and the persistence of necessitous relations would diminish accordingly.

Let us summarise what is ultimately at issue between mechanistic and radical or critical interpretations of the international system. In its search for the distinctive qualities of relations between independent states, the mechanistic theory of international relations ignores differences between one historical epoch and another. The modern states-system, for example, reflects the more general phenomenon of international relations and exhibits the characteristics which distinguish politics between from politics within states. Exponents of a critical theory of international relations on the other hand were less concerned with eliciting the recurrent patterns of thought and action present within all states-systems than with confronting a moral problem peculiar to the modern experience of international relations. It was their particular sensitivity to the way in which the modern world valued the ideas of humanity and self-determination, yet frustrated their political expression by remaining committed to self-regarding states, which led them to produce their novel international theory. For Kant and Green, a solution to the problem of international relations could not consist simply of balancing the power available to states; it required the radical reconstruction of modern political life so that the tension between moral self-consciousness and political practice might be eliminated entirely. Accordingly, to prescribe principles of foreign policy without any allusion to the cultural background of modern international relations was to create seriously one-sided recommendations. Given the possession of the idea of humanity, the problem of international relations could not be solved simply in a mechanistic fashion which aimed to identify the ingredients of a stable order among egotistical sovereign states; what was necessary was the construction of an order sensitive to the human capacity to shape social relations in accordance with the goal of autonomy, and expressive of modern concepts of moral community. To allow an order based on an equilibrium of power to be the principal determinant of human conduct would be to preserve a conflict between moral theory and political practice.

Many political theorists, concerned with the problem of men and citizens in its domestic sense and desirous of recovering that integrated moral community evidently missing from the modern world, have commented upon the problem of obligation in international society. Clearly the tension that exists between men and citizens has troubled them. How is that community to be recovered within a domestic framework whose equilibrium may be disturbed at any time by the appeal of universalism? Christianity with its vision of a community more fundamental and embracing than the state posed an inevitable problem. Recognition of the opposition between religious individualism and universalism and the performance of civic obligations troubled Rousseau for whom the tension must be dissolved in a civic religion 'without which a man cannot be a good citizen or a faithful subject'.[35] Later writers had to confront the potentially subversive role of a secularised cosmopolitanism, the secular faith of humanity. Although attracted by the idea that rights were attached to sheer humanity, and prepared to regard this notion as the basis of modern as opposed to ancient community, they were reluctant to articulate a theory of international relations on the same foundation. In opposition to Kantian cosmopolitanism, Hegel stated that

> A man counts as a man in virtue of his manhood alone, not because he is a Jew, Catholic, Protestant, German, Italian, etc. This is an assertion which thinking ratifies and to be conscious of it is of infinite importance. It is defective only when it is crystallised, e.g. as a cosmopolitanism in opposition to the concrete life of the state.[36]

Rousseau, characteristically ambivalent towards the phenomenon of cosmopolitanism, maintained that 'the feeling of humanity evaporates and grows feeble in embracing mankind', and urged that 'our humanity should confine itself to our fellow-citizens' if it is to be 'active'.[37] The absence or undesirability of an association of mankind, the lack of determinate relationships or concrete forms of international life, rendered the idea of humanity vacuous or idealistic. Durkheim's lengthy statement upon this theme is worth quoting at length:

> On the one hand, we can scarcely help conceiving of moral ends that are loftier than national goals; on the other hand,

> it seems quite impossible that these loftier ends can be embodied in a human group perfectly adequate to them. The only way of resolving this difficulty, which troubles public thinking, is to seek the realisation of the human ideal through the most highly developed groups that we know, through those closest to humanity as a whole, but without confusing the two – that is to say through the efforts of specific nations. To eliminate all such contradictions, thus satisfying the requirements of our moral consciousness, it suffices that the state commit itself as its main goal not to expanding, in a material sense, to the detriment of its neighbours, not to gaining greater strength than they, or to becoming richer than they; but to the goal of realising among its own people the general interests of humanity – that is to say, committing itself to an access of justice, to a higher morality, to organising itself in such a way that there is always a closer correspondence between the merit of its citizens and their conditions of life with the end of reducing or preventing individual suffering. From this point of view, all rivalry between different countries disappears and, consequently, all contradiction between cosmopolitanism and patriotism.[38]

These are representative reactions to the problem of men and citizens.

Some realisation of the tension between men and citizens is preferable to no acquaintance with it whatsoever. But what is surprising is the fact that within theories of domestic political community the tension has often been noted but then ignored and abandoned as if the theorist believed he had digressed too far from his principal concerns. Theoretical attempts to make good citizens out of modern men failed to the extent that they formulated their solutions in such a way as to exclude the concurrent problem of international relations. When characterised adequately, the conflict between citizenship and humanity reveals dissatisfaction with the impediments to human freedom which issue both from the character of the sovereign state and the constitutive principles of the international states-system. For this reason Green's theory surpasses not only mechanistic interpretations of international relations but domestic theories of the dichotomy between man and citizen. To develop this further, it is worth returning to Hegel's account of the distinction between ancient and modern political community.

For Hegel, the emergence in ancient Greece of the claim to be men as well as citizens revealed dissatisfaction with the parochial nature of social and political life. The Greek's challenge to traditional and customary morality expressed his aspiration to live in a world which embodied human reason. Social and political morality was not to be simply 'an affair internal to a particular community';[39] now it had to express man's awareness of the nature of rational conduct.[40] If this more free social world was to develop, Hegel argued, the individual's estrangement from his customary morality was essential.[41] This estrangement was necessary in order to realise a higher understanding of self-determination than that attained either in those cultures in which members thought their social relations rested upon natural sanctions or in which they enacted their moral obligations uncritically and spontaneously. It was this demand for a higher level of self-determination, expressed in the contrast between man and citizen, which ultimately proved to be subversive of Greek political life. Nevertheless, individualism itself could not provide, in Hegel's view, the sufficient condition for a free social world. Individualism, especially when it was the rationale for the pursuit of private interests, became an obstacle to the development of a social environment subject to collective control. The product of individualism was a condition in which individuals were increasingly subjected to impersonal laws operative within their societies.[42] To attain a higher level of self-determination, it was necessary to allow men to pursue their separate individual ends while enjoying integration into a rational state which expressed their capacity for collective self-determination. In this way the reconciliation of that opposition between men and citizens, which had been so necessary to progress beyond the parochialism of Greece, would be accomplished.

However, this theory had the resources for characterising the division between men and citizens in international relations in a similar way. The modern state may offer its citizens freedoms unavailable to members of earlier forms of association; it may make available greater opportunities for individual self-determination and for taking part in the process of controlling the immediate social and political environment. Nevertheless, states separately can only imperfectly realise the human capacity for collective self-determination. The possession of citizenship alone is not sufficient to enable the individual to participate in the control of his total political environment. As Rousseau observed, the citizen's ability to live an autonomous life within states is limited severely by the disruptive power of international events. Refuge from a form of heteronomy, which had its source outside the state, could be found only in autarchic states.[43] The anarchic nature of the states-system subjects citizens and states alike to a further set of impersonal laws. Due to this phenomenon the conflict between men and citizens acquires fundamental importance in the theory and practice of international relations. For, as we have seen, what the existence of a realm of human obligation does, is challenge the state as a particularistic moral community which generates heteronomous relations in its external affairs. It may be suggested that the form of estrangement which is exhibited in the division between men and citizens is as necessary in the experience of the world of states as it was in the life of the Greek *polis*. It may be regarded as a division which is integral to the movement from relations of intersocietal estrangement and domination to relations based on respect for human freedom and equality. This division may be interpreted as a development which contains intimations of a higher form of political life at both the domestic and international level.

Any political theory which ignores the problems created by our double existence as men and citizens is no longer adequate to the conditions of modern political life; for it fails to attempt to harmonise all aspects of modern moral and political experience. A political theory acquainted with the problem of men and citizens should proceed to construct a vision of an integrated social and political life within a theory of the international system. On the other hand, a theory of international relations which overlooks the fact that modern citizens possess concepts of humanity fails by offering only a mechanistic interpretation of the states-system. We may conclude by claiming that if it is true that 'the need for philosophy arises when the unifying power has disappeared from the life of man',[44] then that fragmented moral experience specific to the modern states-system provides the issues with which the political theory of international relations must begin.

Having identified the importance of the dichotomy between citizenship and humanity, we can now give direction to the immediate task of formulating the most central categorial frameworks within the present argument. What is required is an analysis of the precise composition of each element of a fragmented moral experience. At a later stage, we shall attempt to determine how we are to choose between them. It was noted earlier that the division between men and citizens contains intimations of a higher form of political life. We must now seek to ascertain what this division anticipates, and what it would have us leave behind. In the next chapter we set out two categorial frameworks containing diametrically opposed conceptions of the relations between insiders and the outside political world.

3 Internal and External Concepts of Obligation in the Theory of International Relations

> The history of the human species as a whole may be regarded as the realisation of a secret plan of Nature for bringing into existence a political constitution perfect both from the internal point of view and, so far as regards this purpose, from the external point of view also; such a constitution being the sole condition under which Nature can fully develop all the capacities she has implanted in humanity. (Kant)

> They moralise from without instead of understanding the nature of the state from within. (Meinecke)

This chapter aims at a closer understanding of the nature of the conflict between two moral perspectives present in the structure of the modern state. It focuses upon three postulates of modern political life: the belief that the sovereign state is legitimately the basis of world political organisation; the conviction that the morality pertinent to the conduct of foreign relations must be different from that observed by citizens in their social relations; and the assumption that international cooperation can only be undertaken if there is good reason to believe that it will satisfy the state's pragmatic considerations. We shall be particularly concerned to show how these postulates were defended within contractarian thought, and we shall consider the fact that they were contested within universalist perspectives linked with the Stoic–Christian tradition. An understanding of these two positions and their conceptions of international relations facilitates grasping the bifurcated nature of modern moral and political experience.

Doctrines which support the above three postulates will be referred to as internal concepts of moral and political obligation; competing perspectives will be called external concepts of obligation. As alternatives, we shall refer to ethical particularism and ethical universalism or, following Kant, to internal and external points of view. Each doctrine is a way of defining proper relationships between the members of a particular society and those persons or groups which collectively form the outside social world. These doctrines may be of two types: they may either be ongoing social moralities whose imperatives make explicit the rules of conduct which ought to be observed by members in the area of their external relations, or they may be theories which seek to legitimise, or criticise, the postulates underlying these social moralities. The initial sections of this chapter make some observations about the general properties of the two points of view in practice; later sections discuss the way in which contractarianism and universalism have been crucial elements in the theories of modern social and political relations.

In practice, as an element in an actual social morality, an internal concept of obligation seeks to defend and perpetuate the belief that members owe their most fundamental obligations to the society into which they were born, or to which they belong. Their society or political system is described as the highest and most embracing moral community, the outer limit of significant moral concern, the fundamental sphere within which moral claims may be advanced and satisfied. This perspective either states that outsiders are beyond the boundaries of moral consideration altogether or, where obligations to outsiders are recognised, claims that these are secondary or residual in comparison with those which issue from membership of a particular way of life. In either event, a clear priority is established between the individual's moral obligations, and social systems thereby ensure that primary responsibilities to insiders are reinforced. An actual social morality with this composition informs its subjects of the respects in which insiders and outsiders exhibit morally significant differences (because of religion, race, kinship or citizenship, for example);

and these distinctions serve to identify those who have and those who have not the special status of being recognised as moral claimants against the group.

The precise composition of an internal concept of obligation, the specific content it has at any time or place, is as variable as social structures and belief-systems themselves. Tribal groups, the states of ancient Greece or China, the modern state in its various manifestations between the Renaissance and the present day all reveal nuances in their respective conceptions and enactments of the internal point of view. Although we cannot develop this theme further here, these conceptions will be important determinants of their external relations. Any group of societies, or system of states, will structure the world of international relations in its unique way as a consequence of the dominant postulates about social and political life which are common to their members. A specific society within such a structure may act upon a particular variant of the internal point of view which is at odds with other members', and this will have to be grasped in order to understand the identity of any states-system or international social system at any particular time. These are observations which suggest certain empirical undertakings which cannot be executed here. Let us simply say that midst the diversity within a system of states, or despite the differences between one system and another, there is a recurrent feature which is that any separate community which wishes to preserve its social institutions and exclusiveness must display some variant of the internal point of view expressive of its traditions and experience.

An external account of moral and political obligation arises only in those societies which include particular persons who articulate their sense of being located within a much wider set of moral relations and ethical responsibilities than those which are associated with their particular community. The distinguishing identity of this perspective is the conviction that there is a moral framework which extends beyond the one surrounding insiders, so necessitating ethical as opposed to merely pragmatic orientations towards relations with outsiders. Separate societies can, and have continued to exist, without any vision of obligation and responsibility extending beyond the traditional moral boundaries recognised between members. Indeed, the emergence of moral universalism, or even the extension of moral community through the recognition of additional moral claimants, is one of the more remarkable elements of historical development.

In practice, external approaches to moral and political obligation have had various manifestations. At the most elementary level, we may identify a form of universalism which regards the social practices of other groups as reprehensible or uncivilised because they contravene universal moral principles. A more elaborate form seeks to extend the boundaries of moral community by limiting demands on outsiders and by responding sympathetically to their moral claims. More complex still is the vision of a moral community of mankind and the ideal of the incorporation of the entire species within a single political society. Conceptions of political unification are at the end of a series of images of universal moral community.

Our claim is that the modern state embraces two moral perspectives – both ethical particularism and ethical universalism. It does so because the modern state recovered the values of political separateness and civic virtue while preserving the notion of a wider moral community to which men, as opposed to citizens, continued to owe obligations. We are concerned here however with the way in which this dualism was represented at the level of theory. To give an account of moral conflict within modern theories of international relations, it is necessary first to present an ideal-typical description of two modes of moral experience. We do not assume that these are the only ways in which modern moral and political experience have been described in political theories; but they were the principal concerns of the earliest theorists of international relations. One of these approaches presents the individual with contractual obligations which underpin the importance of the separate community; the other tradition, linked with the Stoic–Christian perspective, asserts that the rational obligations which all men should honour extend beyond their particular communities and embrace the whole of mankind. These two perspectives are selected initially because they reflect at the level of philosophical inquiry the peculiar constitution of the modern state: the fact that its individualism reflects its break, while its universalism reveals its continuity, with the medieval order. In the second principal section of this work, we shall discuss the way in which each perspective was incorporated within the structure of rationalist theories of international relations.

The first mode, contractarianism, was employed by political theorists to account for political obligations and to justify the primacy of obligations among fellow-citizens. Civil society was conceived to be the outcome of individual negotiation. Individuals surrendered their inherent, absolute rights of liberty in order to obtain a condition of civility conducive to their utility. Because of their natural equality and liberty, society could be constructed only through free, individual exchanges of equivalent benefits; reciprocity made social life possible, and consent gave force to obligation. Because a universal political association was unnecessary and unobtainable, contracts were concluded not by the whole of humanity collectively but separately within emergent political groups. Individuals left the state of nature by granting one another determinate rights and duties, the rights and duties of citizens. Between their respective communities, however, the state of nature continued to exist. Since individuals were not parties to contracts with outsiders, they were free from international moral responsibilities; states, moreover, owed obligations only to those who had consented to their establishment. By their contract, individuals specified the nature of obligations between citizens within associations whose sovereignty expressed the closed nature of moral life.

This world-view is specific to the political experience of the modern state. What is especially interesting is the fact that no cultural divisions or antagonisms prevent a person in principle from attaining citizenship of a state: only the fact that once men have contracted to form a viable political association, there is no imperative to involve other individuals within their system of reciprocal obligations. Potentially, obligations could be established between all the individual members of mankind, were the need there. Relations within the state are the fundamental concern of most members, and relations between states are conceived principally in instrumental terms, as means whereby the state may enhance its particularistic interests. Nevertheless, these goals themselves can lead to an extension of the system of reciprocal relations into the sphere of international intercourse. The fact that there are no cultural obstacles to the formation of obligations between different communities means that a state based upon contractarian principles can engage in social forms of external relations. That type of ethical particularism based upon the idea that domestic social relations should conform with the principle of reciprocity can generate a form of international egalitarianism which is wholly inadmissible within those societies whose views of their own racial or cultural supremacy allow only feudal, hierarchical or imperial international relations.[1]

The contractarian perspective offers an integrated theory of the sovereign state and its rights, the division between private and public ethics, and the justification and limits of international cooperation. Walter Ullman's claim that the move from medieval to modern politics was a shift away from a 'descending' and theocratic to an 'ascending' and individualistic conception of government is particularly important here.[2] For the medieval world,

> governmental authority and law-creating competency descend from one supreme organ; power is distributed 'downwards', again in the shape of a pyramid, but so that whatever power is found 'down below' at the base of the pyramid is not, as in the ascending theme, an original power, but one that is derived from 'above'.[3]

For the modern world, 'governing authority and the law ascend from the broad base in the shape of a pyramid';[4] legitimacy is derived from the consent of the people. The contractarian perspective exhibits precisely this 'supersession of the descending by the ascending theme'. The legitimacy of the state is not derived from a higher authority which retains the prerogative of withdrawing it, but from the consent of individuals who have granted government power over them.

An ascending conception of government underlies the critical element in the contractarian theory of obligation, namely sovereignty. Firstly, the concept refers to that juridical separateness or legal autonomy which arises from the fact that some men have abolished the state of nature among themselves while remaining in that condition with others who are without legal claims upon them. For this reason the notion of a state of nature as a system of free and equal individuals is often considered the most convenient device for referring to the essential features of the international political system.[5] Like individuals in their original condition, the state is a person, a collective personality, free from other than self-imposed legal limitations upon its conduct. Secondly, sovereignty denotes the institutionalisation of the distinction between insiders and outsiders, and reflects the fact that the former have granted each other a special status which is not possessed by outsiders. The exclusive nature of their contract, and their ensuing obligations, is especially evident within Bodin's thought:

> It is not the rights and privileges which he enjoys which makes man a citizen, but the mutual obligation between subject and sovereign, by which, in return for the faith and obedience returned to him, the sovereign must do justice and give counsel, assistance, encouragement and protection to the subject. *He does not owe this to aliens*.[6]

The same is true, of course, of relations between citizens generally. Thirdly, sovereignty suggests complete liberty of action in the sense of freedom from binding moral obligations to outsiders. The sovereign's right to promote the interests of his separate association, by force if necessary, is the international analogue of the original right of self-help in the state of nature. This is the necessary outcome of the ascending conception of authority. A theory which begins with the rights of individuals to advance their interests must proceed to develop a series of rights which facilitate the attainment of individual ends. Thus, the right to associate politically and to construct sovereign power follows from the individual right to promote self-interest; and the right to use force, to whatever degree necessary, follows from the right to live in a sovereign association. The sovereign's 'right to everything', as Hobbes described it, his right to 'seek, and use, all helps, and advantages of Warre'[7] is a necessary part of an internal concept of obligation founded upon an ascending conception of authority.

Let us now consider the contractarian approach to the

morality of private persons and sovereigns. Crucial here is the fact that the principles which come to be accepted by contractors cannot be applied more extensively in the area of relations between states. Each citizen relinquishes his right of self-help against other citizens and acknowledges the rule-governed nature of their social interaction, but he does not regard their social principles as binding upon human beings as such. To do so would be to abstract these principles from their place within an actual form of social life; it would be to detach them from the social arena in which they derive their meaning, to break their inseverable connection with agreements made between specific men.

Citizens, therefore, cannot appeal to supposedly absolute principles of international morality in order to evaluate the conduct of their state, or as a basis from which to refuse it their allegiance. Nor can they claim on the basis of their allegedly inalienable human rights that they may make claims on the world stage for assistance against their governments. Their moral rights are defined in relation to, and are entirely enclosed by, the sovereign state. While it provides them with a level of security unavailable to them in the state of nature, they owe it, on their part, an unqualified obligation to participate in promoting its interests.[8]

Their sovereign representative, on the other hand, possesses a certain liberty of action in the area of foreign relations. This liberty of action against outsiders is a product of his specifically contractual obligations to fellow-citizens; it flows not from the retention of his natural, individual right of self-help but from the requirements of a socially constituted morality. Highly specific responsibilities are assigned to the sovereign within the contracted political framework of the sovereign state. The sovereign is entrusted with all previously individual rights of self-help, and it is his fundamental duty to act solely on behalf of those who have transferred their rights to the political community and its representatives. Like his fellow-citizens, the sovereign cannot detach the principles of political life from their basis in the will of contractors. To apply domestic principles to the realm of external relations would be to infringe the constitutive principles of his office.

The sovereign is the trustee of the community and, as such,

it is his responsibility to commit acts which have been outlawed from relations between citizens. The specific nature of the sovereign's obligations is best discussed in relation to that form of particularism which tolerates the individual choice of international ideals or private international moralities such as pacificism. A particular society may allow citizens the liberty of adopting these ideals, but it cannot allow that its sovereign will share the same freedom of choice. To use Max Weber's terminology, the sovereign cannot select 'an ethic of conviction' or 'an ethic of ultimate ends', but only 'an ethic of responsibility' which precludes the adoption of any ideals which might ultimately endanger the interests of the state.[9] Before all else, it is the sovereign's duty to be prepared to have recourse to 'morally dubious means',[10] or to be willing 'to learn how not to be good'[11] in the realm of international relations. The statesman must be prepared to commit acts from which others might flinch; he must either 'take upon himself the responsibility for sacrifices of value in order that others, as a nation, may protect or attain the things they treasure',[12] or accept that he must turn his back on politics.[13] In all conceptions of particularism, the sovereign is prevented from making certain ethical commitments contrary to the principles of his office. This proscription issues from the recognition that he must be prepared at times to impose considerable costs on outsiders if he is to serve his state well. Within a contractarian perspective, therefore, to be constrained by international ethical considerations is to be guided by a descending rather than an ascending conception of government.

International obligations are not incompatible with the idea of the sovereign state or the division between a private and public morality. The importance of a relatively stable international condition may induce the formation of a variety of international practices. Diplomacy, international law and the balance of power (crucial elements of the modern states-system) reflect the capacity of particularistic political entities to articulate their separate interests. Through the operation of mutual consent states can extend the web of social relations. Reciprocity facilitates the development of a society of states, but the reason for states is a constraint upon the level of sociability which they can exhibit in their external relations.

Because of the structure of domestic political obligation, the state cannot conceive of international obligations as permanently binding, just as it cannot dismiss out of hand any act of duplicity or violence outlawed within domestic society. Were it to do so, it would predicate its conduct upon an external not an internal concept of obligation.

We have seen what it means to characterise international relations as a state of nature analogous to the one which social contract theorists presumed to have existed formerly among individuals. This interpretation, deeply embedded within the Western political tradition, continues to be reflected within contemporary accounts of the structure of international society. Nevertheless, the categories of the contractarian perspective, and those derived from or similar to it, are not sufficient to give a complete account of the modern experience of the world of states. To grasp the total picture it is necessary to include the international political implications of ethical universalism.

The modern experience of international relations has not assumed that the states-system consisted solely of insulated moral enclaves. Additionally, it has posited the existence of a primordial moral community co-extensive with mankind itself. Western external concepts of obligation emanate from what Carlyle called 'the most decisive change in political thinking . . . which came some time between the days of Aristotle and Cicero, and proclaimed the fundamental equality of men'[14]. The emergence of the idea of moral equality divided Western concepts of morality and international relations between two dominant perspectives. According to one conception of moral life, the individual should understand morality as 'an affair internal to a particular community';[15] his separate community is the source of his concrete ethical life and the particular object of his political loyalty; the states-system is the inevitable product of man's division into a variety of particularistic social moralities; the idea of humanity, moreover, lacking expression in the roles and responsibilities of a form of life, exerts little or no constraint upon relations between states. From this perspective, the state is the sole moral constituency and the states-system is an unproblematical form of world political organisation.

According to the second conception, 'the moral law binds

men as men and not as members of any particular community';[16] individuals may employ their rational faculties to determine the rights and duties which necessarily govern them all; the state is an incomplete moral community, too limited to satisfy the individual's sense of his moral responsibilites, and the states-system is an obstacle to the institutional expression of the human race. On account of a primordial, if latent, moral community obligations to citizens cannot constitute the outer parameter of the individual's moral experience; and vertical divisions between states, accordingly, cannot be unchallengeable characteristics of a system of states.

All forms of universalism possess a concept of progress in which the moral unity of mankind overcomes the purely arbitrary divisions of the human race. In St. Simon's words, they have confidence in 'the continual extension of the principle of association', in the desirability or inevitability of 'a still vaster association comprehending the whole race'.[17] Some versions of universalism posit the necessity of a cosmopolitan community in which all cultural and other divisions are finally submerged. But apart from Enlightenment thinking, for which there is no reason for societies maintaining their differences,[18] few traditions of universalist thought hold that historical progress will culminate in the dissolution of all social differences within a universal association. Members of modern states have been responsive to universalism, but principally as a brake upon the possible excesses of statecraft; modern versions of universalism, or at least the more powerful of them, have been internationalist rather than cosmopolitan.

Typically, modern universalists express their confidence in the human capacity to transcend those social and cultural differences which previously stood in the way of extensive schemes of social and political cooperation between states. Universalists hold that since these differences are not natural, but social and historical, human sociability can in principle be extended indefinitely. The sentiments attached to modern universalism are very similar to those expressed by Alberico Gentili in his comment on the Greek political temperament. Having quoted Philip of Macedon's belief that the Greeks and the barbarians were eternally enemies by nature, Gentili observed that

> the Greeks and the barbarians were trained to be enemies one of the other. That is a different reason, and perhaps it is not very far from being a natural one, for it is the result of education, which is a second nature.[19]

Gentili denied that differences between other groups – Palestinians and Jews, Christians and Saracens, Romans and foreign nations – were natural and eternal, 'for, on the contrary, we are by nature all akin'.[20] It is this confidence in the existence of a reality deeper than that formed by social and cultural differences which is the more pronounced element in modern types of universalism.

To be committed to universalism is to claim a status which transcends that of membership; it is to be incapable of total identification with the community to which one belongs, to demand recognition of one's humanity as well as one's citizenship. Universalism is revolutionary in intent insofar as it desires what no morally exclusive community can supply, namely a politics of impartiality which takes the welfare of all humans into account irrespective of the society to which they belong. Its aspiration is the replacement of relations of estrangement and conflict with relations of familiarity. It is not surprising that this remarkable development of human consciousness should be directed, first of all in historical terms, against the more manifest forms of intersocietal conflict which men experienced, the threat, or actual use, of the instruments of war. Consideration of the principles defining the morality of warfare is therefore the original area of application of the belief in a wider moral community than the particular state. These principles remain one of the great legacies of universalism; they are the clearest example of a form of universalism which seeks to mitigate some of the harsher consequences of statecraft and war. Universalism, however, poses a more fundamental challenge to the postulates of the sovereign state and the international states-system. To discuss these it is best to begin with a brief statement of medieval international relations thought. Not until the writings of Vitoria and Suarez is this universalist disposition the basis of a comprehensive theory of the legitimate principles of world organisation. Few subsequent traditions have offered equally systematic accounts of the implications of universalism for the structure of international society.

The medieval theory of international society, which is an internationalist rather than a cosmopolitan theory, is profoundly influenced by the belief in the need for a variety of social institutions, each capable of providing for some aspect of the individual's material and spiritual well-being. If the individual person's development is to be promoted effectively, each of the social institutions to which he belongs must be in harmony with the others. Ultimately, however, the individual and his institutions are the basic elements of an association co-extensive with the entire human race. The state, the most fundamental political association, is bound both by the need to respect the balance of institutions within its jurisdiction and by the duty of not disturbing the promotion of the common good elsewhere. It is under an obligation both to conform with moral and legal obligations in its external relations, obligations which, according to the descending conception of political authority, have their ultimate source in God, and to refrain from demanding of the individual that he perform acts which would alienate him from his membership of the larger human society. Let us now consider how this theory of associations led to a distinctive account of the state, the division between private and public morality, and international cooperation.

Francisco de Vitoria's theory of the world community denies the sovereignty of the state as modern Europeans have come to understand it. Not only does the state owe a moral responsibility to the rest of the world; it can, indeed, be bound by the consent of the larger society of mankind, the *ius gentium*:

> International law has not only the force of a pact and agreement among men, but also the force of a law; for the world as a whole, being in a way one single state, has the power to create laws that are just and fitting for all persons, as are the rules of international law. Consequently, it is clear that they who violate international rules, whether in peace or in war, commit a mortal sin; moreover, in the gravest of matters such as the inviolability of ambassadors, it is not permissible for one country to refuse to be bound by

> international law, the latter having been established by the whole world.[21]

For Vitoria the whole human race constitutes a moral unity with a common good which can in principle override the particular good of any independent state. This dimension of medieval universalism is expressed in Vitoria's remark that

> one nation is a part of the whole world, and since the Christian province is a part of the whole Christian state, if any war should be advantageous to one province or nation but injurious to the world, or Christendom . . . for this very reason, that war is unjust.[22]

Furthermore, the appeal to the welfare of the human race means that, contrary to the dominant attitudes and practices of the time, Christians themselves are bound to apply Christian principles to their relations with the Spanish American Indians. There cannot be one standard of conduct among Christians and another between Christians and the newly discovered peoples.[23] All are bound by a common set of moral principles, for all are the common creation of God. No single group or nation can detach itself from the purposes of creation without contravening the very laws of being.

The moral supremacy of international society suggests the need for authoritative international institutions capable of promoting the common good of the whole world and able to balance that good with the respective ends of other communities. For Suarez,

> just as within a state some lawful power to punish crimes is necessary to the preservation of domestic peace; so, in the world as a whole, there must exist, in order that various states may dwell in concord, some power for the punishment of injuries inflicted by one state upon another.[24]

Nevertheless, the establishment of international institutions is 'hardly possible',[25] while to allow the power of punishment to 'reside in the sovereign power of the injured state'[26] is to create a condition in which 'the same party in one and the same case is both plaintiff and judge', and in which the punisher may 'exceed the bounds of justice'.[27]

Nevertheless, there is within the writings of Vitoria and Suarez the philosophical basis for arguing that states should submit to a higher authority if favourable conditions present themselves.[28] Evidently, while particularism is reconciled to the existence of the sovereign state and the practices of the states-system, universalism exhibits a profound disquiet with them. For universalism, unlike particularism, there is a gulf between theory and practice, and a concomitant sense of the need to overcome the distance between the practical arrangements amongst citizens and the morally desirable arrangements amongst men.

It follows that the distinction between private and public morality is not given in the nature of social and political life; it is rather an obstacle to the realisation of political structures which conform with human obligation. Considered alongside the belief in universal reason, the separation between public and private ethics is a reflection of the incomplete and one-sided nature of moral life. The division between the two moralities depends upon a prior decision to confine the moral constituency to the boundaries of contracted political association; on account of the supposed rationality of this decision, morality can be separated into two realms without believing that this dichotomy disturbs the unity of citizens' moral lives. The contractarian perspective commits the error of forming

> a plan of geographical morality, by which the duties of men, in public and private situations, are not to be governed by their relation to the great Governor of the Universe, or by their relations to mankind, but by climates, degrees of longitude, parallels, not of life, but of latitudes.[29]

If the states-system is an artefact superimposed upon a given international morality, the attempt to legitimise the division between the two moralities must be denied. The sovereign cannot simply be the trustee for those who have contracted together and who authorised him to promote their interests. Also drawing on the medieval legacy, Gentili argued

> what Plato and those expounders of the law say of private citizens we feel justified in applying to sovereigns and nations, since the rule which governs a private citizen in his own state ought to govern a public citizen, that is to say a sovereign or sovereign people, in this public and universal state formed by the world.[30]

There is a denial then of the rights of peoples to constitute themselves in the form of sovereign states with absolute rights against one another. Artificial boundaries between states create limitations within moral experience, whether apprehended or not.

Furthermore, a community cannot assume that the only important moral problems arise within rather than between states, and that international relations confront the community with problems of a merely pragmatic or technical order. On the contrary, moral universalism asserts that a person should be concerned to develop an 'all-encompassing sphere of cosmopolitan sentiment';[31] the moral self-consciousness of individuals and societies should develop to the point at which 'a violation of right in one place of the earth is felt all over it';[32] a violation of right anywhere in the world is not an isolated affair since it plays its part in determining the extent to which a civil society of mankind is made more or less possible. For any particular citizen, universal obligations can grant him the *prima facie* right of disobeying his state if its conduct of external relations exhibits its self-assertion as an autonomous moral entity; the citizen may also invoke the principle that outsiders have obligations to him, even to the point of assisting him against the actions of his own state. For any sovereign, universal obligations confront him with a 'double function',[33] that of promoting the welfare of his community while mindful of his role as cultivator of an enlarged, potentially universal moral community.

The performance of this role involves engaging in whatever forms of international cooperation may be needed in order to extend the boundaries of the moral constituency. Universalism challenges the state's particularistic basis which permits the creation of a civil society at the domestic level while international relations are abandoned to chance and left outside the sphere of binding legal and moral relations.

Cooperation at the international level should not be subject to calculations whereby more or less egotistical political entities determine how they are to satisfy the interests of their uniquely placed members. International cooperation is to be promoted not merely because it is fair that moral equals should respect one another's rights, but because it is only through cooperation that men can transform the political conditions of their existence, the constitutive principles of world political organisation which make up the international states-system itself.

Thus, while the internal concept of obligation regards the state as a conclusive association, the last product of the inalienable right of association belonging to those who wish to pursue their interests together, the external concept of obligation regards the state as a temporary association suspended between, for example, a supposed state of nature and a condition which would fully express the human capacity to develop more inclusive moral relations. Universalism denies that self-interest is the sole basis of social experiment. It is an anti-individualistic doctrine which highlights the human capacity for sociability (whether natural or otherwise) and the possibility of its indefinite extension.[34] The establishment of a state can only be a stage in a historical process which would culminate ideally in a society which embraced the entire society of mankind. As Fichte wrote:

> A small state of two or three persons, therefore, would be in contradiction with the concept of right. There is not perfect security – and perfect security that concept demands – possible in it. Nor is any such security possible in any absolutely limited state. A commonwealth which is to afford perfect security must embrace the whole globe, or at least, in order to be conformable to the concept of rights, must contain the possibility of uniting the whole of mankind.[35]

We can discern therefore two contrasting accounts of progress within the structure of the modern state. From one of these perspectives, progress is understood as a process internal to the state, as the enhancement of the conditions of civility; the internal point of view takes the postulates of international relations for granted. Therefore, to the extent that a concept of international progress exists, it is defined narrowly as the formation of international arrangements which will promote the interests of the state. Universalism, as an extension and modification of the medieval vision of international community, challenges the postulates of a world founded on the institution of sovereignty and defines progress as the creation of international structures designed to promote the welfare of all. The enhancement of the conditions of civility within the state is but one step within a much more broadly conceived historical process which culminates in the granting of political expression to the idea of humanity. For particularism, the state and the states-system are to be seen as a 'climax'; for universalism, they are simply the 'dominant' forms of modern political life.[36] One position holds that there is no need to consider ways in which the state might be incorporated within a larger association, just as the family and other associations have been accommodated and integrated within it. The state stands at the end of a chain of associations. For exponents of the competing perspective, states can realise their proper functions only by being included within a universal moral community. In a similar way, the Aristotelian imagined families readjusting their responsibilities and obligations in order to be integrated at a higher level, namely the village; and villages in turn reconstructing their place in the world of associations in order to be integrated within a more perfect political association, the *polis*. For universalists, there is a final stage in the process of associating, where men comprehend their separate political associations as the elements of a universal community, and so reach a condition in which their humanity is more perfectly expressed.

To conclude: modern societies have not been content to enact only internal concepts of obligation, and they have shown resistance to having their moral and political experience represented simply in the language of ethical particularism. Their members are responsive to the idea that by virtue of their humanity other men may have moral claims upon them. Obligations between the individual members of humanity are, for the most part, honoured through the mediation of the states to which they belong. As Hedley Bull has shown, the constitutive principles of the modern states-system are not uncritical of the belief that individuals have rights and duties to one another which may override their obligations as members of states. Furthermore, these principles are antagonistic to concepts of human obligation which threaten the existence of international order or seem capable of subverting its essential ingredients.[37]

The confusions of practical moral and political life find expression at the level of political theory. We have already noted the juxtaposition of rather different concepts of obligation in extracts from the writings of Rousseau, Hegel and Durkheim, and we have sought to describe the general traditions to which these different propositions belong. Divisions between our traditions of political theory are manifestations of much deeper divisions within our culture; they disclose a great deal that is imperfect in the structure of modern social and political life.

Part Two

From Rationalism to the Philosophy of History

Introduction to Part Two

We have paid particular attention above to the existence of that development whereby citizens dissolved their complete identification with their particularistic communities in accordance with their perception of themselves as men to whom important rights and duties are necessarily attached. Although modern citizens maintain an identification with their respective sovereign states, by depicting themselves as men they create the possibility of articulating general principles for the purpose of regulating their relations with each other. The last chapter aimed to clarify the difference between an international theory based simply upon a morality of citizenship and an alternative philosophical framework which seeks to incorporate the elements of a morality among men. We have observed that the modern state, and various diplomatic forums in modern times, provides a focal point for the expression of quite different moral claims arising from antagonistic conceptions of international society. With the emergence of an external account of obligation, the modern citizen's uncritical acceptance of the unqualified rights of the sovereign state, the division between a public and private ethic, and a pragmatic conception of interaction with outsiders becomes problematical. Accordingly, it is essential that a philosophy of international relations ought to explore the bases of these competing theories and moral claims in addition to executing the larger task of ascertaining the principles whereby the tension between men and citizens can be overcome.

The second part of this argument begins with the analysis of three approaches to the state and international relations which attempted a theoretical integration of two perspectives whose competing accounts of international society were described earlier: contractarianism and universalism. We shall examine the theories of Pufendorf (1632–94), Vattel

(1714–67) and Kant (1724–1804) in order to understand the way in which these perspectives were integrated in the classic writings of the modern states-system. What is especially striking about these approaches is the detailed attention they give to the problem of defending the sovereign state within a theory of international obligation. These three thinkers are comparatively rare among legal and political thinkers simply because they investigate assumptions about sovereign states usually taken for granted within other writings. Their intrinsic historical importance apart, these writings deserve discussion as a means of understanding the issues involved in attempting to proceed to construct a coherent political theory of international relations.

The first three chapters of part two discuss the existence of a dialectical development of thinking about international relations from the writings of Pufendorf to Vattel, and from Vattel to Kant. Each progresses beyond the other. Pufendorf begins with a defence of the primordial moral community of mankind but proceeds to justify a state-centred world. By employing ethical universalism as a basis for the idea of a society of states, Vattel overcomes several weaknesses inherent in Pufendorf's work. We shall find, however, that Vattel's theory of the sovereign state also fails to provide a coherent theory of the relationship between the moralities of men and citizens. Various inconsistencies within these earlier approaches are finally overcome in the Kantian theory of international relations.

The remaining chapters aim to defend two claims. The first is that the critique of rationalism makes it impossible to preserve the philosophical foundations of Kantian international political theory; the second is that the principal critics of rationalism within the historicist tradition also failed to supply an adequate, alternative basis for a theory of international society. Our critique of rationalism and historicism lays the groundwork for constructing that theory in conjunction with an analysis of the historical development of human freedom.

An acceptance of the fundamental principles of philosophical history is not a complete break with the elements of Kant's position, but a development of the form which Kantian rationalism was adopting in its later stages. Indeed, within a theory of history we can locate a more secure basis from which to defend those internationalist aspirations present in one form or another within each of the rationalist perspectives which we shall have examined. From an analysis of rationalism we derive new principles better fitted to execute its stated purposes.

4 Pufendorf's Theory of International Relations

> The collective egoism of particular associations raised into ethical categories. Such also is the morality of the state founded upon the theory of social contract. (Bakunin)

An international political theory considers two issues ignored by traditional philosophies of politics. It confronts the problem of the legitimacy of man's division into separate, sovereign states, and it examines the justification for the belief that obligations to the state are more fundamental than obligations to any wider society of men. These issues receive their earliest and most detailed consideration in Pufendorf's writings,[1] an interpretation of which is salient to the development of contemporary international theory in three respects. Firstly, it indicates the way in which the classic theory of the modern states-system made explicit one of the central tensions of Western culture; secondly, it reveals the failure of that account to resolve the opposition between two concepts of obligation; and thirdly it highlights the difficulties which contemporary international relations theorists face in their attempt to construct a modern theory of politics. Pufendorf's system can best be examined by distinguishing three parts: its description of the state of nature and the natural law which binds all individuals within it; its attempted justification of the sovereign state, of a civil society which unites only one part of humanity subject to a common moral framework; and its analysis of the types of behaviour which are appropriate within a system of states.

One of Pufendorf's few commentators states that he aimed to effect a 'compromise' between the theories of Grotius and Hobbes.[2] Pufendorf sought to preserve the notion of a universal law of reason while accounting for the state in essentially prudential terms. His theory begins by affirming the existence of various rights and duties, which have their foundation in human nature itself, and by rejecting forms of domination, such as slavery, which are incompatible with the natural equality of men.[3] Pufendorf's description of man's condition in the state of nature is consequently at variance with that provided by Hobbes. The former defends the existence of horizontal moral ties within international society and, therefore, criticises the citizens of those states which would enact only an internal concept of obligation. Pufendorf writes that

> even though some man may be unable to work me any benefit or harm and has in himself nothing for me to fear or desire, yet it is nature's will that even such a one be considered my kinsman and equal, and this reason alone, were there no others, lays upon the race of men the cultivation of a friendly society.[4]

Politics in the ancient world are condemned because

> most men had so completely forgotten the principle of the natural law, namely, that all men are related to each other by nature, and that it is wrong, therefore, for one to do violence to another except for some preceding offence, that it was generally believed the duties of humanity should be exercised only towards one's fellow-citizens, and that foreigners were no better than enemies, whom we could injure whenever it appeared to be to our advantage.[5]

The first stages of the argument suggest the development of an uncompromising critique of those exclusive vertical obligations which also exist within the modern states-system.

However, for Pufendorf, universal morality does not suffice to render human relations entirely harmonious. Human beings are rarely disposed to assist each other out of 'mere humanity and love', and prefer that assistance take the form of exchanges of equivalent benefits:[6]

> The duties thus far set forth derive their force from that common relationship which nature established among all

men even before any act was exchanged between them. But it is not enough to confine within such a circuit the duties which men owe each other. For not all men are so constituted that they are willing to do everything, with which they can help others, out of mere humanity and love, and without assuring themselves of some hope of receiving their equivalent; while it is often the case that the things which can come to us from others are of such a nature that we cannot have the boldness to ask that they be done for us gratis. It is often also not fitting for our person or lot that we be indebted to another for such a kindness, and so in many instances another person is unable to do us a kindness, and we are often unwilling to receive one, unless the other person receives its equivalent from us. Moreover, it often happens that other men do not know how they may serve our interests. Finally in view of the finite power of man being unable to extend itself to all persons at the same time and with the same force, it is surely reasonable that such actions as are not yet covenanted for by former obligations are bound over to those who, by agreements, have secured for themselves a prior right to them. And so, if mutual offices, the real fruit of humanity, are to be practised more frequently between men, and by a kind of set rule, it was necessary for men themselves to agree among themselves on the mutual rendering of such services as a man could not also be certain of for himself on the mere law of humanity. Therefore, it had to be determined beforehand what one should do for another, and what he should in his turn expect from another, and demand on his own right. This is, indeed, accomplished by promises and agreements.[7]

A deep sense of independence, which accounts for a reluctance to be placed in moral debt, also leads men to prefer reciprocal arrangements, and the ensuing duties of citizenship, to unconditional acts of benevolence. Pufendorf does not adopt Grotius's view that 'the very nature of man . . . even if we had no lack of anything would lead us into the mutual relations of society'.[8] When a man 'volutarily seeks civil society, it must be that he has had regard to some utility that he will derive from it for himself'.[9] Following Hobbes's political theory Pufendorf maintains that the concern for individual protection propels men to seek refuge in sovereignty. Both the insecurity of life in the state of nature and the futility of individual efforts to make life more secure combine to demonstrate the necessity of the state and the rationality of political obligation. In particular, the individual leaves the state of nature for the benefits of a condition where obligations are 'perfect' because they may be enforced ultimately by higher authority.[10] In common with Hobbes, Pufendorf states that

> the complaint of the masses about the burdens and drawbacks of civil states could be met in no better way than by picturing to their eyes the drawbacks of a state of nature. These are properly understood by those who have accepted as a proverb the saying: 'were there no courts of justice every man would devour his neighbour'.[11]

It may be noted then that Pufendorf's second series of statements about obligation discuss it in the language of pragmatism and prudence.

A search for the guarantees provided by sovereignty is uppermost in the minds of men when they contract to establish civil society. Faced with the 'great multitude of those to whom every right is worthless',[12] men cannot suppose that the natural law alone will enable them 'to live quite safely in natural liberty'.[13] Indeed, there is no hope of order, of 'continued agreement and concord in a great group of men, when there is no sovereignty', when there is an absence of legitimised coercion and perfect obligation.[14]

The deficiencies of the state of nature arise from the fact that:

> what we owe under the mere duty of humanity differs from what is owed by virtue of a compact or perfect promise especially in this respect, viz., that things of the former class are properly asked, and honourably performed; but when the other has failed of his own motion to perform, I can complain merely of his inhumanity, barbarity or harshness; but I cannot compel him to perform, by my force or that of a superior. This is my privilege however when he does not of

> himself perform what is due in accordance with a perfect promise or a compact. Hence we are said in the former case to have an imperfect right, in the latter, a perfect right, as also to be obligated imperfectly in one case, and perfectly in the other.[15]

Sovereignty is the indispensable foundation of social life since it transforms unenforceable obligations (morality) into enforceable ones (law). It is 'the most efficient cure' that men could discover for their ills; it is 'sacrosanct' since its establishment puts to an end 'the infinite miseries of the state of nature'.[16]

However, men must give ample consideration to a variety of circumstances which have an impact upon the contract they will eventually conclude.[17] The most important of these circumstances makes it impossible for men to seek security within a global political association. First of all 'in view of the finite power of man being unable to extend itself to all persons at the same time and with the same force' it is rational to enter into a contract to form a group within which particular men, one's fellow-citizens, are assigned 'prior' rights. Further, since a man cannot know how to advance the interests of all others, a compact is best confined to those with the kind of information about one another which facilitates the specification of determinate rights and obligations. A limited social contract is necessary since

> the numbers of the human race and the infinite multitude of transactions have not allowed men to unite into one body, forasmuch as that one body, in such huge dimensions, would be threatened through internal disturbances by the same inconveniences as those which exercise the human race, and almost greater ones, divided, as the race is, into a large number of smaller governments.[18]

International government would abolish inter-state wars only to be handicapped by civil ones. For these reasons the state 'is considered the most perfect society, and is that wherein is contained the greatest safety for mankind, now that it has grown so numerous'.[19]

The size and complexity of the human race compel men to

seek their security within a variety of political associations founded on the principle of reciprocity. The human race therefore divides as men superimpose a variety of contracts upon their original human community. Specific obligations of citizenship are superimposed upon diffuse obligations to humanity; vertical divisions confront horizontal ties. Although the principle of reciprocity leads a man to establish

> a special bond to some particular society, nevertheless, with all men, even those who live outside of that society, he should cultivate universal peace as far as they may allow him to, and he should exhibit the services of humanity which he can conveniently.[20]

The enterprise of constructing a commonwealth should proceed therefore with the intention of harmonising two requirements. Contractors must consider the most effective means of establishing a legal system with 'perfect' obligations among themselves while observing their primordial moral obligations to the wider society of men. The tension between these two requirements emerges clearly with the attempt to establish a political association which is economically and politically viable. Pufendorf maintains that 'want was neither the only nor even the main cause for the establishment of states' and points by way of illustration to those states which 'seek abroad the means to supply their needs or pleasure and yet ... do not feel it necessary to combine with those with whom they trade into one state'.[21] Legal bonds are qualitatively different from economic arrangements and unmistakably superior to them. Nevertheless, the central purpose of contractors may be thwarted if they are unable to establish a viable form of association. They must be concerned with the relative economic and political power of their association if they are to realise their goal of having the protection of a legal system. Pufendorf emphasises that

> the agreement of two or three cannot afford that sort of security against other men. For it is easy for so many to conspire to overthrow those few, that they can insure for themselves a perfectly certain victory over the others; and the hope of success and impunity will give them confidence

> for the attack. Therefore, to this end it is necessary for a considerable number of men to join together, that the addition of a few to the numbers of the enemy may not be of appreciable moment in helping them to victory.[22]

Pragmatic reasoning suggests that the 'just size of a state should be measured by the strength of its neighbours'.[23] Contractors must have considerable power at their disposal with the consequence that 'others afterwards may be induced to join them out of fear'.[24] Evidently the impossibility of establishing a global form of association appears to set in motion a chain of events with the outcome that obligations to outsiders matter less than the realisation of unconditional viability. The construction of the sovereign association is marked by a competition for power; the means of securing protection within the state appear to jeopardise the possibility of observing principles of natural law in relations with outsiders. The first of the major transitions in the move towards a world characterised by vertical divisions is a compromise rather than a synthesis.

A crucial feature of Pufendorf's contractarian approach is that citizens are able to define both their internal arrangements and the rights attached to their association without any form of coordination with outsiders. The fact that the state and its rights are established by a contract restricted to only part of the human race indicates most clearly the way in which Pufendorf compromises the Grotian foundations of his thought. The state is constructed by a three-part social contract.[25] Firstly, each man agrees that he 'is desirous of entering into a single and perpetual group, and of administering the considerations of their safety and security by common council and leadership'. Citizens then proceed to determine the nature of the government which will rule over them and finally confer authority upon a particular individual, so establishing the 'finished state'. The sovereign derives legitimacy from citizens alone and is conferred with those rights which citizens have chosen to surrender. The nature of the acquisition of sovereign rights has immediate and direct bearing upon relations with outsiders who remain in the state of nature *vis-a-vis* the established political association. Most fundamentally, 'just as a king owes his sovereignty and majesty to no one outside his realm, so he need not obtain the consent and approval of other kings or states, before he may carry himself like a king and be regarded as such'.[26] As non-citizens are uninvolved in the act of authorising the powers of the sovereign it would be an 'injury for the sovereignty of such a king to be called in question by a foreigner'.[27] The rights of sovereigns are not determined through a process involving the joint consent of the peoples of the world but are the products of independent compacts whereby citizens transfer their rights to their respective governments. A concern for structuring political life in accordance with obligations to humanity would suggest that a further social contract is required for the purposes of determining both the principles of international society and the rights and duties of political associations. Pufendorf, however, assumes that fellow-contractors, who are also fellow-citizens, may unilaterally establish the rights inherent in their political community. By virtue of this dubious step, Pufendorf is able to uphold the position that vertical divisions within international society indefinitely separate communities which are absolutely sovereign.

Pufendorf emphasises the importance of power to contractors aiming at the security of a legal system, but he does not recognise its implications for the development of his argument. Sovereignty is described as 'sacrosanct' because it allegedly ends 'the infinite miseries of the state of nature'. But this judgment is hasty and inconclusive, and Kant's decision to include Pufendorf among the 'miserable comforters' concerned with the law of nature is perfectly just.[28] Pufendorf acknowledges that the flight from the state of nature is the occasion for a competition for security through the amassment of power, and that it generates new reasons for fear, but he is remarkably imperceptive about the nature of this development in man's condition. He proceeds to affirm the rationality of the states-system without considering the likelihood that the miseries encountered in the transition from the natural to the civil condition will become permanent features of political life. The argument lacks Rousseau's insight that the various contracts to form political societies will bring a new and more terrible state of nature into existence.[29]

Indicative of Pufendorf's realism is his tendency not to

overlook or trivialise the competition inherent in the establishment of states and necessary to their existence. Within the argument there is explicit recognition of the limitations which man's concern for reciprocity places upon social and political organisation. But there is no awareness of the sovereign state's inability to eliminate the 'miseries of the state of nature' completely. The weakness of Pufendorf's argument becomes apparent when it is compared with Kant's statement:

> What avails it to labour at the arrangement of a Commonwealth as a civil constitution regulated by law among individual men? The same unsociableness which forced men to it, becomes again the cause of each Commonwealth assuming the attitude of uncontrolled freedom in its external relations, that is, as one state in relation to other states; and consequently, any one state must expect from another the same sort of evils as oppressed individual men and compelled them to enter into a Civil Constitution regulated by law.[30]

Pufendorf, by comparison, attempts to reconcile men both to their citizenship and the experience of living in a states-system without proposing any solution to the problems they will necessarily encounter. There is no recognition, as there is within Kant's philosophical history, that the state overcomes some of the problems of the original state of nature only to require supersession itself by some international arrangement capable of exercising control over its power.

It is evident that Pufendorf would have rejected the possibility that men might circumvent these problems by seeking protection through the immediate establishment of a global political association. What is less easy to discern from his writings are his reasons for excluding the possibility of future adjustments of the states-system in order to establish a form of world political organisation more able to satisfy human purposes and more compatible with man's natural obligations.

Arguably, Pufendorf's conception of the states-system cannot be fully comprehended without identifying the limits of his individualism and rationalism. Within the parameters of his natural law doctrine, the rationality of man's division into separate states seems problematical because it appears to compromise man's natural duties. Pufendorf does not overlook this aspect of the states-system as the following critical passage indicates:

> Now as for the further objection: 'If man loved man in the course of nature, that is, as man, no reason could be given why each single individual should not love each other single individual, as being equally a man, or why he should the rather frequent those in whose society honour and advantage are accorded him beyond others.' To meet this it should be known that all men, indeed, have been brought together by the similarity of their nature . . . Now, in truth, a number of circumstances are added to that common nature which are responsible for one loving this one more than that one; suppose, for example, that there was between them a greater harmony of dispositions in regard to special inclinations, or else that their birthplaces were not far apart. But then and only then could no reason be given, if all men had grown out of the earth together like fungi, without any relationship to one another, or if they had among one another a similarity of dispositions at every point. But such a state of men has never existed, so no conclusion can be drawn from supposing it, contrary to what the actual facts show.[31]

Indeed, for Pufendorf, a state of nature comprising solitary individuals 'never actually existed' and mankind was at first 'divided into different family groups' which later established states.[32] Men have therefore always been differentiated by their membership of distinct societies; they did not grow 'from the earth together like fungi'. From this point of view the states-system acquires rather different features from those identified by a rationalist style of argument. It is not the most that men can accomplish if their natural capacity and tendency to associate within a global political structure is currently frustrated. Man's political division is made necessary by the absence of a consensus about the rights and duties which would enter into the constitution of a world political organisation. And although Pufendorf states that the natural law itself is insufficiently precise to allow men 'to deduce from that one source all that men were entitled to receive to advantage from one another', there is a suggestion that the cultural values employed in different societies to interpret that law is one major source of their difficulty.[33] Accordingly the states-system is superimposed upon existing vertical divisions of a social or cultural character and its rationality stems in part from its capacity to give expression to the profound fact of human diversity.

Pufendorf appears to believe that the diverse characteristics of men should find expression in the fragmentation of mankind into several civil societies. Men have the right to choose the societies to which they will belong:

> Such societies nature has altogether wished to have among men, although it has been left within the free choice of men, and so is to be determined by pacts, just what individuals are to be united to what society, or who is to be set at their head for governing them.[34]

But their freedom of association does not exclude obligations to the wider society of men, although it may well qualify them. Pufendorf maintains that:

> definite individuals unite to form a definite kind of society . . . either in consequence of a special harmony of dispositions or of other qualities, or else because they imagine that they can obtain some special end better with these persons than with those. Now it is by no means necessary for all men to coalesce into one society in which all are equal to one another; but it is sufficient if the same persons get together in several and distinct groups, which are, nevertheless, by no means altogether mutually unsociable, but refrain from unjust injuries towards one another, and, as far as they are permitted by closer obligations, share with one another their advantages and blessing.[35]

Belief in the existence of obligations to humanity remains, therefore, too important a part of Pufendorf's argument.

It may appear unfair to assert that because of this belief the states-system should have seemed defective to Pufendorf in a second way; that it should have appeared as an intermediate form of political organisation poised between man's original condition, where he could not safely enact his natural obligations, and a future international arrangement where the rights and duties of humanity were formulated and implemented universally; that against this moral background the states-system was a partial realisation of the human capacity to specify determinate rights and duties in accordance with the natural law; that it was merely an imperfect expression of rationality. But Pufendorf's theory of international relations cannot be excused simply on the grounds that he was attempting to reconcile social differentiation with man's ability to identify and sympathise with others of his species. Ultimately, Pufendorf's failure to characterise the states-system in the above ways is a function of his decision to allow the Hobbesian dimension of his thought to become predominant.

Morality does not exist alone, but competes with man's concern for his ineluctable self-esteem and with his natural preference for grounding relationships upon a principle of mutual self-interest. In his discussion of human motivation Pufendorf maintains that man both 'loves himself and his interests to the utmost degree' and assesses the value of institutions with regard for his perception of their 'utility'.[36] Underlying the decision to enter into a contract is the consideration that 'whatever I have done with another man in agreements, I have done not so much for his advantage as for my own'.[37] Pufendorf's willingness to endorse this form of prudential reasoning renders both the compromise between the Hobbesian and Grotian elements of his thought, and the belief that services of humanity should survive man's division into sovereign states, somewhat suspect. Relations between states become problematical given the conviction that the states-system is superimposed upon horizontal moral ties. Conversely, an unreserved defence of the states-system presumes either that these ties do not exist or that they may be outweighed by man's more important concern for his own interest. Pufendorf hesitates to adopt the former position but his acceptance of the second line of argument has the same consequences. It leads to the point at which Pufendorf advances a criticism of the Greek city-state's conduct while subverting that criticism's basis. Only Pufendorf's willingness to privilege the Hobbesian element in his thought can account for the manner in which he characterises the state and its international relations.

Vertical divisions between sovereign associations arise from contractors' self-regarding concern with the viability of their associations. Once they have acquired the economic and political conditions which are favourable to the maintenance of their legal system they appear to wish to minimise unrewarding connections with, or obligations to, outsiders, and sovereignty is the instrument at their disposal. Self-interested reasoning informs their attitude to their external relations and is clearly exemplified in their assessment of the value of international law and cooperation. Legal obligations between sovereign associations are not 'perfect'; international law is merely a law of coordination between states, and for Pufendorf not law properly so-called. To understand treaties as legally binding is to 'confuse a law with a pact'.[38] It is to overlook the fact that agreements can be revoked by states unilaterally and with unqualified right since

> they have been established by the special order of the individual legislators in the individual states, and so can be changed by one people without consulting others, and are frequently found to have been so changed.[39]

The same principle applies to particular pacts to form inter-state associations which Pufendorf names 'systems of states'.[40] A system exists where several states are 'so held together by some special and strict bond that they appear to form one body'. This condition may arise because individual states are governed, albeit temporarily, by a common king. But on his death 'there returns at once to each of the peoples the right to decide as it will on its own form of government' and to exercise this right 'without consulting the others'. A second type of system exists where various political associations have agreed to cooperate because they 'wished to preserve their autonomy and yet had not sufficient strength to repel their common enemies'. In this form of association, states attempt to proceed by common consent and may establish a 'permanent council' to conduct relations with outsiders. Nevertheless, the Hobbesian moment is uppermost in the minds of 'confederates'. Thus the institution is constrained by the constitutive principle of world politics which maintains that

> the liberty of a state, which is nothing other than the power to decide on its own judgment about matters pertaining to its own self-preservation, is unintelligible in case it can be forced by another, acting with authority, to undertake something against its will.

By implication, no state can be compelled to remain within the association when its utilitarian calculation suggests it may receive greater 'advantage from separation than from union' and when it views its allies as 'more of a burden than an assistance'.

This conception of the sovereign state is the necessary outcome of earlier illegitimate transitions in Pufendorf's argument. Despite the initial stages of the argument with their emphasis upon the natural moral ties which cut across man's division into separate societies Pufendorf's principal theoretical conclusions support the priority of obligations which centre around the sovereign political association. Accordingly, Pufendorf's discussion of the morality of the private citizen and his sovereign representative manifests the dissolution of this horizontal type of morality and its replacement by one which is unambiguously state-centred. The importance of the state requires that the sovereign should act from the conviction that 'the welfare of the people is the supreme law';[41] it also demands that the citizen adopt the view that his

> duty towards the whole state is to have nothing dearer than its welfare and safety, to offer his life, property and fortunes freely for its preservation; to exert all the strength of his mind and industry to add to its fame and promote its interests.[42]

In a further expression of the dissolution of natural obligations Pufendorf observes that

> the height of mortal achievement has been attained, when security rests upon the strength of the entire state, and where one recognises no man on earth to be his superior.[43]

With the conclusion that the state rather than the natural law should be central in determining human conduct the substitution of vertical divisions for horizontal ties, the morality of citizenship for the morality of men, is complete.

This substitution is tantamount to the assertion that the state and not the individual is the fundamental personality in world politics. Pufendorf's characterisation of the state is clearly incompatible with the principle that contractors were

> still subject to the natural law, and so were obligated, of course, to draw up only such rules of sovereignty and civil obedience as were agreeable to that law and to the lawful ends of states.[44]

The law of nature may be relatively imprecise but its proper application to the determination of the principles of international society would tend to support the argument that the individual retains particular rights, which the international community may defend, against his state, while the sovereign retains particular obligations to other political societies. The subversion of the Grotian dimension of Pufendorf's thought undermines an alternative political condition where

> the rights of each man can be asserted on the world political stage over and against the claims of his state, and his duties proclaimed irrespective of his position as a servant or citizen of that state.

If these are taken seriously

> then the position of the state as a body sovereign over its citizens, and entitled to command obedience, has been subject to challenge, and the structure of the society of sovereign states has been placed in jeopardy. The way is left open for the subversion of the society of sovereign states on behalf of the alternative organising principle of a cosmopolitan community.[45]

The tension between the Hobbesian and Grotian components of Pufendorf's thought is ultimately a tension between two incompatible visions of world order, or between an internal and an external theory of obligation. Pufendorf succeeds in showing that one of these visions of world order cannot take the form of a cosmopolitical community. But what his premises forbid him to argue is that a world of separate political systems must therefore be a world of self-interested sovereign states. Since these political systems are supposedly superimposed upon a pre-existing moral community, the single most fundamental deficiency of Pufendorf's theory is its failure to construct a philosophy of world political organisation which seeks to give institutional expression to man's horizontal ties. The theory cannot perform this task since it allows contractors to determine the rights inherent in their political association. Contractors privately appropriate a decision-making process which should involve the whole of humanity. And thereby the theory presupposes what it requires to establish, the legitimacy of the sovereign association and the rationality of the division of mankind into separate sovereign states.

ADDENDUM

It is a curious feature of the contractarian tradition that those of its thinkers who argued that the state of nature contained some semblance of moral community should prove so negligent in discussing the transitions from that original condition to a world of structured political life. The transitions within Pufendorf's argument are susceptible to that critique of contractarianism suggested by Filmer.[46] The particular areas of vulnerability within Pufendorf's thought are those areas of transition which aim to justify the substitution of horizontal ties with allegedly more fundamental and compelling vertical obligations. To provide a satisfactory account of the structure of international society Pufendorf's theory would require a mechanism for the expression of universal consent to the principles of international relations. Without it Pufendorf's argument simply perpetuates the moral tensions within Western thought.

A discussion of the contemporary relevance of Pufendorf's thought may begin by stating that the need to resolve the conflict between the vertical and the horizontal, between two conceptions of obligation, and between antagonistic theories of world order, continues to be overlooked by traditional political theorists. Rawls, having introduced the broader issue of how separate societies should be related to one another, is the clearest example of a contemporary writer who repeats some of Pufendorf's arbitrary transitions.[47] His theory may appear as a substantial improvement upon the argument advanced by Pufendorf. Most noticeably it makes the important separation between the social contract which constitutes government and the contract which establishes the principles of international society. Nevertheless, this innovation is ultimately less important in assessing the degree of progress beyond Pufendorf's system than Rawls' similar examples of arbitrariness. Barry states that

> Rawls does not and cannot defend the assumption that principles will be chosen in the original position by men as members of pre-existing societies rather than by men as men who may wish to form sovereign states or may wish to set up an overriding state.[48]

Pufendorf understood the necessity of explaining why men would make certain divisions amongst themselves prior to selecting their principles of government; Rawls simply assumes that 'the community already exists and its members have merely forgotten various things about its character and their place within it', thus introducing 'an arbitrary move that cannot be defended within the theory'.[49] However, Rawls, having introduced the idea that the principles of international society would be selected by the representatives of separate societies behind a veil of ignorance, produces a list which presupposes the legitimacy of the sovereign state and the rationality of the states-system. This list, which on Rawls' admission contains 'no surprises', includes the principles of the equal liberty of states, the right of self-determination, the duty of non-intervention in the internal affairs of other states, the right of forming defensive alliances and the principle *pacta sunt servanda*.[50] It is not evident that contractors would opt for these principles unless it is presumed they already accept the legitimacy of sovereign states. Rawls makes a transition from the division of humanity into separate societies to the allegedly corresponding division into a world of separate sovereign associations. It may be said of Rawls as of Pufendorf that the constitutive principles of such a world 'are no more than a fraction of what would be agreed upon, if indeed they would not be superseded altogether'.[51] Interestingly, Rawls does not make use of the principles of justice as a foundation for an alternative account of world political organisation; more revealingly, the absence of any significant progress in the development of international relations theory is manifested in the fact that some of the more vulnerable stages of Pufendorf's argument re-appear within Rawls' system.

5 Vattel's Society of States

> It will perhaps be said that society is so formed that every man gains by serving the rest. That would be all very well, if he did not gain still more by injuring them. (Rousseau)

Pufendorf argued that it was impossible for men to construct now or in the future a universal society adequate to their higher conceptions of natural law. Self-regarding conduct, the primordial fact of social diversity, the inalienable right of free association and the sheer size of the human race itself contributed to making a universal civil society impossible. All men could not be brought together within a single society with the authority to make determinate and secure their common natural rights and duties.

But if there cannot be an inter-individual morality, enacted within a cosmopolitan society, there might at least be the possibility of establishing a society of states. Pufendorf acknowledged the fact that states owe obligations to one another as equally free associations, but the developments to which this idea gives rise are not systematically elaborated within his theory. Its tolerance of the egocentric sovereign state, responsible to the interests of its citizens, and its defence of the discretionary rights present within sovereignty itself, lead to the dissolution of the moral framework of international society. The importance of Vattel is that, using similar resources to those employed by Pufendorf, he aims to defend the moral obligations which all states ought to honour as members of 'the natural society of nations'.[1] As equals, Vattel writes, sovereign states have obligations to preserve the natural order of the society of states, and to assist one another to become more perfect. This alone is an important and necessary step beyond the theory of Pufendorf. The issue here, however, is whether or not the notion of a society of states is capable of effecting a reconciliation between the moralities of men and citizens. To what extent does this perspective blend universalism and contractarianism in such a way as to eliminate the conflict between the internal and external concepts of obligation?

Vattel's theory closely resembles Pufendorf's in several respects, but particularly by operating with an individualistic theory of the state, or an ascending concept of government. It also begins with an original state of nature in which individuals can neither live safely nor perfect themselves. The legitimacy of the state, therefore, has a utilitarian basis; it does what individuals cannot do by themselves. Further, Vattel agrees with Pufendorf that there is not the same necessity for a universal society as for the conclusion of a compact which establishes the state:

> It is true that men, seeing that the Laws of Nature were not being voluntarily observed, have had recourse to political association as the one remedy against the degeneracy of the majority, as the one means of protecting the good and restraining the wicked; and the natural law itself approves of such a course. But it is clear that there is by no means the same necessity for a civil society among Nations as among individuals. It cannot be said, therefore, that nature recommends it to an equal degree, far less that it prescribes it. Individuals are so constituted that they could accomplish but little by themselves and could scarcely get on without the assistance of civil society and its laws. But as soon as a sufficient number have united under a government, they are able to provide for most of their needs, and they find the help of other political societies not so necessary to them as the State itself is to individuals.[2]

In addition, Vattel clearly believed, as did Pufendorf, that states are sub-divisions of the human race, and that their members are united together by virtue of their common moral obligations:

> Since the universal society of the human race is an institution of nature, itself, that is, a necessary result of man's nature, all men of whatever condition are bound to advance

> its interests and to fulfil its duties. No convention or special agreement can release them from the obligation. When, therefore, men unite in civil society and form a separate State or Nation, they may, indeed make particular agreements with others of the same State, but their duties towards the rest of the human race remain unchanged; but with this difference, that when men have agreed to act in common, and have given up their rights and have submitted their will to the whole body as far as concerns their common good, it devolves thenceforth upon that body, the State, and upon its rulers, to fulfil the duties of humanity towards outsiders in all matters in which individuals are no longer at liberty to act, and it peculiarly rests with the State to fulfil these duties towards other States.[3]

As a rationalist, Vattel restated the existence of two loyalties, two realms of obligation. Once again, the problem arose of reconciling duties to the state with duties to humanity, a problem which could be solved if states regarded one another as equal members of an international society.

Both Pufendorf and Vattel held that all men were moral equals, and that no man had the right to claim for himself that which he would refuse others.[4] This principle of human equality was grounded in natural, pre-contractual obligations. The state is a legitimate political association established by a group of men wishing to improve their condition. And, since the right to conclude a contract is an inherent right of every man, it followed that each state had the duty to treat all others as its equals, and to assist them wherever possible to promote their individual ends. What Pufendorf had failed to develop systematically, Vattel emphatically asserts. In a famous passage, Vattel writes that:

> Since men are by nature equal, and their individual rights and obligations the same, as coming equally from nature, Nations, which are composed of men and may be regarded as so many free persons living together in a state of nature, are by nature equal and hold from nature the same obligations and the same rights. Strength or weakness in this case counts for nothing. A dwarf is as much a man as a giant is; a small republic is no less a sovereign State than the

most powerful kingdom. From this equality it necessarily follows that what is lawful or unlawful for one Nation is equally lawful or unlawful for every other Nation.[5]

There are various means by which the members of a natural society of nations can assist one another in matters relating to their political independence and economic viability. Should a nation be 'suffering from famine, all those who have provisions to spare should assist it in its need'.[6] States ought to be prepared to protect each other's natural independence, and therefore the structure of international society itself, from the encroachments of any aggressive power. Therefore,

> if a Nation were to make open profession of treading justice under foot by despising and violating the rights of another whenever it had an opportunity of doing so, the safety of the human society at large would warrant all the other Nations in uniting together to subdue and punish such a Nation.[7]

Unlike Pufendorf, Vattel cannot condone the actions of egocentric sovereign states; and he refuses to do so because of his powerful attachment to the principle of a natural society of free and independent states which each community is obliged to preserve and enhance.

The fundamental principles of Vattel's international theory require that substantial limitations be placed not upon sovereignty itself but upon its exercise. International society should be composed of sovereign entities, legally free to determine their own conduct, but constrained nevertheless by their own awareness of moral obligations. Vattel's vision is of an 'anarchical society' in which states enact these fundamental obligations of their own free will.[8] Vattel claims that:

> A Nation must, therefore, render to others what is due to them, leave them in the peaceful enjoyment of their rights, repair any harm caused or injury done to any of them by itself, render them just satisfaction for any injury that cannot be repaired, and give them reasonable securities where they have had just grounds of fear as to what the Nation might do.[9]

But if the moral law is to be properly binding it would appear irrational, as Kant later observed, to defend the liberty of states in these matters. A more complete perspective would entail arguing that states ought to have recourse to international adjudication to settle disputes between themselves; and that, ultimately, states should be incorporated within international structures with responsibility, for example, for the goal of world distributive justice. But Vattel does not argue for a move beyond the international states-system so that natural obligations may be enforced among states, just as they are among the individual members of a particular political society. All of the major distinguishing features of Vattel's position stem from his belief that the natural morality which survives the division of mankind into sovereign states will be enacted only at their discretion. It is at this point of his thought, moreover, in his attempt to balance sovereignty and international obligation, that we can locate the source of Vattel's failure to provide that coherent form of international political theory for which we are searching.

To comprehend Vattel's doctrine we must first understand his use of the idea of imperfect obligation. Obligations between states are merely imperfect; prior to the intervention of consent they cannot be enforced. A right is

> always imperfect when the corresponding obligation depends upon the judgment of him who owes it; for if he could be constrained in such a case he would cease to have the right of deciding what are his obligations according to the law of conscience. Our obligations to others are always imperfect when the decision as to how we are to act rests with us, as it does in all matters where we ought to be free.[10]

The concept of an imperfect obligation, so vital to Vattel's thought, immediately weakens the moral framework which holds together the natural society of nations. Vattel argues that a nation in the throes of famine may request aid from others, but it cannot compel the granting of aid without undermining the freedom of those associations into which the human race is naturally divided. Assistance is an option which must be retained by any potential donor. It would not be an 'injury' or an 'act of aggression' to refuse aid; but it would be an injury to compel others to provide it.[11] Imperfect obligations may be transformed into perfect enforceable obligations only by the consent of states. By this process alone can one state grant another a perfect right to receive assistance; and only under these circumstances may a state be compelled by another signatory to honour the obligation expressed in the treaty between them.

Vattel believed that each state should recognise the others' rights to determine whether or not to transform imperfect into perfect obligations. Each state should value its own liberty and respect that of its neighbours, the ensuing condition being preferable to one in which states could compel one another to assist in their perfection. In that alternative condition, states would be in constant danger of war; their concern for receiving justice from one another would represent a continual threat to international order. And, as we have seen, Vattel rejected any international authority with the power to compel states to enact their natural obligations, a condition which threatened individual and collective freedom.

This particular vision of international society is one in which states promote each other's welfare as far as possible within a form of world political organisation based upon respect for the sovereignty of all. Thus far, it may seem little different from Pufendorf's theory of the international states-system. However, Vattel wields the notion of a natural society of nations in order to criticise the egocentric state which would ignore international obligations at will, or violate the rights of others whenever it chooses. Vattel's defence of international obligations, even imperfect ones, is so powerful that he will argue that any policy which places trivial advantages for the state before major benefits for world order must always be wrong:

> We know that, in general, duties toward self prevail over duties towards others; but this is only to be understood of duties which bear some proportion to one another . . . What idea should we have of a prince, or of a Nation, who would refuse to yield the smallest advantage in order to gain for the world the inestimable blessing of peace?[12]

And, in this respect at least, Vattel's system is more internally coherent and genuinely universalist than Pufendorf's.

Nevertheless, we must discover some explanation for Vattel's similarly state-centred international theory. Although we cannot underestimate the importance of the principle of proportionality, which each state must observe by virtue of its membership of the society of nations, it is the defence of the liberty of nations which is the keystone of Vattel's doctrine and the basis of his early fame. The following passage is crucial to the understanding of his system:

> In consequence of that liberty and independence, it follows that it is for each Nation to decide what its conscience demands of it, what it can or cannot do; what it thinks well or does not think well to do; and therefore it is for each Nation to consider and determine what duties it can fulfil towards others without failing in its duty towards itself. Hence in all cases in which it belongs to a Nation to judge of the extent of its duty, no other Nation may force it to act one way or another. Any attempt to do so would be an encroachment upon the liberty of Nations.[13]

To an important extent, an explanation of the pronounced state-libertarianism of Vattel's doctrine need look no further than his use of an ascending conception of government. From this perspective, no man can be subjected to political authority without his prior consent. Each man has the inalienable right to perfect himself, and to associate with others in order to improve his condition; but it must be his own act of deliberation which finally commits him to entering civil society. The remainder of humanity has no right to prevent a man from entering the civil society of his choice, or to interfere with the form of constitution which a people wishes to adopt. Furthermore, once the constitution of the state has been determined, no other state can have the right to impose its will upon it. Each state is the product of the natural right of free association; each state has particular responsibilities to those who wish to belong together. As a consequence of their separate contracts, states possess a natural freedom in relation to one another which is analogous to the condition enjoyed by individuals in the original state of nature. Since a group of individuals have an absolute right to form an association together, their sovereignty, the very basis of their association, will be imperfect if they can be compelled as of right to perform actions desired by others. Their contract establishes a form of ethical particularism, albeit one which is responsive to the existence of the independent interests of other associations. While states do have duties to one another, it is fundamental to the principles of their association that they pay particular attention to the interests of their members. Vattel has no urge to instruct men 'to learn how not to be good'.[14] It is his wish that states respect obligations to others as their equals; but since the state must be responsible for its own welfare first, it always has to measure the extent to which it can honour obligations to outsiders against this fundamental standard:

> If the rights of a Nation are derived from its obligations they are chiefly derived from those which the Nation owes to itself. We shall likewise see that its duties towards others mainly depend upon, and should be regulated and measured by, its duties towards itself.[15]

However, the contractual basis of political association in the theories of Pufendorf and Vattel suggests the existence of a deeper problem in human life. It is the uncertainty attached to the natural law which makes it necessary for men to establish amongst themselves the precise content of the rights and duties which bind them together. The social contract not only makes certain rights and duties enforceable; it makes them determinate; it solves the problem of their content. Undeniably, a form of ethical scepticism, less pronounced than those current since Hume, exists thinly disguised within the contractarian approaches of Pufendorf and Vattel. And, if we need to have recourse to this concept to find a deeper explanation of the reasons for states, so we need to recall it in order to understand Vattel's radical state-libertarianism.

Vattel's dissolution of the moral framework of international society (his 'subjectivising' of the natural law by allowing every state the liberty of deciding what it can or cannot do) rests on rather different assumptions from those held by Pufendorf. Vattel does not wish to press the essentially self-interested dimension of human conduct or the unwillingness of men to perform obligations without the expectation of some equivalent benefit in return. It is the prospect of an objective morality being used to subvert the liberty of nations which is his most pronounced concern. Such a morality might be employed to justify intervention in another state's affairs or to subordinate the state to an imperialistic power or the Papacy.[16] The division of humanity into separate sovereign states was not simply the consequence of the impossibility of administering a world-wide political association. More positively, and here Vattel is in agreement with Kant and Gibbon, the division of men into states is held to be one of the preconditions of human freedom.[17] Because of this belief, Vattel advocated acceptance of the natural society of nations and held that freedom was not compatible with states judging one another's conduct or punishing one another in accordance with the ethical imperatives of some allegedly ascertainable universal morality. The natural society of nations and ethical scepticism therefore go hand in hand; state sovereignty and ethical subjectivism are two sides of the same coin.

When Vattel's more emphatic versions of this theme are pressed to their most likely conclusions, the very notion of an international morality is itself subverted:

> When differences arise each Nation in fact claims to have justice on its side, and neither of the interested parties nor other Nations may decide the question. The one who is actually in the wrong sins against its conscience; but as it may possibly be in the right, it cannot be accused of violating the law of the society of Nations.[18]

Here, the liberty of the state is clearly a consequence of an absence of consensus about international ethical standards. Although this inclines towards some form of realpolitik which Vattel had no desire to embrace, the tensions within his thought become even more profound. What Vattel also proposed was that state sovereignty or state-libertarianism was not simply the outcome of an absence of an international ethical consensus, but morality's very core:

> The liberty of a Nation would not remain complete if other Nations presumed to inspect and control its conduct; a presumption which would be contrary to the natural law, which declares every Nation free and independent of all other Nations.[19]

Three incompatible perspectives can be discerned within Vattel's theory; firstly, the doctrine that states, albeit sovereign, are bound both to preserve the welfare of that society from which they have seceded and to continue to enact those natural obligations whose subjects previously were individuals; secondly, that disputes over the content of those natural obligations make it preferable that each independent state should determine how it will behave, but always with respect for a principle of proportionality; and lastly the doctrine that international morality itself prescribes state-libertarianism, or endows states with a considerable range of discretion in the conduct of their external affairs. These different perspectives cannot be accommodated within a single theory. Their juxtaposition reveals, however, that Vattel has contradicted his original purpose. Vattel is committed to arguing that, as members of the natural society of the human race, states have the duty of not enforcing those horizontal moral ties which had preceded their establishment; and they must not comply rigorously with those natural duties because to do so would jeopardise the more substantial principle of social and political freedom. Duties among citizens are ultimately more important than duties among men.

Clearly, for Vattel no state has the entitlement of violating another state's right to a free existence. But under those circumstances in which a state faces a choice between harming another or suffering some substantial injury itself, it will have little choice but to promote its own interests. Although a state has the duty to preserve the natural society of states, it is by no means certain that it can respect the equality and independence of all. Vattel's concern with this problem, and it is a genuine concern which reveals both his internationalism and his progress beyond Pufendorf's system, leads him to defend the institution of the balance of power. International equilibrium is understood to be the practice which harmonises duties to the state with obligations to humanity.

Vattel writes:

> We are here presented with a celebrated question which is of the greatest importance. It is asked whether the aggrandisement of a neighbouring State, in consequence of which a Nation fears that it will one day be oppressed, is a sufficient ground for making war upon it; whether a Nation can with justice take up arms to resist the growing power of that State, or to weaken the State, with the sole object of protecting itself from the dangers with which weak States are almost always threatened from an overpowerful one. The question presents no difficulty to the majority of statesmen; it is more perplexing for those who seek at all times to unite justice with prudence.[20]

Vattel's solution is that a state confronting such a nation is 'justified in forestalling a danger in direct ratio to the degree of probability attending it, and to the seriousness of the evil with which [it] is threatened'.[21] It cannot resist exercising its power without running the risk that it will delay 'averting [its] destruction until it has become inevitable';[22] and this the sovereign as guardian cannot do 'out of magnanimity and generosity'. But neither can the sovereign use 'means that are contrary to justice and honour' on the grounds that 'the welfare of the people is the supreme law of the state'.[23] There are, however, 'gentler means, which are always lawful. The most efficacious of these is an alliance of other less powerful sovereigns, who, by uniting their forces, are enabled to counterbalance the sovereign who excites their alarm'.[24]

Vattel imagines a voluntaristic international order in which free states collaborate to preserve their natural freedom. Moreover, it is in the Europe of his day that Vattel perceives the operation of that system of equilibrium which most conforms to his celebrated notion of a society of states:

> Europe forms a political system in which the Nations inhabiting this part of the world are bound together by their relations and various interests into a single body. It is no longer, as in former times, a confused heap of detached parts, each of which had but little concern for the lot of others, and rarely troubled itself over what did not im-

> mediately affect it. The constant attention of sovereigns to all that goes on, the custom of resident ministers, the continual negotiations that take place, make modern Europe a sort of republic, whose members – each independent, but all bound together by a common interest – unite for the maintenance of order and the preservation of liberty. This is what has given rise to the well-known principle of the balance of power, by which is meant an arrangement of affairs so that no State shall be in a position to have absolute mastery and dominate over the others.[25]

For Vattel the balance of power is an instrument for preserving the liberty and equality of separate states while maintaining an order among them. He does not characterise it as a consequence of the actions of a separate, egotistical association attempting to reach a condition of preponderant power only to be thwarted in its efforts by the responses of others. As Hinsley has argued, the balance of power was not understood as an essential part of any international system 'in which egotism was limited by nothing but consideration of egotism'.[26] Vattel belonged to a group of thinkers who 'assumed that the relations between those states were moderated by the recognition that they were members of a common civilisation, no less than by expediency'.[27] Through the operations of the balance of power states could promote their various interests while preserving the fundamental value of the civilisation to which they belonged, liberty.

What is particularly prominent in this defence of the balance of power is the belief that it combined, better than any other arrangement, justice and prudence. Particular regard was shown for England

> whose wealth and powerful navy have given her a very great influence, without, however, causing any state to fear for its liberty, since that power appears to be cured of the spirit of conquest – England, I say, has the honour to hold in her hands the political scales. She is careful to maintain them in equilibrium.[28]

A state which acts to uphold the balance of power, even where it has no immediate interest at stake, safeguards the liberty of others, enacts its duty to preserve the natural liberty of all and maintains an environment in which other states are likely to come to its aid should it be the victim of aggression at a later stage. Indeed, 'if all sovereigns were constantly aware of their true interests',[29] they would be prepared to preserve the international balance at all times, for it is only in this way that they can reconcile their obligations to themselves with their obligations to outsiders:

> Thus, when a neighbouring State is attacked unjustly by a powerful enemy which threatens to crush it, if you can defend it without exposing yourself to great danger there is no question but that you should do so. Do not raise the objection that a sovereign has not the right to expose the life of his soldiers for the safety of a foreign Nation with which he has not contracted a defensive alliance. He may happen to have like need of help; and therefore by putting into force the spirit of mutual assistance he is promoting the safety of his own Nation. Statecraft thus goes hand in hand with obligation and duty, for princes have an interest in checking the advance of an ambitious ruler who seeks to increase his power by subduing his neighbours.[30]

Enlightened self-interest would enable sovereigns to operate the balance of power in a way which effected a remarkable synthesis of prudence and justice, of duties to men and duties to fellow-citizens. Who, indeed, would do less than celebrate any international arrangement capable of eliminating the timeless conflict between duty and self-interest? But it seems that Vattel is too sanguine when he imputes such an alchemic function to the balance of power. Experience has taught that statecraft is more complex than this. The balance of power is not necessarily capable of reconciling an international order, based upon the liberty of states, with the equal freedom of each of them; recourse to intervention is merely one of the instruments by which this synthesis of order and justice may be easily fragmented.[31]

We cannot counter these remarks by invoking Vattel's desire for a more sociable international system than that within which the balance of power has been situated in more modern periods. While Vattel's universalism cannot be denied, the more powerful component of his doctrine is the principle that the state must always be judge of the extent to which it can honour its imperfect international obligations. In an environment in which the commitment of others to a common objective cannot be assumed, a state must always be tempted to promote its own interests rather than those of others, lest in performing its obligations to outsiders its own position is seriously and irredeemably damaged; it is the generalised condition of insecurity which demands that it be so. For this reason Rousseau's famous parable is particularly telling. Why should a man cooperate with five others to capture a stag when through his own efforts he can capture a hare – not because the interests of others are of no concern to him but because each of the others is at liberty to do the same?[32] It is this form of insecurity, essentially related to the liberty of states, which most damages the prospect of harmonising obligations to fellow-citizens and fellow-men. What Rousseau's parable underlines is the inevitable imposition of particular uncertainties and calculations likely to destroy that very sociability which Vattel regarded as critical for the maintenance of international order, uncertainties which make it unlikely that the freedom of each state can be compatible with the freedom of all. Natural liberty and sociability appear as competing or opposing elements rather than as the dual foundations of a stable and enduring international order.

It is not surprising that Vattel should have found favour in the contemporary world at a time when the freedom of states from the imposition of the ideologies of other powers is widely agreed to be a necessary condition for the maintenance of order. Hedley Bull's argument that in an ideologically diverse world, order must have priority over justice, (since the pursuit of competing theories of justice would undermine order) has its roots in Vattel's theory of international relations.[33] Bull credits Vattel with having helped to establish the 'pluralist' as opposed to the 'solidarist' approach to international society.[34] In opposition to the Grotian or 'solidarist' approach, the 'pluralists' maintained that states

> are capable of agreeing only for certain minimum purposes which fall short of that of the enforcement of law. In the

> view it takes of the area of actual or potential agreement among the member states of international society it may be called pluralist where the Grotian doctrine is solidarist; and the rules it prescribes for relations among them are such as to reflect this difference.[35]

There is a sense in which the principles advanced by Vattel deal with a unique context formed by a group of states which form a society insofar as they recognise certain common moral principles while acknowledging that nothing more than limited agreement should be expected in relations between them. Where states are ideologically divided, it is evidently more desirable that they establish a minimal order among themselves than attempt to impose opposing conceptions of justice upon one another. An agreement upon the need to preserve the natural liberty of states would be no mean achievement in such a condition.

Bull, who reproduces Vattel's pluralism, states that

> although the solidarity exhibited by international society may increase in the future, just as it may decrease, it can still be argued that in the twentieth century the Grotian conception has proved premature.[36]

If the Grotian conception is premature rather than absurd or incoherent, then we shall have to go beyond Vattel for a more complete theory of international relations. After all, Vattel does not propose that his theory be applied only in that contingent set of circumstances where states are unable to agree on fundamental rules for the regulation of their interaction. Although this may have been a preferable position for Vattel to have adopted, ultimately it does him less justice than he is due. Vattel is fundamentally opposed to the development of an association larger than states, as is apparent from his explicit rejection of Wolff's *civitas maxima*; and he is opposed to the emergence of a different form of international society not on the grounds of its temporary unattainability but on the basis of a theoretical appraisal of the necessary and unalterable prerequisites of social and political life.

It is not the approach which a theory adopts in relation to

the complex practical problems of statecraft which reveals its identity, but the degree to which it is acquiescent or resistant towards the conditions which makes these problems possible. Earlier we drew a distinction between those theories which accepted the structure of an international society consisting of sovereign states, and radical or critical theories of international relations. Clearly, it is necessary to draw a sharp contrast between Vattel's theory and the systems advanced by Rousseau, Kant and Green. Vattel's theory is a defence both of the sovereign states-system and universal moral obligations. But it fails to appreciate the nature of the conflict between the moralities of men and citizens; and it overlooks the fact that the enactment of an external concept of obligation is especially difficult to maintain under conditions of insecurity when it is more likely that the state will be forced back upon its internal notion of duty. The tensions between these perspectives are suppressed in Vattel's theory. Indeed, its defence of the liberty of states ensures the prematureness of Grotius and the solidarist ideal; Vattel's conception of the state itself obstructs the emergence of a properly international society which allows the reconciliation of competing views of obligation and the presentation of a coherent statement of our moral and political experience.

A method which attempted to ground the principles of international society upon universal consent would overcome many of the difficulties discernible in the works of those representatives of the contractarian tradition who discussed the realm of relations between states. This is so since

> if we are to speak of our obligations as members of the society of humanity as a whole, the theory requires us to say that there are some classes of action regarding which it is in the interest of every man on the surface of the earth to make a contract with every other.[37]

Such a strategy is more compatible with Kant's belief that the principle of equality, which had been so blatantly disregarded by the classical theorists of the states-system, should serve as the main constituent of the organisation of international relations. It is a method which, of all the contractarians, Kant was alone in applying in his transformation of the rationalist tradition of international relations. Kant's new synthesis of contractarianism and universalism would produce a critical account of the world of international relations. Here rationalism embraces the critical theory of international society and specifies for the first time the conditions under which men can attain a coherence in their moral and political experience.

6 Kantian Ethics and International Relations

> Grotius, Pufendorf, Vattel – miserable comforters all of them. (Kant)

Kant's savage criticism of his immediate predecessors within the rationalist tradition supplies the key to his distinctive type of international political theory. Neither Pufendorf nor Vattel had shared Kant's aspiration of paying 'the Stoic–Christian ideal of the unity of mankind the supreme compliment of taking its political consequences seriously';[1] each had failed in Kant's opinion to appreciate that rationalism required a progressivist interpretation of international relations which conceived the perfectibility of world political organisation as a sublime historical goal. Rationalism had been severely compromised by the toleration of that condition in which obligations to humanity were second to obligations to the state. Under these circumstances, the deceptively simple supposition that wholly free states could produce a just and stable international order among themselves was as naive as it was dangerous.

Kant held that all men were bound together by the necessary obligation to so arrange their social and political lives that they could gradually realise a condition of universal justice and perpetual peace. These goals were not hypothetical goals, ones which men would be obligated to pursue if they were to satisfy the contingent ends they had set for themselves. On the contrary, they were essential or categorical ends which men were under an unconditional obligation to promote by virtue of their rational nature.[2] There was an unconditional obligation to further a 'systematic harmony of purposes',[3] to create a condition in which each person's freedom to promote his purposes was compatible with the equal freedom of all others. Reason legislated that if this universalist objective was ever to be attained, the entire human race had to submit its social and political affairs to governance by a world-wide system of law.

A radically different statement of human purposes separates Kantian theory from its immediate predecessors. For Pufendorf and Vattel, men in pursuit of their self-regarding ends resorted to the establishment of political societies. Their capacity to promote their purposes without forming a universal political association explained the separation of humanity into sovereign states. And although there is a natural morality which survived this division, it does not demand that citizens should consider the gradual formation of an international civil society as a matter of intrinsic importance; nor is the state obliged to relinquish gradually that freedom of action at its disposal for the purpose of satisfying the interests of its members. While there is an obligation to respect the moral framework which exists naturally, morality is only properly effective within the boundaries of sovereign states. Had it been necessary for men to associate at the global level a more determinate system of moral rights and duties would have existed universally. The degree to which man's natural morality is made effective depends upon the calculations which determine the precise boundaries of political community.

One of the recurrent features of Kant's thought is his opposition to those approaches which make the effectiveness of morality dependent upon various assessments of how individuals can best advance their interests. Although it is undeniable that individuals choose to promote different goals, it is equally true for Kant that as moral beings they have rational ends which they ought to respect. According to Kant, man is a member of two worlds – a world of desire in which he seeks satisfaction of his inclinations, and a world of rationality in which reason determines the moral ends which men must pursue. The preservation of his life and the satisfaction of his desires are ends which man shares with the rest of nature. But through enactment of a morality, whereby he acts in accordance with principles which are true for all, man curbs his animal inclinations and affirms his freedom and dignity. By acting in accordance with moral principles prescribed by his own reason, man asserts his independence from the natural world and establishes what is distinctively human in his nature. The ordering of his life in accordance with moral rules is the manner in which he unfolds his uniquely human characteristics, his non-natural being, his freedom. Purely natural beings are condemned to behave instinctively; humanity exists and unfolds as men curb their animal inclinations and act freely or autonomously out of respect for those moral principles inherent within their rational nature.

Kant is at odds with Pufendorf and Vattel because they reverse the proper order of things, because they allow the world of reason to be subservient to the world of inclination. Those thinkers had failed to construct a vision of political life in conformity with the ends which they maintained all should pursue by virtue of their rational nature. On the contrary, they considered the world of politics in purely instrumental terms, as a set of mechanisms which men would be wise to establish if they wished to protect their individual interests. Morality is therefore only effective within states, not in relations between them. In opposition to Pufendorf and Vattel, who had tied political life to the realm of inclination, Kant connected it to the world of rational nature. Political order provided important guarantees for the security and property of persons, but more importantly it created sufficient safety for them to proceed to perfect their moral lives.

Therefore, Kant's project begins by establishing the ends which men have an unconditional duty to promote as rational beings with the capacity to escape from the world of natural determination; and he proceeds to argue for a radical transformation of the political world in the direction of that condition in which all human beings live in conformity with the imperatives grounded in their common rational nature.

To reconstruct Kant's theory of international relations it is necessary to set out as briefly as possible the ethical principles which all rational beings are required to observe; then it is important to recognise that Kant's more systematic statement of universalism subverts the foundations of the international political theories of Pufendorf and Vattel; finally, we shall consider how the opposition between Kant and his immediate predecessors finds expression in a more rigorously developed theory of international relations.

Kant makes it plain in a statement of his objectives that he is not attempting to establish new ethical principles. It would be arrogant, Kant alleged, for the theorist to assume that he was in the process of discovering principles previously concealed from the human race. For this reason it is unacceptable to hold that Kant was in favour of principles which were binding in all circumstances irrespective of the consequences of acting upon them. Indeed Kant's single most important ambition was to begin with man's experience of himself as a moral agent, and to proceed to articulate the propositions which made this experience possible and intelligible. His task was then to make explicit the postulates which underlie moral experience, to bring its presuppositions to light.

Kant states that there are three necessary and universal principles underlying all moral conduct – these are the principles of universality, treating others as ends in themselves, and acting autonomously (to which is connected the idea of membership of a universal kingdom of ends).

The principle of universality enjoins us to 'Act only on that maxim through which you can at the same time will that it shall become a universal law'.[4] This first formulation clarifies the fact that to act morally a person must act upon a principle of universal applicability. When stating this point, Kant has in mind all rational beings, a category which includes more than simply human persons. For it is conceivable that there are beings which are so constituted that, being absolutely rational and perfectly good, they always act upon principles which are valid for all. But man, on the other hand, belonging to both the worlds of reason and inclination may be tempted to 'take the liberty of making an exception' to a principle in order to satisfy a personal interest or inclination.[5] A moral agent must therefore strive against instinct to act on impartial and impersonal principles which treat similar persons acting in like circumstances equally.

The formula of universality is a formal test which certain principles of conduct will fail. We know that any principle of action, which we are unable to universalise, will not be moral. Thus, if a person acts on a principle, which he could not wish another person to employ in his actions towards him, that principle is not a moral one.

But another formulation of the principle of morality is

implicit within this test, since to govern one's conduct by universal principles is to acknowledge rules which take the ends of all persons into consideration. If a person acts in such a way as to promote only his own interests then the ends of others mean nothing to him; others may be treated simply as means to his own purposes. But to observe universal laws is to perceive oneself as one actor among many; it is to recognise others as ends in themselves whose purposes cannot be excluded from any consideration of how to act. To submit to universal principles is to regard the ends of others with respect or to affirm the value of rational nature. The point of universality is not consistency for its own sake; it is to further the principle

> that man . . . exists as an end in himself, not merely as a means for arbitrary use by this or that will; he must in all his actions, whether they are directed to himself or to other rational beings, always be viewed at the same time as an end . . . Rational nature exists as an end in itself.[6]

Kant is therefore correct to infer that a second formulation of morality is already contained in the first. It is the injunction to

> Act in such a way that you always treat humanity, whether in your own person or in the person of any other, never simply as a means, but always at the same time as an end.[7]

To respond to limitations inherent in recognising others as ends in themselves is tantamount to understanding that it would be improper to treat another in accordance with a principle which he could not consent to as a rational being. When acting morally therefore we draw upon a third principle, that of recognising 'the will of every rational being as a will which makes universal law'.[8]

Two consequences follow from this proposition. Firstly, human beings do not submit to a morality which has its source outside them. Indeed, 'the will is therefore not merely subject to the law, but is so subject that it must be considered as also making the law'.[9] Kant's criticism of some earlier thinkers is that they failed to recognise the full implications of the fact that men were subject to laws not only made by themselves but universally valid.[10] Since men are capable of dominating their inclinations, because they are free from the complete determinism which pervades the natural order, they can act in accordance with the principles of their reason alone. Compliance with 'the laws of freedom' need depend upon no other incentive than respect for the rationality immanent within them.

However, earlier thinkers had not seen that reason is the sole source of moral imperatives, and that submission to reason was equivalent to realising one's capacity for free action. They had

> thought of man merely as subject to a law [whatever it might be], and the law had to carry with it some interest in order to attract or compel, because it did not spring as a law from his own will: in order to conform with the law his will had to be necessitated by something else to act in a certain way.[11]

But to argue that man cannot follow the promptings of moral reason alone (an assumption common to both Pufendorf and Vattel) is to undermine that very freedom from natural determination which is central to the concept of a moral agent. The concept of morality presupposes the capacity to stand above inclination, to ensure that its satisfaction does not violate universal principle; it would be pointless directing moral approval or disapproval at a being incapable of acting differently. The capacity to follow reason alone is necessary if we are to subscribe to the notion of morality; and it is recognition of this capacity in others which underpins our membership of a universal kingdom of ends.

A second consequence of recognising 'the will of every rational being as a will which makes universal law' is the awareness of participating with others in a law-making community. Underlying our conduct is the third formulation of what is implicit in moral behaviour: it is the imperative of acting 'as if [you] were through [your] maxims always a law-making member in the universal kingdom of ends'.[12] This moral community, or kingdom of ends, harks back to Rousseau's vision of direct democracy, to that condition in which 'each, while uniting himself with all, may still obey himself alone, and remain as free as before'.[13] Kant's indebtedness to Rousseau is manifest in his remark that

> a rational being belongs to the kingdom of ends as a member, when, although he makes its universal laws, he is also himself subject to these laws. He belongs to it as its head, when as the maker of the laws he is himself subject to the will of no other.[14]

Rousseau's endorsement of the inalienable sovereignty of the people is reflected in the Kantian notion of a kingdom of ends as a condition in which rational beings obey only the laws they make themselves, where obedience to law is not submission to authority but expression of human freedom. This condition is what Kant calls 'a systematic harmony of purposes', a moral community in which the ends of rational beings are harmonised in accordance with rational principles imposed upon themselves.

When Kant maintains that it would be improper to treat another in accordance with a principle to which he could not consent, he means that a rational being would not allow himself to be used as a means to the satisfaction of another's personal inclinations. He is not denying that under certain circumstances a person might consent to being so used – because of impaired rationality for instance. Therefore, when Kant states that we might test public laws by considering whether or not contractors could assent to them, it is rational contractors that he has in mind.[15] Within his writings we can discern a conscious attempt to eliminate that gap between contractarianism and universalism which we found in the theories of Pufendorf and Vattel. The fiction of a social contract, which Kant employs in his analyses of just domestic and international arrangements, overcomes the distinction between the actual consent which empirical men might give and the rational consent which they would give if they fully observed the moral law. Here the contract will be used to determine what would emerge from the rational consent of autonomous individuals. This reconciliation of contractarianism and universalism removes the inconsistencies present in the thinking of Pufendorf and Vattel; it is not a form of contractarianism which will permit the slide from an external to an internal concept of obligation.

One of the traditional objections to Kantian ethics – an objection which has its source in Hegelian thought – claims that it is purely formal, incapable of specifying determinate rights and duties.[16] To the extent that this criticism focuses on the principle of universality alone, it is unfair to Kant. This principle, and those to which it is attached, govern all rational beings, a category which includes but is not exhausted by human beings. Kant states that the concept of duty holds 'for all rational beings . . . and only because of this can it also be a law for all human wills'.[17] But because of this degree of generality, the principle of universality is not sufficient to determine what it is that humans should do. For this reason, Kant distinguishes between his formal moral philosophy, which specifies the tests to be performed by all rational beings, and his material moral philosophy which seeks to apply these tests to the specifically human condition in order to derive concrete rights and duties. Kant is well aware, as a recent commentator has stated, that

> to know that we should treat all rational beings as ends in themselves is not to know a great deal. . . . For what we want to know now is not simply what in general counts as rational action for any rational being, but rather what counts as rational action for humanity.[18]

To apply the moral law to human beings we must take account of specifically human purposes and circumstances. In his attempt to define these, Kant resorts to his recurrent theme that humans belong to the worlds of reason and inclination. Because humans have needs which they must satisfy it is impossible for them to share the circumstances peculiar to perfectly rational beings, beings with a 'holy will';[19] since they inhabit the world of reason and have the capacity to promote their moral lives, they cannot regard themselves simply as natural beings, and they cannot seek satisfaction of their animal inclinations alone. Kant holds that one of the 'essential ends' of humanity must be to develop its capacity to elevate itself above nature.[20] Neither a being with a holy will nor an animal could be said to have the duty to perfect itself.

While the former is perfectly rational, the latter is condemned to live in a world of complete natural determination. The concept of perfectibility has significance only with reference to a being which can transcend the natural element within its self. This is true also of another of man's essential ends, the capacity to integrate his purposes into a systematic whole, a condition which Kant calls happiness.

Although a person is at liberty to pursue the ends which give him happiness, he should not be indifferent to the happiness of others.[21] For moral agents are obliged to govern their conduct with rational principles which provide each person with an equal liberty to pursue his ends.[22] Although persons have no obligations to perfect others (since this would constitute an intrusion upon their moral lives) they have a duty to enact universal principles which prohibit impeding others from promoting their self-realisation. Those principles, moreover, should be reinforced with the sanction of law. Indeed, 'the first decision' that a person must take 'if he does not wish to renounce all concepts of justice, is to accept the principle that one must quit the state of nature in which everyone follows his own judgment'.[23] There is a fundamental obligation to enter into

> a condition of society in which what is to be recognised as belonging to him must be established lawfully and secured to him by an effective power that is not his own, but an outside power. That is, before anything else, he ought to enter into a civil society'.[24]

Universal moral principles which seek to enhance the conditions of human freedom must receive the protection of political authority and law.[25]

Unlike Pufendorf and Vattel, who had grounded political obligation in the previous consent of contractors, Kant derived obligation immediately from moral duty. The duty to belong to the state emanated from the fact that the pursuit of any one man's happiness and security should not be incompatible with the equal liberty of others. And because this was so, the state could not be considered a sufficient juridical community; the primary importance of justice required that outsiders too be brought within a common moral framework.

Once the state is established, therefore, it is a duty to continue to ask whether or not a principle upon which we propose to act could assist or delay the realisation of that condition in which the ends of men are systematically harmonised. An action's ability to bring about a systematic harmony of purposes among all men is for Kant a simple test whereby moral agents can clarify what they ought to do.[26] Insistence upon duty led Kant to redirect the rationalist tradition away from acceptance of those circumstances in which the state's pursuit of its own welfare or security might jeopardise the welfare of others. What Pufendorf and Vattel had accepted, thereby compromising the spirit of rationalism, Kant refused to condone. In conclusion then, at the heart of his conception of domestic and international politics is a vision of a condition in which men are equally at liberty to promote their ends within a common framework of universal principles which emanate from their wills.

Pufendorf, Vattel and Kant incorporated ethical universalism into their theories, but it is only Kant's theory which produced a radical critique of the international states-system. We may explain this difference as a function of Kant's more rigorous statement of ethical universalism and his insistence that all principles with universal validity must be expressions of rational consent. Moreover, if Kant's version of ethical universalism develops into a political cosmopolitanism absent from the writings of Pufendorf and Vattel, it is because it allows no place for the latter's way of drawing the distinction between perfect and imperfect obligations.

It will be recalled that Pufendorf believed a man could not be compelled to do what was required by 'a mere duty of humanity'. An obligation could only be enforced between men who had jointly determined what they were willing to perform among themselves and had consented to submit to a common sovereign. Moral obligations were not perfectly obliging in relations between states since these had refrained from consenting to submit to a common sovereign. For Vattel individuals or states established perfect obligations when they were convinced that these were compatible with obligations to themselves. From these perspectives, states are granted an absolute liberty of determining the scope of their obligations, a liberty which is clearly at odds with the principle that they should treat one another as equals under the same moral law. It is this distinction between perfect and imperfect obligations which transformed ethical universalism into a doctrine holding that the states-system was a 'climax' rather than a 'dominant'.

From our preceding statements, it would seem unlikely that Kant could accept this distinction.[27] The essence of morality is its constraining influence upon agents tempted to place their personal inclinations and interests before other persons'. Kant argued that there would be no point to morality if it were constantly subject to the interpretation of individuals referring to their particular interests. If a person had a moral right then, in Kant's view, he was authorised to use coercion to protect it, since ' "right" [or "justice"] and "authorisation to use coercion" mean the same thing';[28] a person could not allow his right to be infringed by any other person who found the corresponding obligation in conflict with his self-interest or perfection.

But this is precisely what Pufendorf and Vattel allowed. Although they regarded the principle of universalisation as a test of right action, its strictness was immediately relaxed by allowing individuals or states the liberty of deciding the extent to which they could honour their moral obligations. This libertarianism could not be acceptable to Kant. Here, empirical ends such as perfection or happiness are transformed into tests of the extent to which agents can perform their moral obligations.[29] The proper approach would operate in reverse by subordinating the world of inclination to reason.

It is important to consider further the bearing of Kant's ethical conclusions upon certain arguments which Pufendorf and Vattel believed to be fundamental to their defence of sovereign states. In Pufendorf's theory two arguments may be criticised from a Kantian perspective. The first holds that the sovereign state is responsible first and foremost to itself; the second holds that a state cannot be perfectly obliged to another without the assurance of receiving an equivalent benefit in return.

If the first argument is regarded as a universal principle, it becomes a form of ethical egoism;[30] egoism because the state pursues its interests regardless of the consequences for others, ethical because it grants that others have the same rights, or because egoism is universalised. However, if a state universalises its egoism, it is committed to recognising that others may pursue their interests to the point at which its own welfare is harmed. Egoism, therefore, cannot be universalised without the generation of a contradiction.

There is no obvious way of resolving this contradiction present, for example, in a system of states where each association enacts its specific form of particularism. A state based upon an internal concept of obligation may hope that others will not exercise their entitlement to pursue their interests irrespective of the consequences for others, thus allowing its egoism to prevail. It may contract to form a pragmatic arrangement with other states whereby each achieves something of what it desires. But an arrangement like this can never be wholly satisfactory for the state because it is aware that if others did not exist, or were not to pursue their interests, it would gain as a result. If it is egotistical, others must always appear as obstacles to the complete realisation of its ends. Moreover, if a state takes the purposes of others into account only insofar as they contribute to its own satisfaction, it can be accused of failing to treat others as ends in themselves. This perspective would be in contradiction with what it means to behave ethically, assuming Kant is correct in arguing that morality is not simply reverence for logical consistency but regard for the equality of others. And if a state does treat others as equals, and limits its actions accordingly, it has transcended the limitations of egoism; it has moved from an internal to an external point of view.

Pufendorf's second argument that states have a right to become perfectly obliged only when it is in their interests to do so is equally defective. While it shares some of the deficiencies of the first argument – most noticeably by failing to regard the ends of others as independently valuable – it generates its own particular contradictions.

Pufendorf supposed that it is not in the interests of a man to establish reciprocal arrangements with every other man on the face of the earth. Men have nothing to gain from entering into a civil society of mankind. Underlying this argument is the belief that there is no perfect obligation to help another poorer than oneself, however defined, unless there is a prospect of a benefit in return. Although Pufendorf does not advise men to act only on this uncharitable maxim, it is evident that this belief strongly influences both his argument for separate states and his conception of how they ought to conduct their external relations.

The problem is whether or not an egotist can live without contradiction in a condition in which unconditional obligation is non-existent. An egotist believes that as long as he does not require assistance, there is no need to extend help to others. But if the egotist's circumstances change, he could not reasonably refuse the unconditional assistance of others without contradicting that self-concern which is egoism. In other words, a person or state would not be an egotist if he were unprepared to be the beneficiary of an unconditional act of kindness; therefore, egotism as a doctrine, and certainly universalised egotism, can work against the interest of any of its particular adherents.

Pufendorf's two principles of self-interest are therefore unacceptable. But neither the view that individuals cannot assist all men to the same degree nor the view that men cannot know how best to help one another, nor the view that the moral law is insufficiently precise to order political relations, can provide sufficient justification for the argument that humanity should be divided into sovereign states, each possessing the right to advance its own interests. Without the concepts of self-interest and reciprocity, Pufendorf's account of the legitimacy of a world of sovereign states is untenable. And since on Kantian grounds there are good reasons for rejecting these principles, Pufendorf's defence of particularism and its political consequences must be judged invalid.

Vattel argues that duties to others must always be measured against more fundamental duties to the self; perfect obligations, therefore, may be avoided if the state believes they are incompatible with what it owes to itself or to its members. For Kant the concept of a duty to one's self, in Vattel's sense, is contradictory. It carries the connotation that 'the one who binds could always release the one bound from the obligation'. If this is so, 'if both are one and the same subject', then a person 'would not be bound at all by a duty he imposes on himself, and this involves a contradiction'.[31] From the Kantian perspective, the perfection of the self or the satisfaction of its interests cannot be considered in abstraction from the welfare of others. Vattel does not employ his universalist ethic to determine whether the ends of states are compatible with the emergence of a systematic harmony of purposes. Indeed, Vattel's pluralist account of international relations depends upon the dissolution of that moral framework which might place substantial constraints upon the actions of states. Therefore, the idea of a duty to the state is really equivalent to a freedom from moral ties to outsiders. But, on Kantian grounds, the status of state-libertarianism is problematical; it could not be agreed to by rational agents since it allows the state a freedom to ignore the ends of equal persons. If the concept of a duty to the self, and the ensuing distinction between perfect and imperfect obligations, cannot be supported, then the whole basis of Vattel's pluralist theory must be judged wanting.

Prior to setting out the Kantian theory of international relations, it is necessary to consider one possible line of argument which might be used to defend Pufendorf and Vattel. Inconsistencies certainly exist within their theories; nevertheless, it may be argued, their perspectives contain fundamental insights into the conditions in which states must act, insights which ought to be incorporated within any international political theory. For states act in a peculiar context in which only limited agreement is possible and where the Kantian question 'what if everyone did that?' is inappropriate: everyone is doing 'that' already.[32] Under these circumstances, states have little choice but to look to their own interests first and foremost, and to conduct their relations on a principle of reciprocity. It is not a condition, in other words, in which a statesman should be encouraged to act unilaterally in accordance with the categorical imperative.[33]

The issue is whether or not concepts of justice have application in the international state of nature. It was argued previously that a theoretical account of our experience of the states-system should include such concepts; what the Kantian perspective develops is the fact that our practical experience can accommodate them also. Morality need not be suspended or held to be binding merely in conscience.

Rational agents in a state of nature can establish what may be called rules of proportionality.[34] To give an example, a state which has broken a treaty in order to save itself from aggression can hardly accept that the society of states has a reasonable right to punish it severely. Exceptional circumstances release it from the obligation which would otherwise exist. Actors in a state of nature can determine the general conditions which would release them from conventional moral expectations; and they can ascertain what would count as unreasonable or disproportionate departures from normally binding rules. Furthermore, rules which are usually observed in the state of nature may be examined to discover whether or not they are reasonable departures from those which would apply ideally, in a fully rational condition.

We need not assume that a state of nature is a condition for which only an autonomous statecraft is appropriate. Vattel himself urged the importance of a principle of proportionality in the conduct of external relations, although ultimately the precise definition of proportionality is a matter for the subjective determination of the sovereign state. However, not only may rules of proportionality apply in the state of nature, but such rules may be objectively ascertainable and universalisable. Foundations for this argument are, I shall argue, present in Kant's thought. In his theory, not only is the formulation of these rules right in itself; it is an important step in the transition from the state of nature to a condition in which ideal rules apply universally. And if such considerations were not observed it would be difficult to imagine how states could ever leave that state of nature which reason requires them to abandon.

What Kantian theory possesses, therefore, is a concept of the progressive development of the conditions of sociability, first at the domestic and later at the international level. It does not merely set out the tests which rational agents should observe under ideal conditions, but the tests which ought to be recognised in preceding stages. We shall now discuss how this moral philosophy is applied to the structure of international relations.

Clearly, Kant's moral philosophy is fundamentally opposed to the earlier contractarian foundations for an internal concept of obligation. Each of the features of that perspective – its defence of the absolute rights of the sovereign state, the separation it makes between a public and a private morality, its pragmatic approach to international cooperation – clashes with the Kantian vision of a universal kingdom of ends. Kant's international political theory sets out to accomplish three tasks: to provide a critique of the international states-system in its conventional form and to describe what kind of transformation it must undergo if human moral capacities are to be fully realised; and, since we inhabit a world in which the internal concept of obligation is dominant, to provide an account of the processes whereby this world may be transformed into one expressive of the moral law inherent in rational nature. Each of these themes will now be considered in turn.

In his portrayal of international relations, Rousseau maintained that with the emergence of states, men 'committed more murders in a single day's fighting . . . than were committed in the state of nature during whole ages over the whole earth'.[35] Rousseau's pessimism, which profoundly influenced Kant, is exemplified in the latter's outright repudiation of the contractarian solution to the problem of order. The 'same unsociableness' which brought men into states would continue to bedevil them in the international state of nature.[36] But Kant could embrace neither Rousseau's pessimistic conclusion that there was no escape from the international state of nature nor that radical-utopianism in Rousseau which called for the states-system's immediate and total reconstruction. Rousseau was 'right to criticise historical institutions, but they [were]the germs of future good ones'.[37] Further, Kant argued that

> it would manifestly be contrary to that political expediency which is in agreement with morals, to destroy the existing bonds of National and Cosmopolitical Union before there was a better constitution ready to take its place.[38]

It is this emphasis upon gradual, painstaking historical progress which finally separates Kant from the most significant political influence upon him.

In Kantian thought, freedom, if governed by a universal principle, 'is the one sole and original right that belongs to every human being by virtue of his humanity'.[39] Because this is so, individuals have the obligation to establish a legal framework which protects their equal freedom. And, on the same principle, the state's barbaric freedom, which issues from the contract whereby a people imposes a constitution upon itself, is in contradiction with the principle of right. The sovereign state, of itself, is incomplete and in need of the constraints of law to curb the exercise of its own natural liberty. It cannot claim the right to promote its own interests without concern for any wider moral constituency, or to ground its external relations simply upon reciprocity or power. The state of nature is a

> state of war [the right of the stronger], even though there may not be an actual war or continuous fighting [hostility]. Nevertheless [inasmuch as neither side wants to have it better], it is still a condition that is in the highest degree unjust, and it is a condition that states adjoining one another are obligated to abandon.[40]

Reason demands that rights receive guarantees which are not available in the state of nature; and states, like individuals before them, are obliged to relinquish their 'wild, lawless freedom'.[41]

But it is not necessary that they surrender their freedom to an international state. Kant's liberalism breeds a cautious concern for the despotic tendencies of large, distant governments.[42] Moreover, differences of language and religion are obstacles to the incorporation of all peoples within a single, political society. But what is crucial from Kant's perspective is the fact that the necessity for an international state decreases as civilisation progresses; for what develops in the more advanced historical epochs to offset linguistic and religious differences is a greater 'unanimity in principles' and a 'mutual understanding of the conditions of peace even in view of these differences'.[43] Kant believed that if an international order could not be constructed from the consensus of its parts (and here he is absolutely in agreement with Vattel) then it could not be constructed at all. The progress of history produced the conditions which made this consensus possible. Respect for the moral law and the high value placed upon human freedom formed a consensus which enabled states themselves to agree upon the conditions of their sociability. With the emergence of an international ethical consensus, states could conclude a specific form of contract which would put an end not to any war in particular but 'to all wars forever'.[44] The development of moral capacities led to the consensus that war was not the means which states should rely upon in order to preserve their rights;[45] it would be agreed that nations should 'settle their differences in a civilised way by judicial process, rather than in the barbaric way [of savages], namely, through war'.[46] A free federation would exist among nations, an organisation which would not

> aim at the acquisition of any of the political powers of the state, but merely at the preservation and guarantee for itself, and likewise for the other confederated states, of the liberty that is proper to a state; and this would not require these states to subject themselves for this purpose – as is the case with men in the state of nature – to public laws and to coercion under them.[47]

Although the growth of cosmopolitical tendencies expressed the flourishing of uniquely human capacities, man's development involved more than the gradual creation of a universal kingdom of ends; the unfolding of human powers was also reflected in progress towards anarchy, towards a condition in which coercion by law gradually receded to be replaced in time by a form of self-constraint engendered by reverence for freedom and morality alone.

Kant did not contend that this cosmopolitical society would be the creation of human rationality only.[48] Rather, its development was a complex product of the interplay of rational and irrational influences. In their original condition of wild, lawless freedom men acted on impulse; the experience of conflict and competition between them stimulated the development of reason to the point at which men recognised the prudence of submission to the constraints of the state; only later did they begin to substitute moral for legal, internal for external, constraints. And so it is with international history – nature or providence employs the passions and inclinations of states in its design of unfolding human rationality. Competition and conflict between states teaches men by experience what they would have known by reason had they not had to undergo self-education through the painful lessons of history.

The devastating consequences of modern warfare prompted human reason to begin 'to arrange for a great future political body, such as the world has never yet seen':

> Finally the war itself comes to be regarded as a very hazardous and objectionable undertaking, not only from its being so artificial in itself and so uncertain as regards its issue on both sides, but also from the afterpains which the state feels in the ever increasing burdens it entails in the form of national debt – a modern infliction – which it becomes almost impossible to extinguish. And to this is to be added the influence which every political disturbance of any state of our continent – linked as it is so closely to others by the connections of trade – exerts upon all the states and which becomes so observable that they are forced by their common danger, although without lawful authority, to offer themselves as arbiters in the troubles of any such state. In doing so, they are beginning to arrange for a great future political body, such as the world has never yet seen. Although this political body may as yet exist only in a rough outline, nevertheless a feeling begins, as it were, to stir in all its members, each of which has a common interest in the maintenance of the whole. And this may well inspire the hope that after many political revolutions and transformations, the highest purpose of Nature will be at last realised in the establishment of a universal Cosmo-political Institution, in the bosom of which all the original capacities and endowments of the human species will be unfolded and developed.[49]

An important precondition of the development of world political society is the republican constitution.[50] Naïvely, no doubt, Kant presumed that a citizen body involved in decisions about warfare would be 'very loth' to commit itself to taking part in 'all the horrors of war'.[51] But there is another dimension to Kant's doctrine of republicanism which is important in the development of perpetual peace. Republicanism is a product of man's aspiration to have the freedom to which he is entitled as a rational being expressed in the practices of his community. But, when they established the republican regime men were doing more than gaining recognition of their own rational nature; they were creating a political society more able than any of its predecessors to be incorporated within an international political community. A republican constitution, in which men *qua* men are treated as ends in themselves, would by its very nature provide a core around which other states would gather to form a free federation of nations. A man who takes his place within a republican constitution can perceive himself as taking part in that historical process which will culminate in a political structure which treats all men, not merely those within the state, as ends in themselves.[52] Moral progress at the international level depends upon 'a long internal process of improvement' within each commonwealth;[53] it depends upon more than a mechanical re-arrangement of relations between states, namely a redefinition of obligations to outsiders. Insofar as a separate state has nothing in its nature which makes it inevitably prone to conflict with others, and everything in its nature which makes it predisposed to become incorporated within an international moral community – it would have to be a republic. And it has this tendency because its very constitution is predicated upon the proposition that men are ends in themselves.

Irrationality alone cannot bring a universal kingdom of ends into existence. Thus, the higher stages of the historical process are distinguished by the gradual purification of action. Growing awareness of rational capacities leads to the eradication of inclination from history as men subject the remaining dimensions of their political world to reason and principle. The idea of the rational consent of the world acquires shape as the determinate test of inter-state conduct.

In the course of their history states transcend the conception of outsiders which determined the structure of their internal points of view. Sovereigns therefore cannot consider themselves obliged to act solely as trustees for those who have traditionally associated together; nor can they apply standards 'based on the experience of those who have hitherto found [them] most to their advantage'.[54] Their approach to international cooperation

> must not start from the prosperity and happiness that are to be expected in each state from following them [principles of

> international relations], nor from the end which each of them makes the object of its will as the highest empirical principle of politics; but they must proceed from the pure conception of the duty of right or justice, as an obligatory principle given a priori by pure reason.[55]

Reverence for moral law informs the wills of sovereigns:

> If certain defects which could not be prevented, are found in the political constitution, or in the relations of the state, it becomes a duty especially for the heads of the state to apply themselves to correct them as soon as possible, and to improve the constitution so that it may be brought into conformity with natural right.[56]

Many of the more remarkable and frequently overlooked passages from Kant's writings clearly indicate that theoretical integration of contractarianism and universalism which defines his uniquely ethical theory of international relations. These passages specify the considerations which sovereigns should bring to the task of establishing a cosmopolitical society in keeping with rational obligations. What is crucial in that development is an increased sensitivity to the maxims underlying foreign policy. Both the solution to international conflict and the foundations of successful international cooperation require a conscious effort to act in accordance with maxims which can be universalised. To judge whether a maxim of foreign policy is right or wrong, it is necessary to test it by considering whether or not its universal enactment would hasten or postpone the realisation of a world-wide systematic harmony of purposes. Kant writes:

> But what, then, is an unjust enemy according to concepts of the Law of Nations, which holds that every state is a judge in its own cause as in a state of nature in general? An unjust enemy is someone whose publicly expressed will [whether by words or by deeds] discloses a maxim that, if made into a universal rule, would make peace among nations impossible and would perpetuate the state of nature forever.[57]

Individuals and states alike are obliged to conduct their affairs not on the basis of 'one-sided maxims',[58] for which there is no moral justification, but on the basis of rules conducive to the realisation of a universal kingdom of ends.

One of the principles which Kant regards as absolutely fundamental to the test of right action is the principle of publicity. If secrecy is necessary for an act of foreign policy to succeed, we must presume that act to be unjust:

> For a maxim cannot be a right maxim which is such that I cannot allow it to be published without thereby at the same time frustrating my own intention, which would necessarily have to be kept secret entirely in order that it might succeed, and which I could not publicly confess to be mine without inevitably arousing thereby the resistance of all men against my purpose. It is clear that this necessary and universal opposition of all against me on self evident grounds, can arise from nothing else than the injustice which such a maxim threatens to everyone.[59]

There are two possible criticisms of Kant's principle of publicity, but it may be reconstructed to overcome them. Firstly, it may appear that action conforming with the principle of publicity runs all the risks commonly associated with ethical conceptions of foreign policy. A state may have to withhold its intentions from others, either in peace or in war, to preserve itself from the unjust designs of its enemies. To expect this state to publicise its intentions is to impose wholly inappropriate demands upon it. Secondly, it might be suggested that in a variety of empirical circumstances a state might be able to publicise virtually any intention without fearing a hostile response from others – when, for example, it has such commanding power at its disposal that no other state is prepared to antagonise it. The principle of publicity might appear then as neither a necessary nor a sufficient test of the morality of inter-state conduct.

But these objections may be overcome if the principle of publicity is considered more sympathetically in the context of Kant's complete moral philosophy. We noted earlier that Kant sought to integrate contractarianism and universalism in a way which overcame the deficiencies of earlier rationalist positions, namely by positing a contract which elicited the rational consent of moral agents.[60] Arguably, the moral adequacy of foreign policy in the state of nature is to be determined not by referring to what actual and perhaps imperfect agents would choose, but by considering what would emanate from the wills of rational contractors.

Nor does Kant assume that the test of foreign policy is to be discovered by deciding what rational contractors would accept in an ideal condition. Right conduct must be determined with due regard for the empirical circumstances in which states must act. Kant was perfectly explicit that states must progress gradually rather than endanger what they have achieved already by 'overhaste';[61] the latter would almost certainly be the case if states were to ignore 'gradual reform according to fixed principles'.[62] In *Perpetual Peace*, Kant's distinction between two types of principle reveals his concern to take account of empirical circumstances without 'losing sight' of the ends which ought to be realised eventually.[63] Kant refers to 'strict laws' which are 'valid without distinction of circumstances, and press immediately for the abolition of certain things'; and rules which have a 'certain subjective breadth in respect of their application' as 'they imply a regard to circumstances in practice'. Those rules which Kant describes as strict include the duty to avoid endangering 'mutual confidence', the duty of non-intervention and the obligation to conclude peace treaties without any secret intention of restarting the war; those rules which have 'subjective breadth' include the duty not to acquire other states as 'property', the duty of avoiding 'national debts' and of abolishing standing armies 'in the course of time'.[64] The content of this list is less important for present purposes than the reasons for its existence; its antiquated, even idiosyncratic character, should not blind us to the subtle relationship between ethics and politics which it embodies.

Kant argued that men ought to be treated as members of a universal kingdom of ends; but he also acknowledged that if progress were to be made without jeopardising what had been achieved already, then states must have some latitude regarding the fulfilment of their rational obligations. With this purpose in mind, Kant made use of the concept of a broad or imperfect duty, but he denied that the selfish interest of a state could justify the non-fulfilment of these. Non-fulfilment itself could be tested to discern whether or not latitude was proportionate. If the distinction between perfect and imperfect obligations had operated traditionally to defend the liberty of the state, now it functioned within a theory of the moral development of world society; what had been employed within a non-progressivist account of international relations was now revised to meet the demands of a theory of international progress. By taking universalism seriously, by arguing for the humanisation of international relations, Kant fulfilled the latent aspirations within earlier strands of the rationalist tradition.

7 The Dissolution of Rationalist International Theory

> Man feels himself to be, first of all, German or French, and then only man as man.
>
> The unhappy attempt to transform the multiplicity of European life into the arid uniformity of universal sovereignty has produced the exclusive sway of nationality as the dominant political idea. Cosmopolitanism has receded too far. (Treitschke)

Although Kant must be located within the rationalist tradition, his greater sensitivity to the fact of human, historical development clearly distinguishes him from his immediate predecessors. Indeed, Kant's adoption of an historical perspective is critical to his attempt to rework and redirect the rationalist persuasion; it is essential to his task of overcoming those major inadequacies which had prevented rationalism from providing a coherent account of moral and political experience. Kant's theory cannot be dismissed lightly as yet another utopian peace plan. It offers considerably more, namely a profound statement of the kind of reorganisation of the world political system which must be undertaken if citizenship and humanity are no longer to suggest contradictory forms of behaviour.

Kant's theory is a supreme example of the principle that given the existence of 'a primordial moral community', 'the work of the political theorist begins in subordination to moral philosophy which seeks to establish the scope of the moral community, a man's claims on other men'. It also exemplifies the conviction that 'the political theorist's own proper province opens' not with a discussion of the rights and duties which bind men to one another as citizens but with

> a finding of the grounds on which men may . . . give priority to some of their fellows over others, of the terms on which they are required and entitled to segregate themselves from others in separate states, and of the obligations to all mankind which may be renounced and those which continue.[1]

With Kant's method, and with his substantive doctrine of obligation, rationalism may be said to achieve a certain perfection.

Nevertheless, various difficulties are associated with rationalism and the Kantian solution to its traditional problems. To state these, it is necessary to recall that the dominant trends in the political theory of the late eighteenth and nineteenth centuries were hostile to the individualistic and universalistic components of rationalist international thought. Critical of the belief in the uniformity of human nature and the supposed timelessness of moral principles, a new tradition of political thought refused to acknowledge that rationalism had identified the substantive problems of international society and the appropriate political method. This radical development stressed first the cultural and historical variability of moral beliefs and, later, the incommensurability of moral systems and the inevitability of conflict between them. It came to be argued that procedures for justifying or criticising either beliefs or actions would vary from one society to another in accordance with their diverse, and often mutually antagonistic, belief-systems. No universally true moral code embraced them all. The subversion of that realm of human obligation associated with rationalism produced a radically different conception of international political theory. Because reason was now held to be relative to culture, 'any attempt to turn upon the separate states in which we live and to question them in the name of some alleged reason beyond their history [would be] absurd'. For political theorists, the state had become 'the one, given, substantial thing on which it can get a grip'; from this perspective, 'political theory cannot pretend to criticise [men] and their states from an external standpoint because there is none'.[2]

The argument that no distinction could be made between the values of this time or place and the principles supplied by an overarching reason was, then, an argument in defence of particularism against universalism. But it was equally hostile to the classical contractarian approach to the state and the international states-system. This reconstructed defence of particularism denied that pre-social men had contracted to form predominantly self-regarding states, so fragmenting that natural society to which they had previously belonged. It was claimed that the primordial fact about the human race was its socially differentiated nature; the important point of departure for the political theory of international relations was the observation that humanity was naturally fragmented into a multiplicity of cultural wholes. Moral obligations were not to be conceived as issuing from some transcendent human reason or unchanging human essence; nor could they be understood in the terms in which contract theorists understood them, as the products of specific contracts whereby men organised themselves into several communities. In opposition to both positions, it was argued that obligations were intricately woven into the roles and responsibilities of the forms of cultural life from which individuals derived their diverse social identities; obligations were internal to forms of social life; they were socially produced and particularistic rather than ascertained by individuals and universalistic.

The basis of the revolt against rationalism must be discussed in the course of any attempt to identify the essential categories of an effective political theory of international relations. Three issues need to be discussed. Firstly, it is important to specify what was problematical within the rationalist tradition; secondly, we need to understand that perspective which was the consequence of the attempt to found a new theory of the internal nature of moral and political obligation – that is, we must briefly analyse the historicist contribution to international thought. Thirdly, it is necessary to consider a proposition whose precise meaning will become clearer later in this chapter. This proposition states that rationalism cannot give an adequate account of its own origins and development, or of the conditions of its existence, and that it may be undermined by revealing that its categories are not basic and self-sufficient but abstractions from a more complete categorial system; that while the historicist's concentration upon the social context of all thought and action may appear to lend that theory the completeness which rationalism had lacked, historicism must also be judged one-sided and defective. When we have completed this part of the argument, we shall be better able to identify the essential features of a position which seems capable of overcoming the limitations inherent in rationalism and historicism. Let us begin, however, by defining the problems which came to be associated with the rationalist system of categories.

The classical rationalist theories of Pufendorf and Vattel rested upon three interconnected propositions. Firstly, they assumed that the human race was naturally individuated, that it consisted originally of free and equal human beings. Secondly, they claimed that all individuals were in possession of the same set of human capacities. Certain unchanging and essential human powers or properties could therefore be imputed to individuals in a state of nature prior to the formation of organised social life. Because of these shared capacities, and particularly because it was assumed that individuals had the same moral understandings, it was believed to be meaningful to refer to the natural society of mankind. Thirdly, it was understood that a universal political system had been unnecessary because self-interested individuals had been able to satisfy their pre-social ends by contracting to join smaller-scale political societies. (Kant may be said to have shared the individualistic and universalistic elements of rationalism, albeit in a significantly modified form.) Each of these propositions is vulnerable to criticisms which stemmed from romanticism and were incorporated within subsequent traditions of thought.[3]

Modern social and political theory, influenced by the romantic critique, has been unsympathetic to the rationalist form of individualism, to the claim that we can talk about individuals as though they were

> real by themselves, and it is because of them that [social] relations are real. They make them, they are real in them, not because of them, and they would be just as real out of them. The whole is the mere sum of the parts, and the parts

are as real away from the whole as they are within the whole'.[4]

Early in the nineteenth century, this doctrine appeared as 'a moral version of Cartesian doubt', through which theorists sought to understand their society by breaking it down to 'the simplest, interchangeable parts and then reconstructing it from them'.[5] But as romanticism asserted, to think in these terms, and particularly in terms of an original state of nature, was either to be governed by historical inaccuracy or to be swayed by unnecessary and misleading fiction. For we cannot think in any meaningful way of men creating the conditions of their sociability, *ex nihilo*, in order to gain satisfaction for their naturally existing ends. In the nineteenth century this perspective is replaced with the now familiar claim that individuals and their ends are socially determined. Individualism is itself a cultural phenomenon. As Marx wrote, when individuals first make their appearance it is as a consequence of complex social processes which tear them from the 'umbilical' cords attaching them to their forms of social life.[6] In the beginning, men exhibit 'herd-consciousness';[7] only much later in their historical development do they appear as individuals or form the additional understanding that they are naturally so.

Individualism is a moral religion (it 'is a social product, like all moralities and religions. The individual receives from society even the moral beliefs which deify him');[8] but it is equally a form of alienation in which social powers or properties are imputed to individuals and regarded as their natural capacities. As such, it is impossible to give an account of individualism with recourse only to rationalist categories.[9] Individualism is not self-explanatory; to begin to explain it is to locate it within the social and historical development of men, a notion which is wholly absent from the rationalist framework.

Similar conclusions are reached when attention is turned to the rationalist supposition that there is a natural moral community of mankind. One of the earliest challenges to this tenet may be found in the writings of Vico. Vico stated that 'the three princes of the doctrine of the natural law of the gentes' (Grotius, Pufendorf and Selden) were wrong to assume that men in their natural condition possessed absolute knowledge of the principles of human reason and right association. Those theorists

> believed that natural equity in its perfect form had been understood by the gentile nations from their first beginnings; they did not reflect that it took some two thousand years for philosophers to appear in any of them...[10]

Modern natural law was accused then of wrongly imputing a set of universalistic ethical beliefs to men in their more primitive condition. To think that a peculiarly modern moral perspective was shared by men at the beginning of history was to assume the existence of an immutable, universal set of human moral capacities; and it was therefore to ignore the complex social and historical forces which had made universalism possible.

The rejection of rationalism frequently leads to an emphasis upon the fact that originally men were members of tribal groupings whose moralities were social and invariably exclusive as befitted their needs and experience. In 'the early stages of ethics', it is argued, 'rights and duties do not attach to a human being as such. They attach to him as a member of a group'; for 'morality is in its origins group-morality'.[11] It is not enough to say that men in this condition failed to acknowledge a moral code which governed them and the immediate outsiders with whom they had contact; the very idea of a natural human morality was unintelligible to them, and it was so because the idea had not been created. To understand this is to see the necessity of raising issues which escaped the attention of rationalism; in particular, it involves attempting to comprehend those processes which dissolve particularistic communities and result in the claim that men have rights and duties to one another by virtue of their shared humanity. A more complete theory than rationalism will respond to the existence of social change and moral development by proposing an account of the emergence of universalism.

Individualism and universalism have an historical formation; before anything else, they must be produced. The same objection must be levelled against the terms in which rationalists sought to explain the existence of separate political societies. The ideas of self-interest, reciprocity and contract are historically evolved and culturally specific concepts associated especially with modern ideas about social relations and principles of government. They are neither natural nor universal. Societies were not constructed from the self-interested calculations of independent individuals or from their natural capacity to engage in the creation of reciprocal forms of social relations. The separate calculations of independent individuals neither precede nor underpin the existence of separate, sovereign states. The originally small-scale and exclusive nature of social and moral life, the early estrangement between one group and another, made such calculations unnecessary. Only later in their history did societies develop categories and concepts of social relations which made it possible for them to enter into, and value, more extended communities. Not until considerably later did they believe that a universal society was a natural condition which lacked a single government because of the self-interested calculations, prevalent everywhere, in favour of creating many political communities. But to have come to think so was to impute universality to what was no more than a historically conditioned perspective.

Rationalists had abstracted certain concepts, or particular ways of behaving, from their context and had claimed suprahistorical validity for them. As we have seen, later thinkers were aware that what was assumed to prevail naturally and universally had gained acceptance only within specific social frameworks in the modern epoch.[12] Rationalists, consequently, had failed to see the need to give an account of the origins of their perspective, of the conditions which made it possible. To offer this kind of explanation, moreover, it was necessary to transcend the categories which constituted the rationalist *genre* and underpinned its political theory of international relations. A substantive doctrine with its own distinctive understanding of international relations was developed within the historicist tradition.[13]

Employing the romanticist critique of individualism and universalism, historicists claimed that the capacities of men were linked inextricably with the forms of life with which they were involved. By claiming that moral capacities were similarly dependent, it was believed possible to subvert the belief in a universal moral constituency required by the universality of reason. The latter world-view was predicated upon the wrongful abstraction of individuals from their social and historical contexts. Individuals, it was argued, were not men first, and French or German afterwards; it was not 'true, physiologically or historically, that men come into the world first as men and only afterwards as compatriots'.[14] Only in the West had thinkers become preoccupied with analysing man's condition as it might have been prior to the development of different social and political practices. Nevertheless, that discourse which aimed to depict the natural characteristics of man simply underlined its own cultural limitations; invariably, existing social categories were imputed to the thought and action of natural man. Culture's unavoidable and irreducible qualities were no more evident than in the theorist's ambition to transcend them.

Therefore, it was argued that the fundamental fact about humanity was the existence of cultural individualities. Individuals were not undifferentiated members of a humanity which might attain political unification, but participants within diverse communities of 'intellect and spirit' which had developed in history. The function of states was not to maximise the pre-social requirements of their members but to preserve and enhance the cultures for which they were responsible. Human existence involved cultural pluralism and the necessity of recognising division into states. Historicists believed they had established that a theory of obligations to humanity was problematic; the aspiration to specify the duties between all men was immediately to privilege values dominant only within one culture. But the denial of transcultural or suprahistorical values was not a denial, it was supposed, of a genuinely international political theory. Historicism took humanity to be neither an essence shared by all men nor a set of innate natural tendencies, but the totality of cultural configurations.[15] Humanity was revealed in the various, if not infinite, human expressions which could be discerned only through observation of what men had unfolded in their diverse cultural contexts. No single culture could manifest the totality of human possibilities;[16] since every state had a significant role to play in preserving and unfolding human capacities, separate states did not detract from, but enhanced, humanity.

Historicism produced a distinctive variation upon those themes and concerns which were considered earlier to be the basic elements of the internal concept of obligation. The concept of the absolute sovereignty of the state, the distinction between private and public morality, the pragmatic approach to international cooperation, reappear within it; but now these are predicated not upon an individualistic and contractarian account of the state but upon a theory of the significance of diverse cultural expressions.

It was argued that each culture had the right of access to its own sovereign institutions under the rubric that political separation is essential if cultural pluralism is to be preserved and enhanced. Because of the pre-eminence of cultural entities, states must be conceived to be the outer limits of significant social cohesion and legal relationships; 'the ideal of a state co-extensive with humanity' was, in Treitschke's words, 'no ideal at all'.[17] The state's right to its sovereignty was absolute; its duty to preserve itself, and its honour, by any means at its disposal could not be qualified by any law or morality supposedly higher than its particular will.[18]

Since each state had the right, and indeed the obligation, to enhance its own particular variant on humanity, disputes and differences between states were inevitable: 'international contradictions'[19] could not be superseded by a condition of perpetual peace. And, as the use of force was a necessary part of the state's existence and the statesman's role, the tension between a private and public morality was 'plainly inevitable and as old as world history itself'.[20] Horizontal moral ties between the individual members of world society were simply illusory and our moral and political experience, properly understood, could not display that deep division, present in earlier theories, between the obligations of citizenship and the obligations of humanity.

Nevertheless, despite the absolute sovereign rights of the state, and the distinction between public and private morality, there was a place within the historicist conception of the states-system for the existence of reciprocated rights and duties. International law could evolve within, and was essential to the functioning of, the international states-system. But it was a law which emanated from the wills of sovereigns, and it was a law which each might break unilaterally when it saw fit.[21]

Clearly, historicists consciously attempted to overcome that dichotomy between men and citizens which had been so critical within rationalist philosophy. The rejection of any transcendent reason with far-reaching claims upon the members of sovereign states meant that there were no conceivable foundations for a critique of the system of states. The latter was a climax, not a dominant; it was the most perfect form of world political organisation within which to develop the totality of cultural configurations. Historicism would neither posit the idea of a natural society of mankind, nor share with Kant that vision of a differently constituted international system, one marked by cosmopolitanism and perpetual peace. This, indeed, was the immediate consequence of reducing individualism and universalism to the level of mere abstraction.

The historicist critique of natural law theory appears unanswerable. If, as historicists claimed, reason is embodied within vastly different forms of life rather than present in one single, universal form in the minds of pre-social individuals, then it is not upon the basis of natural law theory that the idea of horizontal moral ties binding together the whole human race, or the critique of the international states-system, can be established. And if no immutable standard of morality is acknowledged by the whole of humanity, but several standards, each expressed within a different cultural whole, then historicism must be deemed an important advance beyond the abstract position of rationalism, even though it throws the traditional bases of international political theory into confusion.

However, despite the initial appeal of historicism, it can be argued that its categories, like those of its opponent, rationalism, are equally one-sided. Historicism subverts itself because it generates its own particular set of limitations and internal contradictions. Rather than dwell on the more familiar form of argument that historicist reasoning is self-refuting, let us focus instead upon certain problems which arise in its attempt to redefine the relationship between specific cultures and humanity.

In order to do this, let us assume the existence of two

cultures which are founded upon antagonistic conceptions of international relations. While one culture accepts the historicist's claim that all cultural configurations help to manifest humanity, and acknowledges obligations to other states on this basis, the other confines obligations simply to members of its own, allegedly superior cultural formation. The historicist argument is that each culture is necessary in order to manifest the diverse range of human possibilities. This observation has a highly specific meaning, since these cultures negate rather than complement each other, namely that they reveal man's capacity to express himself in wholly antagonistic forms of life. To make a different assertion, it would be necessary to choose between these cultures on the grounds that one expressed human potentialities more adequately than the other. Although this point resurrects that very dichotomy which historicism was summoned to deny, it is a division which historicists cannot avoid. For, if we consider the relations between these two cultures, on what basis can the first assert that the second should recognise its contribution to human powers; and, on what basis can it claim that the other should recognise its rightful existence as a separate, sovereign state? It is not possible for the first culture to make its appeal on the basis of the equal importance of cultures. For on the same basis its opponent may claim that its denial of obligations to outsiders is its specific contribution to the full elaboration of cultural possibilities. While historicist reasoning appeared to believe that a principle of the equal importance of cultures was coincidental with the principle that cultures should treat one another as moral equals, it is now apparent that these propositions bear no logical relationship whatsoever. At this point the historicist confronts a clear choice: either the principle of equal importance is advocated, with the consequence that there is no longer the same defence of the states-system, or the principle of moral equality is advocated at the expense of regarding various cultural systems as equally valid. Since the historicists made the decision to advocate the second principle, they reintroduced a dichotomy not unlike that found within classic rationalist theory. In brief, to assert the value of the principle of the equal treatment of cultures in the face of a claim to reject it, is to resurrect a division between a concrete culture and a moral principle which transcends it.

Three further problems complicate the historicist perspective. Firstly, the value of cultural diversity or pluralism is simply presumed within the theory. No defence of this value is provided; no concession is granted to the objection that it is a culturally specific ideal. Indeed, the concept of cultural pluralism is to historicism what individualism and universalism had been to rationalism, an incontestable fact, a natural truth rather than a social and historical development. And since the celebration of cultural diversity has a history, it is no more reasonable to begin here than with the notion of free and equal individuals bound by a universal law in a state of nature. Both rationalism and historicism fail to take account of the fact that their basic categories are not sufficient unto themselves, but need to be considered within a broader, more historical perspective. And this perspective might well contain the observation that, in the beginning, men were estranged from one another by virtue of their membership of particularistic groups, and that it was only in their subsequent development that moral universalism or cultural pluralism came to be conceptualised and highly valued. If this much is granted, some justification ought to be provided for the claim that the development of either of these phenomena ought to be preferred to any of the possible alternatives.

In the second place, historicism may be made the object of a critique similar to the one which it directed against natural law. If the latter abstracted individuals from their historically evolving cultures, the former abstracted cultures (beliefs, values, etc.) from the wider context within which humans and their powers develop. In particular, historicism focused upon culture and cultural development, and omitted the existence of man's social interaction with nature, the production of his material life.[22] Furthermore, the ways in which different societies act on nature leads to the conclusion that some societies are more successful than others; and this invites consideration of whether or not some societies' conceptions of the natural world, and the structure of their productive relations, might be more progressive than others'.

Lastly, historicism maintained that different powers and possibilities were manifested in various cultures. But it did not take account of the fact that culture in the singular, human practice, had to be produced by beings with the capacity for cultural and historical life. Marx's observation that man is part of nature yet able to transcend it is pertinent here. History for Marx is 'the humanisation of the ape',[23] the medium in which there develops the powers of a species with the unique capacity of being able to transcend its origins in nature. By failing to accommodate this fundamental insight, historicists shared the defects of the philosophical position to which they were most opposed.

To develop this theme further: the classical theory of natural law held that all men, by virtue of their common creation, shared the same human nature. Embedded within that nature was the capacity to apprehend permanently valid moral principles. But natural law theorists did not assume that these truths were 'known to all men at all times, in all societies, in an equal degree of perfection'.[24] If different standards of rationality operated at different times and places, then men had not yet come to understand the content of the natural law, a law embedded in their nature, and valid whether they understood it properly or not; the empirical fact that moral practices varied from one society to another was not sufficient then to endorse some version of ethical relativism.

From this perspective, the movement from particularistic to universalistic conceptions of morality meant that men had come to know what had always been true. With this development man's existence and essence now corresponded. Natural law theory proposed a static measure with which to gauge the degree of human progress. By comparing empirical social circumstances with what is permanent in human nature, by referring to the content of the human essence, it was said to be possible to ascertain the precise degree of human development. But various problems are associated with the concept of human essence as this is conceived within the parameters of natural law theory. The belief that men have pre-established or God-given ends moves discussion beyond the scope of what can be philosophically demonstrated and into the uncertain realm of theology. Moreover, reference to the human essence overlooks the more fundamental fact that 'humanity is a matter of degree',[25] or that history is the medium within which distinctively human capacities emerge, or in which humanity itself is formed. Natural law, of whatever kind, disregards the existence of man's gradual humanisation, of the process that is undergone as the animal is transformed into man through the mediation of a variety of changing social configurations. Human nature has a history or formation of a much more radical kind than the natural lawyer can admit. Historicists supersede natural law doctrines in several respects but they do not accomplish a sufficient break with the latter's categories. An adequate political theory of international relations must rest not upon the supposed universality of certain ethical understandings, or upon the presumption that mankind is necessarily divided into various, self-sufficient cultural wholes, but upon the recognition that what is fundamental is the fact of the historical formation of human capacities.

What is necessary therefore is a theory which gives an account not of a nature which is always constant, but a nature which makes history possible and is unfolded within it. This perspective is present within the doctrine known as 'expressivism'.[26] For expressivists, human creations were not to be measured by suprahistorical standards, or judged in comparison with what is constant in human nature; they were expressions of what men believed their nature to be at any given time; and they were the instruments whereby they clarified what they were. Their historical actions and arrangements were the elements of the process of their humanisation. Furthermore, for these theorists the ideal social and political world was not a part of the 'fulfilment of an idea or plan which [was] fixed independently of the subject who realises it'.[27] The gradual understanding of the most adequate form of social life was not the realisation of what best conformed with a human ideal which was 'wholly determinate' beforehand. The structure of the human ideal acquired shape, or became gradually more determinate, as men gained self-knowledge through their activities, through time.

In brief, the expressivist account of history sought to understand the nature and potentialities of human, historical subjects. Its beginning was the belief that history's *a priori* was the existence of a being with the capacity to transcend the world of natural determination. What had to be discerned therefore were those characteristics which explained the emergence and development of a non-natural being, a being distinct from the world of nature. Not surprisingly, this ambition was executed through an analysis of man's early immersion in, or interaction with, the natural world. As we shall see later, theorists of history expanded Rousseau's conjecture that early man was a natural being with the latent capacity for free action and self-improvement. Each shared the belief that history was made possible by the existence of beings which were free. To be free, on this account, was not to be beyond the jurisdiction of law, to be unconstrained as in the state of nature posited by the contract theorists, but to be self-determining or to have the capacity to initiate action. Man was a unique being, a participant within the dimension of history, because of his capacity to set his own ends.

His uniqueness, moreover, stemmed not only from his power of self-determination but from his potentiality for self-development. Man was not a static being; he underwent radical transformation in the course of positing and acting upon his selected ends. What was open to him as an historical being was the ability to enlarge his freedom through ever-increasing rational control of his self and his environment. Indeed, his distinctive human power was the ability to live in a world of his own making, 'a second nature',[28] in which he expressed his own reason and freedom. Through the medium of history, men could come to grasp the adequate goals for free beings together with the conditions most favourable to their realisation. Gradually, they gained a form of self-knowledge which was always theirs' potentially, a form of knowledge which was expressed only in the more advanced socio-political arrangements.

Since the creation of a world of self-determining beings was a gradual historical process, it was inconceivable that all societies could be judged to be equally valid, equally advanced. Different societies could be placed on a scale of types according to the extent to which their members understood and expressed the nature of their power of self-determination. Theorists of history within this tradition proposed principles of 'historical periodisation' which would exhibit the main stages in man's growth to higher forms of understanding. This urge to place different societies on a scale of ascending types is present, as we shall see in the next chapter, in Hegel's analysis of world-historical peoples and in Marx's consideration of various types of socially organised systems of production.[29]

This understanding of man as a dynamic, self-constituting being necessarily takes issue with natural law doctrines and historicism alike. The former were judged wrong to have assumed that the right ends for man were fixed independently of his history because they were given in his nature or pre-determined by his creator. The belief in the immutability of human nature and in the static composition of man's powers overlooked his continuous historical transformation. Natural law doctrines abstracted human nature from the formative role of concrete systems of social relations. Medieval natural law theories with their conception of the universe as a system of interdependent parts, each possessing its distinctive *telos*, confused the natural and normative realms. Laws of nature derived their validity from their existence while laws of social conduct depended for their legitimacy upon human endorsement. A focus upon man's historical development necessitated a division between the repetitive physical world and the potentially progressive world of history.[30] On the other hand, historicists failed to offer any account of the character of a being which existed in a cultural and historical dimension; their theories failed to give prominence to the formation and development of unique human powers.

To a limited extent, earlier theorists suggested that an adequate political philosophy of international relations must be grounded upon a theory of the history of human subjects. For Kant and Green, the ideal political environment gradually acquired determinate shape in the minds of men as they developed their capacity to live in a world governed by rational principles freely imposed upon themselves. To use Kantian terminology, the human species gradually realised its unique capacity to combine its individualisation with cosmopolitanism as it evolved towards that condition in which all men were regarded as co-legislators within an international kingdom of ends. Furthermore, the idea of a scale of forms of approaches to international relations occurs in Kantian thought. Kant claimed that a 'minor motive' for attempting a philosophical history would be the issue of what various societies had contributed to the growth of world citizenship.[31] An expressivist approach to the political theory of international relations raises the prospect of placing different political associations, or systems of states, upon a hierarchy of social and political forms in accordance with their distance from or proximity to a condition in which the idea of self-determination is properly extended into the realm of international relations. The possibility arises of tracing the development of reason in international history, or measuring the levels of humanisation in the world of intersocietal relations.

We noted earlier that the critical theory of international relations included the idea that a states-system in which men aimed to establish institutions which expressed their belief that human beings had 'a claim upon human society as a whole' was more adequate than one in which particularistic social moralities were thought to possess absolute validity. A cosmopolitan culture would occupy a higher place on a scale of social and political types than one in which moral sensibilities were concentrated exclusively upon insiders. On this basis, theorists of history can criticise plans of 'geographical morality' without succumbing to the criticism that they have superimposed an abstracted, suprahistorical ethic upon diverse social systems. They can derive criteria for determining the extent of human progress from the character of man's historical existence alone; nothing exists beyond or outside history as a measure of social development. Certain theorists of history believed that it was possible to regard particularistic moralities as forms of human understanding which would be superseded in time as men grasped the nature of their capacity for self-determination. By developing the resources of the philosophy of history, they made possible the restoration of that mode of inquiry into forms of international relations which had been subverted by the historicist assault on rationalism.

Without anticipating later developments in our argument, it may be suggested that the expressivist tradition provided the basis for a new approach to the division between men and citizens. Philosophical history transformed the meaning of that dichotomy, thereby pointing the way to the means by which it could be overcome. Within the theory of history, the dichotomy between man and citizen is not, as historicism suggested, a feature of an idiosyncratic moral code; nor is it, as rationalism suggested, a conflict between a particularistic social morality and the requirements of an immutable, universal moral code. If historicism sought to subvert the rationalist method of characterising the division between citizenship and humanity, numerous theorists of history responded to the dichotomy by regarding it as an historical product involved with the development of freedom.[32] Therefore, although the dichotomy may arise within particular cultures only, and at certain points in their evolution, its significance is held to be more profound and relevant to the formation of the human species at large. This characterisation of the conflict sees it as an expression of the capacity to apprehend the universality of human nature, and as an awareness of the fact that this universality is frustrated by the division of men between particularistic groups. In modern conditions the conflict between man and citizen reveals dissatisfaction of a specific kind, namely with those impediments upon human freedom and rationality which stem from the sovereign state itself and the constitutive principles of the international system. Philosophical history begins to suggest that the resolution of the conflict within modern moral and political experience requires the transformation of political life so that the human capacity for self-determination can be expressed more perfectly.

The next chapter will consider the relationship between freedom and history in different conceptions of philosophical history. We shall also discuss the way in which different theories of international relations were formulated within this perspective. But we shall find that it is possible to argue that the desirability of a higher form of international political life than the modern states-system can be defended within a theory of history. The latter creates the foundations for that radical critique of the state and the states-system which modern natural law theory was unwilling to undertake, and which historicism was unable to supply.

8 Freedom and History in the Political Theory of International Relations

> Imagination has often pictured to itself the emotions of a blind man suddenly becoming possessed of sight, beholding the bright glimmering of the dawn, the growing light, and the flaming glory of the ascending Sun. The boundless forgetfulness of his individuality in this pure splendour, is his first feeling – utter astonishment. But when the Sun is risen, this astonishment is diminished; . . . Then inactive contemplation is quitted for activity; by the close of day man has erected a building constructed from his own inner Sun; and when in the evening he contemplates this, he esteems it more highly than the original external Sun. For now he stands in a conscious relation to his Spirit, and therefore a free relation. If we hold this image fast in mind, we shall find it symbolising the course of History, the great Day's work of Spirit. (Hegel)

In this chapter I propose to consider the resources which philosophical history makes available to the contemporary theorist of international relations. A more detailed discussion of this perspective allows the formulation of a new approach to the problem of men and citizens in part three.

The attempt to construct an international political theory confronts that impasse which results from the modern antinomy between ethical absolutism and the modern successor to historicism, ethical relativism. Certain problems have already been discerned in those doctrines which assume either that reason is immutable and universal, or that it is plural and culturally relative, partitioned between incommensurable moral systems. Ethical absolutism with its belief in moral universals can be criticised for having neglected the various cultural and historical determinants of human powers. But if we jettison this doctrine in its classical form, we confront the equally unattractive position that there may be as many international political theories as there are ways of life, for no single, common discourse transcends them all. However, ethical relativism is not a satisfactory alternative to ethical universalism. Rightly, it is accused of self-contradiction because it assumed its own privileged immunity from a relativity which allegedly subverts all other doctrines. Relativists argue that there are no transcultural criteria which allow the rational ordering of cultures; but they are committed to arguing that a culture which adopts a relativist perspective is more progressive or adequate than one which does not, and indeed if this conclusion were to be denied it becomes unclear how relativism could claim any greater validity than alternative positions.

Philosophical history may be said to overcome these difficulties. From this perspective, reason is neither uniform nor inevitably plural and diverse; it is developmental, it has a history. Ethical absolutism and relativism appear as sides of a false dichotomy. Neither offers an account of the growth and transformation of both human subjects and the practices in which they are objectified. Theorists of history claimed that a presuppositionless comprehension of man must analyse the historical formation and gradual development of his species-powers; moreover, theoretical history would be accounted for as an element within the processes of human development which it sought to understand.[1]

If human reason has a history the prospect arises of distinguishing several stages in its evolution. Different social formations may be placed on a scale of forms, a hierarchy of types, in accordance with the precise level of rationality embodied within them. Similarly, different conceptions of international relations, different intersocietal arrangements, might be set out on a scale of ascending forms. We shall attempt to execute this task in subsequent chapters, but at this stage we must have a clearer understanding of what is involved in the design of a scale of social forms which attempts to encapsulate the development of freedom.

While theorists of history claimed that history was occasioned by man's unique ability to transcend nature, that history revealed man's power to set himself increasingly rational ends, and that history supplied grounds for the conviction that it was within man's power to appropriate a comprehensive knowledge of the conditions of individual and collective self-determination, they attached different meanings to these propositions. Propositions which are present in Kant's thought undergo a more complex elaboration in the writings of Hegel and Marx; and indeed this is unsurprising since the philosophy of history itself has a history. It is important therefore to consider what these different theories meant when they claimed that reason had a history, or that history revealed the progressive enlargement of the conditions of human freedom; equally, it is necessary to determine how these principles were employed to construct a scale of types of organisation, and what impact they had upon conceptions of international relations. Only when this has been achieved can we begin to apply the resources of philosophical history to problems of international political theory.

The distinctive properties of philosophical history were systematically presented in Kant's political and historical writings.[2] If the principal ethical writings appeared to presume the static nature of human reason, these later writings acknowledge the fact of man's historicity and the development of his reason.[3] Nevertheless, for Kant the proposition that history was progressive could be stated only as a 'regulative' idea, that is, it was brought by the philosopher of history to his study of the past.[4] The idea of progress enabled Kant to determine whether or not the apparent conflict between morality and actual historical action was in the process of being overcome. Decisive proof of progress in history would have to await the appearance of one with the equivalent resources of a Newton or Kepler.

Kant's conjectures on the beginning of human history postulate a condition in which all men are immersed in the natural world, unaware of their uniqueness or potentialities, unaware of their selves, ignorant of both time and death.[5] In the beginning man was only man potentially; he was an animal with latent human powers. The characteristic which distinguished him from the rest of natural creation was his possession of the capacity to reason and imagine. Using this capacity it was possible for man to transcend the natural world of fixed needs and unchanging powers by creating desires which were contrary to natural instincts. By experimenting to discover how far he could transcend instinct, man severed himself from the natural world and was precipitated, painfully at first, into an historical dimension. History was occasioned by, and was the subsequent medium for, the development of man's non-natural powers; it was the medium within which specifically human powers were cast. It was man's peculiar fate, which made him neither a beast nor a god, that he should participate within two worlds, the world of his own making and the world of natural desire; it was his particular and peculiar fate to encounter an ineluctable division within his self, the division between his noumenal and phenomenal self.

Men had freedom by virtue of a process (unexplained within the theory) which resulted in individuals being uniquely endowed with the capacity to select their ends. While they could neither eradicate the natural part of the self nor wholly eliminate the possibility of succumbing to natural inclination, humans could create a world of culture or human practice which revealed their capacity to raise themselves above the repetitive world of nature. Their capacity to produce a world of culture was first expressed in any important sense with the formation of states. Competition and conflict between naturally independent individuals developed human rationality to the point at which individuals recognised the value of submission to law. Their 'unsocial sociability' propelled men to establish a new kind of freedom, civil freedom, which was expressed specifically in legal guarantees for persons and their property. Human freedom achieved its highest expression, however, not merely in the fact of choice (natural freedom) nor in the existence of legal constraints upon inclination (civil freedom) but through the capacity to exercise self-constraint by acting in conformity with moral imperatives legislated by human reason (moral freedom). Kant's typology of human freedoms reveals the important influence of Rousseau; and his statement that man is most free when he obeys morality echoes, as we saw earlier, Rousseau's search for a political condition in which men obey laws while maintaining the freedom they possessed in the original state of nature, that is by obeying the laws which they themselves make.[6]

Through the enactment of moral principles men realise their non-natural powers and unfold what is unique to their species. To act morally was, as we have seen, to recognise other men as ends in themselves, equally transcendent of nature. Membership of a universal kingdom of ends was therefore the highest phase of social life, that condition in which men disclosed more perfectly than ever before the distinctive features of their species, that which differentiated them most of all from merely natural life.

Man's major destiny was to stand over and above the natural world which without him 'would be a mere waste, in vain, and without purpose'.[7] Kant thought in terms of a teleological principle unifying the worlds of nature and history. Nature or Providence

> willed that man should by himself, produce everything that goes beyond the mechanical ordering of his animal existence, and that he should partake of no other happiness or perfection than that which he himself, independently of instinct, has created by his own reason.[8]

Ideally, human history would begin 'with man's partial and end with his total transcendence of nature'.[9] Human history therefore accomplished something without parallel in nature, the emergence and development of a being which came to understand the meaning and preconditions of freedom. Thus Kant announces, and it is the recurrent and distinctive voice of philosophical history, that:

> Man's departure from that paradise which his reason represents as the first abode of his species was nothing but the transition from an uncultured, merely animal condition to the state of humanity, from bondage to instinct to rational control – in a word, from the tutelage of nature to the state of freedom.[10]

Man distances himself most from his natural origins, nature within him, when he recognises that it would be self-contradictory to treat others as means to his own ends; for others are not parts of nature, but equally free beings;[11] and it is therefore his duty to place constraints upon his own conduct so that the freedom of each is compatible with the freedom of all.

There is no need to restate the content of Kant's theory of international relations. Suffice it to say that international progress is defined against the background of the historical development of man from the condition of natural to civil, and then to moral freedom. But what is problematical about this scale and its application to international relations is its expression of Kant's unqualified moral and political individualism. Kant assumed that the human race was naturally individuated, and by so doing his philosophical history did not emancipate itself from those one-sided categories constitutive of rationalism. Progress at the domestic and international level is defined by the extent to which guarantees are made available to individual freedom, 'the one sole and original right that belongs to every man by virtue of his humanity'.[12] But this is an ahistorical position. Kant neglected the fact that individuation is a social process, and his statement that the development of morality is the evolution of the rationality inherent within the individual overlooks the social contexts of individuals and their modes of thinking.

Kantian theory overlooked the possibility of progress within, and in relations between, societies which are not individuated. And having associated historical development exclusively with the activities of free individuals, it lacked an effective theory of change. Change can only be explained within the theory as a function of conflict between independent individuals, or as an outcome of their unsocial sociability. Therefore, whether or not the liberal-individualism of Kant is acceptable, its philosophical foundations are insecure and its implications for the construction of a scale of social forms or international arrangements are too restrictive.

For Hegel, Kantian individualism had to be located within the development of different forms of social consciousness. Like universalism, it was to be understood as a stage, albeit a necessary one, in the progressive development of self-consciousness, a development whose highest expression could be found in the social and political institutions of the modern state. However, the contrast between the realms of freedom and nature is similarly crucial to the structure of Hegel's philosophy of history. Having divested the theory of history of the rationalist tendencies which permeated its Kantian formulation, Hegel proceeds to identify the stages of man's emancipation from nature rather differently. Kant's individualism considered progress as the individual's gradual domination of the natural impulses within him. (For Hegel, Kant had purchased moral freedom at the cost of bifurcating the human personality and establishing an internal despotism, the tyranny of reason over the passions.)[13] Although the Kantian division between reason and nature is not eliminated from the Hegelian theory of the self, Hegel contends that freedom is not attained by dominating natural impulses but through their ordered articulation within a harmoniously constructed personality. But more significantly for present purposes, Hegel characterises the distinction between freedom and nature as a distinction between societies which have and societies which have not severed their connection with nature. The break between reason and nature is a break with the unity with nature which characterised man's early social life. It was an elementary and necessary development if men were to ascend those social stages whereby they gradually formed their distinctively human powers.[14]

Hegel argues that the formation of species-powers required man's transcendence of those societies in which men think they are governed by natural powers and forces and believe that social distinctions have their origins in nature or confront men as naturally sanctioned. In this condition the social world does not appear as a product of human interaction, nor does it seem subject to human modification and control. But this is an alienated form of consciousness for what men are unaware of at this level of social organisation – exemplified for instance by the Indian caste-system – is the fact that it is their cultural framework which endows nature with authority over them; it is they themselves who have conferred social power and meaning upon natural phenomena. Since they are dominated by nature, they can neither exercise any choice over the structure of their social relations nor can they control them. In Hegelian terms they are therefore unfree.

The simplest forms of social development, or of the growth of human powers, consisted of a separation between the worlds of society and nature, between a world which is and a world which is not an expression of human reason and will.[15] It consisted therefore of the knowledge that history is human practice and that social relations may be determined by human deliberations. Under these circumstances a culture produces both historical narrative and political activity. In the Greek *polis*, the principal and most sublime manifestation of this development, the human spirit comes to know 'itself [as] free in its productions';[16] there, moreover, 'the democratic constitution' comes to be regarded as the apt form of political organisation for a being which has acquired knowledge of its capacity to exercise control over its social relations, which has come to know something of what it means to be free.[17]

Nevertheless, the Greek conception of freedom was limited and parochial since Greeks had 'the habit of living for their country without further [analysis] or reflection'. Neither non-citizens nor barbarians participated in the enjoyment of a free life. Spontaneously and uncritically, Greeks enacted those custom-given roles and responsibilities which maintained their limited form of life. Gradually, but with revolutionary impact, the process of individuation took place. Not until the Sophists did men articulate the principle that 'each man should act according to his own conviction'; only then was the individual to claim to be 'in a position to bring everything to the test of his own conscience, even in defiance of the existing constitution'.[18] Critical individualism subverted the citizen's immediate identification with the *polis*, and led both to the deepening of individual life and the flourishing of human reasoning. Freedom demanded more than the knowledge that society issued from human interaction; it required acceptance of the claim that a free form of social organisation should be founded upon rational principles which individuals had self-consciously formulated and adopted.

In the later stages of Greek culture, the range of persons who were recognised to be entitled to a free life was gradually extended. Distinctions between persons became problematical and pressures intensified within Greek culture to recognise that all were free. Later Greek culture witnessed the development of the principle that all men, as beings elevated above nature, or with the capacity to choose, possessed 'infinite worth', and this too contributed to the further dissolution of Greek life. Higher stages in the development of freedom were accompanied by the transcendence of traditional forms of intersocietal estrangement.[19] Particularistic social moralities decayed as the principle developed that rights and duties were inherent in human personality itself. The evolution of human capacities led to the belief in the existence of a universal community which embraced all individuals by virtue of their possession of reason; and it was the modern world in particular, influenced by the Stoic–Christian tradition, which most developed this principle of individual freedom. Accordingly, Hegel characterised the main stages of human development by stating that 'the Eastern nations knew only that one is free; the Greek and Roman world only that some are free, while we know that men absolutely [man as man] are free'.[20]

For Hegel an account of the development of human powers must analyse the emergence and evolution of societies which are based upon rational, critical thinking. The development of human freedom is exhibited in man's increasingly rational control of his self and his environment. In brief, history consists of ascending forms of social life, proceeding from those which introduce the dichotomy between nature and spirit, through those which witness the appearance of individualism and universalism, to those which found laws upon consciously chosen rational principles. The culmination of this process in modern history is the sovereign state. Within this community, within a community of rational law-makers, humans realise the triumph of thought over nature, and express those capacities (particularly the potentiality for free, rational conduct) which are specific to human subjects.[21]

Hegel acknowledged that men had rights as men, rights which they came to regard as adequate to their historically developed powers. But he opposed the crystallisation of this doctrine in the form of a cosmopolitanism which took issue with the roles and responsibilities integral to the state.

Philosophy should seek to discern the rationality which is inherent in existing political practices; it should renounce the rationalist aspiration of setting out the practices which ought to hold ideally. Rationalism disassociated reason from history; it sought to give an account of ideal social and political arrangements independently of the historical processes of their realisation. But Hegel's theory did not detect reason only in the domestic institutions of the state. Among the rational practices developed in the modern world Hegel included the fact that states extend recognition to one another and agree to conduct their hostilities without harming 'persons in their private capacity'.[22] We may wonder whether or not these practices go far enough. The immediate problem arises of the apparent contradiction between the principle of human freedom, which demands the rational organisation of political life, and the actual operations of the international states-system, the coercive or uncontrolled relations which pertain to the life of states. Once again we may inquire whether or not a contradiction begins to reappear between the forms of interaction connected with modern man's existence as a citizen, and his humanity, his nature as a free being.

Hegel has been criticised on the grounds that a 'fully rational and free community' would require the establishment of an international association which articulates the wills of its component parts just as the state articulates the wills of various associations within its particular jurisdiction.[23] In this connection Kant's theory of international relations has more insight because it highlights the negative side of sovereignty and undertakes a critique of the 'wild, lawless freedom' of the state. Although Hegel rejected both Kantian rationalism and associated utopianism, which disassociated reason from history, his famous conception of the retrospective qualities of political philosophy should not diminish his apparent hesitation to declare the states-system the highest form of objective spirit:

> It is as particular entities that states enter into relations with one another. Hence their relations are on the largest scale a maelstrom of external contingency and the inner particularity of passions, private interests and selfish ends, abilities and virtues, vices, force and wrong. All these whirl together,

> and in their vortex the ethical whole itself, the autonomy of the state, is exposed to contingency.[24]

Indeed, it has been argued that ultimately the development of freedom in history involved for Hegel the incorporation of states within a world 'united by culture and reason'.[25] Whether or not this is a correct interpretation of Hegel's thought, his remarks on possible future configurations of the world spirit should cast considerable doubt upon the proposition that the European state represented the highest form of political association.[26] Such a conclusion appears radically at odds with the general system of such a profoundly historical thinker as Hegel. If Hegel wished to avoid detailed analysis of alternative political realities, he certainly did not presume that changes of political structure should be dismissed as improbable.

Hegel detected the elements of ethical life within the European states-system: 'the European peoples form a family in accordance with the universal principle underlying their legal codes, their customs, and their civilisation'. And he observed that this element of sociability within the modern states-system had 'modified . . . a state of affairs [i.e. war] otherwise dominated by the mutual infliction of evils'.[27] These remarks on the nature of international relations reflect those broader ambiguities within Hegel's thought which precipitated the famous split within the Hegelian movement. Within his writings there is the suggestion that the historical development of reason has yet to make any significant impact upon the external lives of states. However, Hegel failed to give philosophical shape to those developments which had led to the emergence of elements of ethical life within the states-system; and he failed, unlike Kant, to identify existing obstacles to, or constraints upon, the further development of rational control of the environment, or upon freedom.

However, Hegel's system is philosophically superior to its Kantian predecessor because it incorporates individualism and universalism within a theory of the history of social and political life. Kantianism breaks down because its categories do not supply an adequate account of the conditions of their own existence, and because its philosophical categories are stated in abstraction from the social conditions which make them possible. Hegelianism, on the other hand, sought to incorporate the history of categories within a theory of the development of their cultural contexts and within a statement of the history of human subjects.

Although Hegel did not overlook the formative role of human labour in the development of mind,[28] man's social interaction with the natural world in order to satisfy his needs does not figure prominently within his account. It was this deficiency within Hegel's theory – the apparent abstraction of mind and human interaction from their natural conditions – which prompted Marx to substitute the idea of man as a natural being who must produce its material life before all else for Hegel's view of man as essentially self-consciousness.[29] Marxist historiography not only emphasises man's social conditions but characterises these in such a way as to reveal or restore their connection with nature; stress is placed upon the social relations of production which mediate between man and his physical environment. The *a priori* of history shifts to the activity of labour, that activity which leads men to interpose between themselves and nature a series of practices expressive of their capacity to develop their non-natural powers. Thus Marx states that:

> Labour is, in the first place, a process in which both man and nature participate, and in which man of his own accord starts, regulates, and controls the material reactions between himself and nature. He opposes himself to nature as one of her own forces, setting in motion arms and legs, heads and hands, the natural forces of his body, in order to appropriate nature's productions in a form adapted to his own wants. By thus acting on the external world and changing it, he at the same time changes his own nature. He develops his slumbering powers and compels them to act in obedience to his sway.[30]

The activity of working upon his natural environment in relations with others distances man from the natural world and enables him to bring 'out of himself all the powers that are his as the species man'.[31]

Like its Kantian predecessor, the Hegelian theory of history fails to supply an adequate statement of its own conditions of existence. It appears as a one-sided doctrine which abstracts developments in self-consciousness from developments within the production of material life. As Marx argued, philosophical pursuits are impossible where an entire community must expend its total collective effort upon production; a sufficiently large surplus product must be available to release certain men from engagement in direct productive activity. Only when such conditions appear natural or normal, when they can be taken for granted, can a philosophy such as Hegel's adopt that alienated perspective which can regard human development as the development of thought. Men have to eat, drink and reproduce their kind before they can do anything else.[32] Therefore an apprehension of history as the development of human powers cannot succeed in isolation from grasping the nature of their interaction with the physical world.

Despite these important differences the dominant characteristic of history as a history of human capacities or species-powers is reiterated within Marx's framework. And the ambition of ordering or scaling societies on the basis of their particular contributions to the development of these potentialities is retained. Thus while Kant approached history with regard to the creation of world citizenship, and Hegel focused upon the emergence of a rationally and consciously controlled, and therefore free, political life, Marx considered the historical refinement of the capacity to control nature and to establish progressively freer forms of social organisation. Systems of production are hierarchically organised then according to the degree to which they develop man's initially 'slumbering' species-powers.

Marx divided human history into three important stages of social development.[33] The earliest forms of social life were characterised by 'relations of personal dependence' in which men were tied to specific persons as in feudalism or, earlier, where they existed as 'a generic being, a tribal animal, a herd animal'. In the simplest forms of social organisation men exhibit 'herd-consciousness' only, since 'each individual has no more torn himself from the navel-string of his tribe or community, than each bee has freed itself from connection with the hive'.[34] Men are immersed in social groups which are estranged from the outside social world. Social life here reflects the awesome presence of a nature barely modified.[35] If the 'law that regulates the divisions of labour in the community acts with the irresistible authority of a law of nature'[36], it is because nature itself 'appears to men as a completely alien, all-powerful and unassailable force, with which men's relations are purely animal, and by which they are overawed like beasts'.[37] Under these conditions human productivity develops 'only to a slight extent'; men have barely developed their capacity to control nature or to express those capacities inherent in their nature which separate them from the merely animal or natural world.

The second and intermediate stage of social development is characterised by 'relations of personal independence'. Here men become individuated; they exist as independent beings; their relations of production have the appearance of freely established contracts. Under capitalist conditions, for example, the capitalist and the labourer confront one another as legally free and independent possessors of the means of exchange: the one capital, the other labour-power. In this social condition there emerges an unparalleled sophistication of human productive capacities and men succeed in dominating nature as they never did before. The productive power of the bourgeois mode of production surpasses all Gothic cathedrals, Roman aqueducts and Chinese walls.[38] Capitalist competition and expansion creates social interconnections which bind the whole species together. Capitalism

> produced world history for the first time, insofar as it made all civilised nations and every individual member of them dependent for the satisfaction of their wants on the whole world, thus destroying the former natural exclusiveness of separate nations;[39] [it] drives beyond national barriers and prejudices . . . as well as all traditional, confined, complacent, encrusted satisfactions of present needs, and reproductions of old ways of life. It is destructive towards all of this, and constantly revolutionises it, tearing down all the barriers which hem in the development of the forces of production, the expansion of needs, the all-sided development of production and the exploitation and exchange of natural and mental forces.[40]

Nevertheless, the paradoxical aspect of this enlarged and unprecedented control of the natural world is man's subjugation by his own social creations – the division of labour, private property, the state and the law-like, impersonal constraints of an expanding world market, etc. The formal equality of individuals conceals their structural inequalities; but, more fundamentally, the tragic aspect of man's domination of nature is his own imprisonment within a system of quasi-physical social constraints; nature is recreated within social life. Nevertheless, capitalist competition, the fundamental source of the intensification and globalisation of alienation is the force behind a third stage of human development, one which unleashes the possibilities inherent in an individuated and increasingly universal form of life.

Capitalism 'forces the development of the productive power of society' and creates the conditions of a future society in which free individuals collaborate in order to subject their interaction to their collective, rational control. The internal dynamic of the second stage of social development makes possible an unprecedented 'higher form of society, a society in which the free and full development of every individual forms the ruling principle'.[41] It is a society in which man has overcome his separation from the development and promotion of his species-specific powers, from conditions favourable to both individual and collective self-determination. Future communist society not only enables individuals to achieve full freedom and equality, and to attain control of their social interaction; it completes the long historical process of unifying the human race. Only in the communist revolution

> will the separate individuals be liberated from the various national and local barriers, be brought into practical connection with the material and intellectual production of the whole world and be put in a position to acquire the capacity to enjoy this all-sided production of the whole earth [the creations of man].[42]

The possibility of overcoming both socio-political oppression and domination by nature (which also includes the possibility of overcoming intersocietal estrangement in the form of man's division between separate and hostile societies) underlies Engels' famous distinction between pre-history and history. The transition from the former to the latter is described by Engels as a step towards a condition in which:

> for the first time, man, in a certain sense, is finally marked off from the animal kingdom, and emerges from mere animal conditions of existence into really human ones. The whole sphere of the conditions of life which environ man, and have hitherto ruled man, now comes under the dominion and control of man, who for the first time becomes the real, conscious lord of nature, because he has now become master of his own social organisation. The laws of his own social action, hitherto standing face to face with man as laws of nature foreign to, and dominating him, will then be used with full understanding, and so mastered by him. Man's own social organisation, hitherto confronting him as a necessity imposed by nature and history, now becomes the result of his own free action. The extraneous objective forces that have hitherto governed history pass under the control of man himself. Only from that time will man himself, with full consciousness, make his own history – only from that time will the social causes set in movement by him have, in the main and in a constantly growing measure, the results intended by him. It is the humanity's leap from the kingdom of necessity to the kingdom of freedom.[43]

At the heart of this conception of history is that contrast between the animal's participation within a law-governed world beyond its control and man's potential participation in a society which is both rationally controlled and responsive to desires for self-determination. It is a condition in which man can develop his species-powers, including his identification with the species, his wealth, for their intrinsic worth.

Marx attempted to overcome the one-sidedness of earlier theories of history by presenting an account of the advance of human freedom (including the emergence of individuation and universalism) within the framework of man's social interaction with nature. Further, he sought to locate the sources of change and the origins of species-powers in the structure of systems of production. Upon this same basis Marx aimed to give an explanation of the processes whereby men overcame their estrangement from one another as members of particularistic and mutually antagonistic societies. Relations between discrete social systems are thus incorporated within a history of the development of species-life; the analysis of the creation and evolution of intersocietal practices is similarly situated within Marx's conception of history as the realisation of freedom. Although Marx shared Hegel's contempt for utopianism (partly because knowledge of future human possibilities could not be established precisely, independently of their realisation, and partly because utopian thought, utopian socialism for example, presumed a static or suprahistorical ethic or set of human needs from which the character of the good society could be derived) he clearly saw philosophy or theory in the critical role of identifying existing obstacles to the further development of man's species-powers.[44] There is in Marx's writings a return from Hegel's passive philosophical disposition to the more critical theory of Kant; and this recovery of criticism, avoiding suprahistorical ethics and steering clear of utopian projects, affects not only the study of productive life but incorporates within that analysis the growth of reason in intersocietal relations.

The control of social life ultimately involves species control of the totality of its relations, and it presupposes the disappearance of a form of estrangement which characterises large periods of human history (pre-history), an estrangement which Marx believed would suffer a significant erosion on account of the globalisation of capitalist commodity production. Marx and Engels observed that social development within pre-history had taken place like natural growth, that is, not subordinate 'to a general plan of freely combined individuals'.[45] Estrangement between human groups other than classes, that is estrangement between the members of separate systems of production, had been a crucial determinant of a historical process which resulted not from conscious human deliberation but from uncoordinated interaction and chance. The structure of world society had been determined by the activities of 'various localities, tribes, nations, branches of labour, etc.'.[46] Marx therefore did not ignore the powerful impact of intersocietal relations upon world history; nor did he assume that an analysis of productive systems could be treated in abstraction from their external relations. Thus Marx claims that in early societies membership of a clan or tribe, for instance, was one of the essential conditions of man's 'production and reproduction' of his life.[47] Marx's reference to warfare illustrates the impossibility within his theory of effecting a legitimate separation between a mode of production and its external relations. Warfare was 'one of the earliest occupations of each of these naturally arisen communities, both for the defence of their property and for obtaining new property';[48] it is, moreover, 'the great comprehensive task, the great communal labour which is required either to occupy the objective conditions of being there alive, or to protect and perpetuate the occupation'.[49] An analysis of the development of freedom includes a focus upon those processes which lead men beyond intersocietal estrangement.

The earliest forms of social life were characterised by the individual's immersion within tribal life and his estrangement from the social world existing beyond his natural community. But for many reasons, such as an increase in the level of population, tribal communities may be unable to generate a product sufficient to satisfy their members' needs. To overcome the deficiencies of tribal organisation, men engage in external relations which in time dissolve or transform the basis of their social life. War, and conquest of the property or persons of neighbouring tribes, may transform the early community into a slave mode of production which necessitates the formation of the state. Trade, occasioned by a surplus collective product, may also set in motion a process which dissolves the natural form of tribal life:

> the exchange of commodities, therefore, first begins on the boundaries of such communities at their points of contact with other similar communities, or with members of the latter. So soon, however, as products once become commodities in the external relations of a community, they also, by reaction, become so in its internal intercourse.[50]

Trade inaugurates the establishment of private property and the division of labour; it too may necessitate the formation of states through the need to manage class divisions and conflicts.

But these are critical transitions in the history of the species since they establish the first social interconnections between primarily independent and mutually estranged societies. Within the theory of history, men cannot be presumed to possess a natural capacity to associate globally, a capacity which results for example from acceptance of a common set of ethical standards or a natural willingness or ability to regard others as members of the same species. The capacity to associate on a more general level than tribal society, and ultimately at the global level, has a history; and its historical nature is itself the expression of particular species-powers. Marx claimed that it was

> certain . . . that individuals cannot gain mastery over their own social interconnections before they have created them. But it is an insipid notion to conceive of this merely objective bond as a spontaneous, natural attribute inherent in individuals and inseparable from their nature [in antithesis to their conscious knowing and willing]. This bond is their product. It is a historic product . . .[51]

It is therefore unsurprising that Marx should state that the interdependence of societies 'is preferable to the lack of any connection, or to a merely local connection resting on blood ties, or on primeval, natural or master–servant relations'.[52] 'The alien and independent character' of their bond proves simply that individuals

> are still engaged in the creation of the conditions of their social life, and that they have not yet begun, on the basis of these conditions to live it. . . . Universally developed individuals, whose social relations, as their own communal relations, are hence also subordinated to their communal control, are no product of nature, but of history.[53]

Marx's reference to the world-historical significance of capitalism needs to be seen against this background. Global capitalism is the driving force behind the suspension of the last vestiges of intersocietal estrangement. The universalisation of capitalist commodity production leads to the nation-state becoming increasingly entangled within the world market and the international division of labour. World society and world history proper are functions of the global expansion of capitalist relations of production. On account of this development individuals are in the process of being 'brought into practical connection with the material and intellectual production of the whole world'. As a consequence of their global interconnectedness men have become 'more and more enslaved under a power alien to them . . . a power which has become more and more enormous and, in the last instance, turns out to be the world market'.[54] The historical product of human labour is a world-system which stands over individuals as a set of quasi-physical constraints. Nevertheless, the species' incorporation within a single, albeit alienating, capitalist world-system is critical to the higher development of human freedom. A critique of the constraints upon self-determination inherent in that system, in connection with the revolutionary activity of the proletariat, makes possible global and 'conscious mastery of these powers, which, born of the action of men on one another, have till now overawed and governed men as powers completely alien to them'.[55] Capitalism, particularly capitalist imperialism, destroys traditional forms of community life in the non-Western, pre-capitalist world and globalises relations of personal independence. All men now confront one another as individual possessors of either capital or labour-power within the world market. But the rights, equalities and freedoms of individuals are contradicted by the unequal nature of capitalist relations of production; the equal nature of bourgeois and proletarian is purely formal. Therefore, in the course of time, estrangement between communities is replaced by estrangement between classes. Marx believed that the necessary outcome of the intensification of conflict between these classes would be the revolutionary triumph of the international proletariat. To control global processes which had towered over them, to make history with 'full-consciousness', men would have to take control of their world-wide system of production; they would recognise through conflict that 'modern universal intercourse can be controlled by individuals, therefore, only when controlled by all'.[56]

Marx may have underestimated the long-term potential resistance by particularistic identities to the supposedly corrosive effects of global commodity production; he failed to recognise that the threat of submergence within a world market could be a force for the intensification and not the dissolution of these identities. Nevertheless, Marxist theory contains the resources for undertaking a critique of forms of particularism whether or not these are in the process of being replaced by a properly universal society. The roots of this critique are present in Marx's theory of alienation and freedom. Within Marx's philosophy of history the principal obstacles to the emergence of a society of species-beings (in control of their social relations and equally able to develop their human powers) were located in the productive relations and economic categories present within the capitalist mode of production. But class particularism exists alongside forms of national particularism for most of human history, and therefore the state and the states-system must also be regarded as obstacles to the universal recognition of men as species-beings.[57] Marx's theory shares with Kant's the desire for a universal society of free individuals, a universal kingdom of ends. Therefore, as one commentator rightly argues:

> the term 'human' applied to post-capitalist society was intended to describe the predominance of humanity over social and national particularism . . . socially divided factors would no longer prevail over those that united humanity. Perhaps even more important is another idea that Marx closely associated with the prospect of the communist revolution, namely the completion of the process by which history became world history as a result of the coalescence of regional societies into a single, world-embracing society that included the whole of mankind.[58]

The designations which had characterised men in the kingdom of necessity must be removed if men are to realise their freedom within a properly humanised society.

In conclusion, within the Marxian framework, control of nature within a set of free social relations involves going beyond intersocietal estrangement, and the abolition of the competitive and conflictual types of interaction which have prevailed between particularistic social groups. Since freedom is understood as global control of social relations in order to maximise species-powers, neither the organisation of material resources nor the management of claims between persons can be monopolised by, or take place within, separate sovereign states. International relations as relations between particularistic forms of organisation give way to a universal society in which members equalise their access to material resources subject to their common ownership and collective control. It is this conception of international society, derived from a distinctive account of the nature of human historical subjects which overcomes the shortcomings inherent within the Kantian or Hegelian systems.

Having identified three different conceptions of philosophical history, it is now possible to specify its relevance for the construction of an international political theory. Its most important contribution is contained in the proposition that reason is neither universal and immutable nor socially relative or culturally dependent. Reason has a history; it develops a determinate and progressive content from its expressions in various forms of social life. This conception of reason and freedom led to a unique philosophical device which distinguishes the philosophy of history from rationalism and historicism, namely the placement of different societies upon a scale or hierarchy of types. It is this idea which we must now attempt to apply to the world of international relations.

We have noted that these theories sought to incorporate an analysis of intersocietal life within their proper focus, the formation of the distinctive qualities of the species. But the implications for international relations, and for a political theory addressed to them, were not fully elaborated. The following implications may be stated here. On the basis of a philosophy of history it becomes possible to approach different types of international relations with a view to determining their contribution to the process of humanisation. And if we assume that relations between as well as within separate societies contribute to the development of species-life, two tasks become possible. In the first place, we may incorporate within the study of international relations the attempt to place different types of international relations upon a scale of forms in order to illustrate the degree of freedom embedded within them. Secondly, it becomes possible to construct a sociology or political economy of international relations which attempts to explain the empirical processes by which international relations move from one level of freedom, one place in the scale, to another. The second task raises too complex issues to be gone into here and it strays from the immediate purpose which is to establish a theory of the relationship between citizenship and humanity. Therefore, in the third part of the argument, with this purpose in mind, we set out a number of progressively adequate accounts of international relations in order to trace the development of freedom within them.

Part Three

A Hierarchy of Forms of International Relations

Introduction to Part Three

The following two chapters try to convert some of the principles of philosophical history into the elements of a systematic political theory of international relations on the grounds that these principles overcome the deficiencies present within rationalist and historicist thinking. By philosophical history we mean not an account of the presuppositions underlying the study and writing of history, but an approach to social and political affairs which seeks to decipher the nature of historical subjects and to describe the conditions most favourable to the realisation of their particular powers. The preceding chapter aimed to show what is included within this form of analysis: the processes whereby men come to distinguish themselves from nature by recognising their own historical being; their capacity to undergo individuation and to recognise the universality of human nature; their ability to create and control institutions and conditions which enable them to promote their individual and social development. The gradual realisation of these conditions is defined in various ways within theories of history as the growth of man's self-consciousness (his understanding of self, society and history), or as the development of his reason or freedom. In Marx's thought particularly, the growth of human freedom involves the replacement of man's sense of powerlessness before nature with the capacity to make nature respond to his purposes and plans; and it involves the replacement of estrangement from others with the inclusion of men within a humanised, and therefore universal, community. Freedom develops as natural and social constraints, the latter issuing from estrangement between men, are reduced. More particularly, the growth of self-knowledge entails first the criticism, and then the abolition, of the forms of necessity associated with the existence of international relations. The philosophy of history creates the basis for a critical theory of international relations of the kind outlined earlier.

But this is not the sole reason for connecting a political theory of international relations with a theory of the history of human subjects. The next two chapters are concerned to correct the dominant bias of many theories of history. For several of these theories, the study of the formation of human powers focuses principally upon changes in the internal structure of social life, as if relations between groups were epiphenomenal. Basic to the remaining chapters is the argument that intersocietal relations as well as internal social relations provide an arena within which human subjects can develop their powers. In the terms discussed above, the analysis of the realisation of human freedom can look beyond the inside of societies to the way in which groups, estranged from one another, come to recognise the possibility of relations based upon equality and justice; it can include an examination of their recognition of the possibility of overcoming their particularism, which issues from estrangement and results in relations of a necessitous character, in the course of discovering and applying universal principles within an inclusive society. We cannot provide very much empirical support in the forthcoming pages for the proposition that human powers have been developed in the area of contact between distinct societies; nor shall we suggest how the study of international relations might accommodate the study of human freedom. These tasks go well beyond the final objectives of the present argument. The following chapters concentrate instead upon the fact that, using the idea of freedom as it came to be elaborated within the theory of history, it is possible to construct various ideal types of international relations in the course of arguing that some embody higher understandings of human powers than others. Within these parameters, we proceed to an analysis of the moral and political claims made on the basis of citizenship and humanity.

In order to clarify these objectives, it is important to state the bases upon which one form of international relations will be distinguished from others, the precise nature of each of the types of international relations to be discussed, and their relationship with one another as elements in a scale of forms of social and political life.

Different types of international relations will be distinguished on the basis of Marx's principles of historical periodisation.[1] Our scale begins with relations of personal dependence. The simplest forms of external relations are taken to involve tribal groups, each enacting its internal concept of obligation, each estranged from its neighbours. Progress will be defined as the growth of relations between individuals from different tribal groups, relations which correspond broadly with relations of personal independence in Marx's system. These relations are accompanied by the production of a body of humanly established intertribal rules. Their culmination is the formation of the state and the development of the idea of citizenship. The state represents a significant advance in the growth of human powers since it is universalistic in comparison with tribal social organisation. However, it remains a particularistic association insofar as citizenship replaces kinship as the basis of an exclusive form of social organisation and as the centre of an internal concept of obligation. Our approach concludes with an analysis of relations of free individuality, with the move beyond the particularism of the state to a universal society of free beings with rights and duties expressive of their identification with humanity. We trace the development of freedom through identifying several examples of international relations which correspond with the typology of social relations underlying the Marxian account of historical periodisation.

Our scale of types of international relations is not drawn directly from historical experience. Although some examples may have a rough correspondence with actual historical forms, although some have a parallel in the history of international relations, each is principally a construct. It will be clear later that the scale of forms of external relations does not correspond with anything that has ever happened. A more complete or profound inquiry might examine the levels of self-consciousness exhibited in the actual history of international relations. In the absence of sufficient historical knowledge and given that this argument is an exercise in political theory, we have been content to employ a set of constructs in order to convey the sense in which different intersocietal relations are stages in the development of freedom.

Finally, it is necessary to clarify the relationship between our forms of intersocietal life. Since these forms are only constructs, it will be clear that their ordering does not reflect their chronological appearance. To quote Hegel:

> What is actual, the shape in which the concept is embodied, is for us therefore the secondary thing and the sequel, even if it were itself first in the actual world. The development we are studying is that whereby the abstract forms reveal themselves not as self-subsistent but as false.[2]

It follows that when one system of external relations is superseded by another in our account, it is not assumed that this is historically faithful or probable if the empirical circumstances are present. It is claimed rather that this supersession is necessary if human subjects are to create a social and political world expressive of their nature. We seek to indicate how changes in the structure of external relations can be said to represent growth in the level of human understanding. The immediate impetus behind the scale is Kant's remark that a 'minor motive' for attempting a philosophical history would be the attempt to answer the question of what various societies have contributed to the goal of world citizenship.[3] The following argument is concerned with the first of these concerns with recourse to hypothetical rather than empirical forms of international relations. It may be read as an initial attempt to explore what it would be for freedom to develop in international history. With these objectives in mind, we have constructed a scale of social and political forms encompassing relations of intersocietal estrangement involving tribes, the development of the state and the international states-system, and a set of universalistic relations expressive of the human capacity to share the conditions of a free life. Within the parameters of a political theory of international relations sympathetic with the principles of philosophical history, we seek to overcome the tension between men and citizens.

9 From Tribalism to Political Society

> At a late moment in man's emergence, he left behind the securities and intimacies and solidarities of tribal existence. . . . At this point an audacious minority, in a handful of specially situated communities, made a daring thrust in a new direction: the experiment of civilisation . . . more far-reaching than man had ever established before, binding together with explicit rules and regulations dissimilar communities and varied local customs. (Mumford)

The advance of freedom in the history of intersocietal relations is connected with two principal stages of social and political development. The first phase comprises the movement beyond relations of intersocietal estrangement between tribal societies towards the establishment of political community. A second stage involves overcoming estrangement and opposition between states, and entails their subsequent supersession by a universalistic community. The growth of freedom in relations between groups proceeds by virtue of three types of community: from a condition in which men have rights in their community as tribal members (and no rights outside it), to one in which they have rights in their states by virtue of their citizenship, to a final condition in which they have rights in a universal political association by virtue of their humanity. This chapter examines the first main stages in a scale of forms of intersocietal life, those which embrace the move from tribal organisation to the establishment of the state.

The most elementary forms of intersocietal life consist of relations between mutually estranged tribal communities. Relations between these communities are simple reflections of their respective principles of social organisation. For tribal members are wholly immersed within particularistic ways of life which they regard as naturally sanctioned and unalterable. While they remain in this condition, men are not yet severed from the 'umbilical cord' whereby they are attached to a seemingly natural order. Given these relations of personal dependence, social behaviour is governed by the fact that membership and status within the group must be preserved before all else. A member's greatest fear, which makes the threat of ostracism the most potent means of social control, is the prospect of losing his place within, and being deprived of protection from, the society of his birth. No member can experience a loss greater than relinquishing his assimilation within the group; not to belong is not to exist.

In this condition, obligations are woven into, and inseparable from, the roles and responsibilities of a distinct society. Social rules derive their authority from custom and they are enacted without question, spontaneously and uncritically. Members enact an internal concept of obligation expressive of their common kinship. Here there is no notion of an obligation to an outsider or non-member, and no such event as a peaceful or equal transaction between insiders and outsiders. Moral constraints upon plundering or killing members of other groups are non-existent, and mechanisms for circumventing or mitigating the consequences of repeated acts of vengeance and endless feuds are not developed. The whole group recognises a responsibility to avenge a harm done to a member, and collective responsibility for an injury to an insider is imputed to members of other groups. In the absence of an intersocietal morality, or of the idea of an affinity with outsiders, relations between groups founded upon distinct kinship lines, can be none other than antagonistic. Tribes exist in a state of permanent tension or war in which apart from the security and protection afforded by the society in which one is at home, there are no rights, 'no mine and thine'.

To regard this form of intersocietal life as the first in a sequence of ascending types is to claim two things: that only the most minimal human powers have been brought forth within the parameters of tribal organisation, and that no fundamental human capacities have been developed through intersocietal contact.[1] It is not assumed that these inter-tribal relations are either the first or the norm historically. All that is claimed is that these relations of personal dependence are a function of man's unawareness of his capacity to transform the conditions of his own existence; and that, similarly, no consciousness exists of the possibility of transforming relations of estrangement into relations of familiarity. Each interconnected sphere of social life confronts members as natural, necessary and unalterable. To repeat a point made by Hegel with reference to those societies in which nature was deemed to be the determinant of social relations: men in this condition are unfree.[2] Within our scale of political forms, they exhibit the lowest form of self-consciousness.

Clearly, many of these forms of social organisation and their corresponding external relations were dissolved at various points in human history. Here we do not refer to the mechanisms which may have precipitated their dissolution or led to their transformation into different systems of social life. We are concerned instead with explaining what it would mean to claim that human powers can develop beyond the point which they have reached at the level of inter-tribal relations. In brief, the development of human powers involves first of all a realisation that the social world is a historical product, created by and subject to the future modification of human subjects. It entails relaxing those supposedly natural prohibitions and constraints upon relations with outsiders. The development of freedom within the realm of external relations will be seen to include the following innovations: the fact that human subjects may engage in transactions despite their cultural divisions, and that they may do so as equals; their realisation that it is within their power to construct a common moral framework for the purposes of regulating the interaction between insiders and outsiders, and the growth of their self-knowledge to the point where they recognise the possibility of their participation within a single social system. They develop their freedom as human reasoning replaces nature or tradition as the shaper of human conduct, and as they begin to determine for themselves what each man may reasonably claim from his fellows.

The development of human powers beyond inter-tribal life can be exemplified in at least two ways. Firstly, a tribe may be unable to satisfy the needs of its members because of scarcity, or on account of the constraints of being organised only around kinship relations, because of limitations of scale. To overcome these problems a tribal society may have recourse to the conquest of other communities, the assimilation of their persons and their wealth. With the foundation of a slave economy, kinship bonds are no longer the sufficient bases of social order; the incorporation of outsiders dissolves the natural unity displayed within tribal society. In the slave economy previously external relations of estrangement are transformed into sources of domestic political conflict which an emerging state apparatus must attempt to control. Under certain historical conditions too complex to discuss in detail here, the attempt to mediate between distinct and historically antagonistic groups may lead to the formation of common rules or principles and the establishment of a new social order. If it attempts to convert relations of intersocietal estrangement into stable or consensual relations, the polyethnic empire must create social rules which transcend the limitations of tribal conventions. Human powers may be said to unfold as the polyethnic empire seeks to clarify the foundations of a more peaceful inter-tribal or international order.[3]

There is a second way in which the limitations of tribal society may generate the development of human capacities. Tribal groups may attempt to overcome economic shortcomings or imbalances through the introduction of commodity exchange. We shall attempt to extend our scale of intersocietal forms in more detail by noting that commerce may not only dissolve relations of personal dependence, as Marx had observed,[4] but also erode the traditional sources of intersocietal estrangement. Commercial exchange can create circumstances in which the formation of a state apparatus becomes necessary in order to manage a variety of social relations and a complex division of labour which can no longer be accommodated and controlled within the kinship structure of tribal organisation.[5] We shall trace the development of a scale of political forms, which expresses the growth of man's self-consciousness, by considering a number of ideal-types of international relations existing between the original condition of inter-tribal estrangement and the emergence of a more inclusive political community, namely the state.

Let us consider a condition in which certain tribal societies begin to relax their ethnocentricity for the purpose of satisfying the needs of their members. Societies move beyond their initially estranged relationships as traditional conceptions of outsiders, and conventional tribal prohibitions and sanctions against contact with them, are eased in order to permit the revolutionary development of exchange relations. A new and higher form of international relations may be said to exist when some members are authorised to conduct relations with outsiders. They do so not on their private initiative and for their individual gratification, but as agents of, or trustees for, the group. They are entrusted with specific responsibilities to initiate contacts which will benefit their society as a whole. This condition may be described as progressive in two respects. Firstly, traditional social rules have been modified to allow the emergence of new forms of social relations between subjects inhabiting different cultural worlds. Secondly, the members of a particular tribe have come to recognise the rule-creating competence of those agents who mediate between them and the outside world. Tribal conventions must be modified to accommodate various practices which are introduced at the frontier in the course of engaging in commercial relations: the institution of promise keeping and rules of reciprocity being among the more important. These developments may be deemed progressive because they entail recognition of the fact that the members of other societies are human subjects with whom there can be fair dealings.

In the circumstances we have described, rules of inter-tribal intercourse allow the creation of non-antagonistic external relations, but they would also pose a considerable threat to group solidarity. The possible extension of sympathy to outsiders, and the intrinsic satisfaction which may be derived from undertaking to engage in relations with outsiders, can distort the stated purposes of cooperation with other groups. If our example of tribal society experiences some weakening of its ethnocentric bias, it does not relax its egocentric concerns. For relations with outsiders are not conducted from any altruistic set of motives, and the welfare of outsiders is advanced only indirectly, insofar as it satisfies the utilitarian calculations of the group. We have not yet gone beyond that level of international relations in which external relations cease, and return to their traditional form, when their utility becomes suspect. Externally created obligations are held to be inferior to those internal obligations shared by members of a natural society. Being an insider remains a necessary precondition of possessing a fundamental moral status. Therefore, if a member places what the group considers a utilitarian rule before an obligation to his kinfolk, or if he feels a tension between his customary social obligations and a developing sense of sympathy for outsiders, social control will be exercised immediately to impress the supremacy of internal obligations upon the one involved. At this stage in the development of international relations, social sanctions are employed to ensure that cooperation does not produce relations of familiarity between distinct kinship groups. The condition to which we have referred exhibits only limited development; we can conceive of still higher expressions of human powers in the realm of international relations.

Progressive though the above conditions are, they have not permitted members the right of engaging in external relations on their own initiative, *qua* individuals; nor have they recognised that outsiders may be regarded as the moral equals of insiders. It may be argued that a higher set of external relations is in existence when a particular claim comes to be made, and then satisfied, on the basis of these social developments: that the opportunity of engaging in relations with outsiders has enabled men to recognise and develop their power of creating rules to manage unprecedented types of human relations, and to acquire knowledge of outsiders through their own individual experience rather than through the collective interpretation of their society. Under these circumstances the possibility of moral experience is enlarged, the capacity for sympathy has been extended, and the process of individuation has begun. A higher social condition comes into existence where members begin to believe that their customary way of life is too parochial to encompass all the social possibilities they would like to have open to them. Characteristic of this higher condition is the emergence of a claim for a further relaxation of group norms, for a greater freedom so that members can conduct external relations on their own individual initiative.

We have defined the development of the human capacity to construct social rules in the realm of intercourse between insiders and outsiders, and the ensuing dissolution of tribal authority, as progressive. The human capacity for self-determination is more advanced under conditions in which it is realised that social rules are alterable, that they are a product of human interaction, even if they have not been consciously created in the past, and where tribal members are less prepared than they were formerly to enact their tribal customs uncritically. Social development entails individuals placing themselves at odds with their societies as they begin to question conventional means of characterising outsiders and to criticise customary prohibitions upon individual relations with them. A higher level of intersocietal life exists if certain men challenge tribal ways in order to elicit recognition for themselves as individuals as well as members; and if they claim the right of initiating more complex relations and of entering binding obligations with those located beyond the tribal frontier. What these individuals require is the extension of that liberty of action which the community had allowed itself, the right of entering into relations with outsiders for the purposes of satisfying interests.

The growth of human freedom involves acceptance of this individual claim and the social recognition of a private sphere within which individuals are free to cultivate relations with outsiders. It requires recognition of the fact that the individual can enter into, and honour, obligations in his private external relations without being harassed by his peers. A higher form of intersocietal relations is characterised by the proliferation of private, external relations; its manifestation within the internal organisation of the tribe is revealed by the drawing of a boundary between that area in which the individual is self-determining, and that realm in which he remains governed by the norms of his society. The establishment of this boundary is positive because it reduces the number of occasions in which individuals come into conflict with their group, or experience a conflict between their internal and external obligations. A society which seeks to draw this boundary aims to recover that degree of social unity which had once existed naturally; it seeks to re-create a condition of social harmony or integration while granting recognition of an important area of liberty to its members. The attempt to determine the boundary between the private and the public itself extends the human capacity to consciously develop the structure of a more adequate social environment.

We have identified a condition in which individuals are not wholly absorbed within their natural, tribal societies, in which they are not simply the subjects of particularistic patterns of thought and action. Within a socially protected realm of interaction the members of a society are at liberty to bring the same moral standards to bear upon their relations with insiders and outsiders. The fact that a person is primarily an associate of a different tribal group is no longer the single determinant of how he is to be treated. What is progressive here is the acceptance of the rights of individuals to act in accordance with universalisable principles which regard cultural or tribal differences as irrelevant to the problem of right conduct within the realm of private, external relations. With the emergence of this principle, relations of estrangement are gradually transformed into relations of familiarity which are expressive of the growth of universalist reasoning, of the fact that moral equality is imputed to insiders and outsiders. At a higher level of intersocietal life, individuals advance the claim to belong to two societies – the natural society into which they were born and the expanding inter-tribal society which they regard as their joint production, the manifestation of their reason and freedom. Tribal society now begins to appear as the local part of a more inclusive and rational social system.

The above stages of international relations have defined progress as the gradual emancipation of individuals from the parochial constraints of their natural societies. In the course of their development, these individuals have gained recognition of a private realm of external relations; their societies have adapted to accommodate their revolutionary claims. Individuals have been liberated from an apparently natural and eternal social order, and they have begun to express their capacity to make it respond to their will. But social development does not cease with their ability to pursue their claims, with the satisfaction of their interests in the erosion of intersocietal estrangement; it involves a more profound change in which similar rights are acknowledged to belong to outsiders, in which tribal society becomes more open and permeated in the course of recognising the individuality of outsiders. Progress in international relations entails the dissolution of the belief that cultural differences are morally significant ones, and the acceptance of the fact that outsiders can enter tribal society to pursue their own ends in their own right. Not to extend this right to outsiders is to remain limited by the previously unqualified existence of intersocietal estrangement. With the recognition of the equal rights of outsiders a transcultural society can come into existence, a society based upon a variety of new practices such as commercial exchange, the migration of persons, exogamy and the proliferation of common beliefs and symbols. Within this sphere of interaction the customary rules of natural societies are insufficient principles of social life. As a consequence men are thrown back upon their own resources as they seek to formulate a common system of rules concerned with managing complex forms of inter-tribal interaction. Participants within this more developed system of relations express their unique powers as they dissolve the supposedly natural constraints of a more simple social order and bring their evolving social framework under reasoned control. The creation of this framework is not a function of their awareness of a latent or dormant reason which was embedded in their nature and simply awaited discovery. It is a medium through which men clarify what they are and develop their powers. Men give shape to their specific capacities and distinguish themselves as unique historical subjects as they begin to determine the character of a social environment based on relations of familiarity, thereby giving new content to their lives.

But the existing condition contains a number of deficiencies which can be overcome within a different set of social and political relations. Three problems make it necessary to construct an image of a higher form of international relations. The first of these arises because of the limited nature of existing forms of social control. In the above system, tribal society exercises jurisdiction over the public lives of its members but it neither wields power nor exercises responsibility over their private, external relations. This situation is a product of the fact that tribal society has made a specific commitment to its members, which is not to intervene in the conduct of their private relations. If the individual is at liberty to enter into obligations of his own making within a new realm of social affairs, equally he is able to dishonour them by placing his individual concerns before the welfare of others. Tribal society made a specific commitment to its members alone; it did not extend guarantees to those outsiders with whom they have relations. This decision to refrain from applying social sanctions within an important dimension of the individual's life must now appear one-sided and defective. The limitations of tribal organisation and its principles of social control can be corrected by creating a new system of authority based upon the desirability of establishing a more extensive range of commitments to insiders and outsiders alike. It involves the construction of an institutional structure whereby outsiders are assured the possibility of redress against insiders. With the establishment of procedures which seek to ensure that principles of justice are observed in relations between insiders and outsiders, we come to that higher level of social organisation which is the state. Tribal society acquired a more rational character when it drew the boundary between public and private life; but its rationality is impaired unless it attempts to exercise some control within the private realm without substantially diminishing the autonomy which has been achieved there. Social development requires the establishment of institutions concerned with the enforcement of universalist principles.

A second problem arises from the fact that tribal society lacks effective means of protecting the interests of those outsiders to whom it is host. But by establishing mechanisms whereby outsiders can seek redress against its own members, a particular society can remove one of the principal shortcomings present within its mode of organisation, one of the legacies of a simpler form of external relations. Until a system of redress is made available to outsiders, the commitment made to them on the basis of the equality of their rights is insufficient. To overcome the legacy of a simpler condition in which it was culturally inconceivable that insiders and outsiders could be regarded as equals, tribal society must ensure that an insider cannot use an outsider as a means to his own ends with impunity. In a higher social condition, with the establishment of new procedures to protect outsiders, society aims to enforce not only tribal law (or what remains of it in this changed condition) but the rules which came into existence with the development of inter-tribal society, rules which pertained exclusively to the conduct of insider–outsider relations. A more rational form of social organisation necessitates the attempt to enforce those principles which emerged at the frontiers of tribal society; it requires the effort to enforce an impartial law which regards insiders and outsiders as equals; it involves the construction of the essential elements of a state apparatus.

A third and final problem arises from the fact that a member may be harmed by the members of another society. While the former's natural society can affect the social conditions which exist within the domestic arena, it has no *de jure* right to ensure that justice is observed within the jurisdiction of a neighbouring society. But if it takes the rights of its individual members seriously, it cannot stand by while their welfare is ignored elsewhere. However, the nature of its assistance is problematical in more advanced levels of international relations. Within the original condition of intersocietal estrangement, an injury to an insider involved the whole group in an act of indiscriminate revenge against outsiders, for all were held responsible for the offence. But with the level of social development which has taken place, society cannot be prepared to spring automatically to the assistance of one of its members. From its modified perspective, a member's claim to act as an individual outside the group cannot be divorced from his duty to accept responsibility for the consequences of his actions. If a society ought to be prepared to assist its members, it cannot offer assistance simply on the grounds that they are members – which would have sufficed before. Prior to offering assistance, fellow-members are required to have sufficient information about the way in which one of their number has behaved. Within a more advanced conception of international relations, they will wish to know if one of their fellows deserves their assistance, since he cannot now claim that they are obliged to provide it on the basis of their common ties and sympathies alone. Therefore, while it is acceptable that a society should accept a *prima facie* duty to extend assistance to one of its members (and it would not respect the rights of individuals unless it did), it cannot be regarded as perfectly obliged if that member is guilty of an infringement of intersocietal law.

Various problems prevent the above stage of social development from being regarded as final. The development of individualism has brought a new state of nature into existence: to the one comprising tribal groups there is now added one composed of private individuals. In the absence of an effective system of protection afforded to insiders and outsiders alike, their relations possess an uncertainty and insecurity, and may indeed be unjust. Until an effective system of social control develops, disagreement between individuals may be transformed into a conflict between societies. In short, the maintenance of traditional instruments of social control involves a failure to perform the tasks required by the emergence of a multiplicity of private, external relations. This problem can be managed in at least two ways: if traditional societies take it upon themselves to give protection to outsiders within their domain by enforcing principles of intersocietal justice, and if they refuse to assist those of their members who are guilty of having contravened the principles which have emerged with the growth of a new social framework. These commitments facilitate the development of a wider moral community than the one which existed naturally; they involve a significant move from a particularistic to a universalistic association. For what traditional society is prepared to accept is an investigation of the conduct of its members on the assumption that they will be punished if they are found guilty of having committed a wrong. What it defends is the principle of defending a person's rights whenever they are infringed, and regardless of the status of the person involved. With this understanding the distinction between an insider and an outsider becomes irrelevant to the judgment which needs to be made. The degree of progress here is best conveyed by stating that those with responsibility for investigating a dispute between an insider and an outsider are concerned only with the character of the act and the circumstances in which it was committed, and not with the membership of those involved; in the original state of nature, in the condition of intersocietal estrangement with which we began our scale, nothing else mattered.

Progress in the sphere of intersocietal relations requires the application of general, international principles to disputes between insiders and outsiders. We may regard the formation of *ad hoc* mechanisms within different societies, or temporary institutions of an inter-tribal character, as important developments which seek to reduce the level of uncertainty surrounding transcultural relations. With the diminishing of culturally based forms of estrangement, with the intensification of economic and social interdependence, each of which carries earlier developments to a new level, the decentralised and uncoordinated nature of those institutions with responsibility for the enforcement of trans-societal law is an obstacle to the effective management of social order. The dissolution of intersocietal estrangement makes it necessary to systematise rules and rule-making institutions within an increasingly unified social system. The maintenance of order at this stage of the development of social life acquires a political dimension: the centralisation of institutions and the monopolisation of the instruments of violence are the necessary elements of an order based upon relations of personal independence. With the appearance of these new structures, formerly separate tribal societies are converted into the parts of a single state.

What we have described above is a set of constructed stages in the development from the 'pre-legal to the legal world',[6] in the move from an internal concept of obligation based upon the tribe to an external concept of obligation which receives expression in the institutions of the state. It is useful to conclude this elaboration of the initial stages of our scale of political forms by describing the contrast between the state and preceding stages of development. Here, in order to do this we have recourse to Hart's description of the nature of the move from 'the pre-legal to the legal world' as a development of the system of social rules.

Neither tribal society nor private, inter-tribal relations in our account contained procedures empowered to give an authoritative interpretation of the basic rules which ought to be observed by members. In the absence of competent institutions, the elementary rules of social life are subject to varying interpretation, and are uncertain. Neither social system possessed structures 'capable of deliberately adapting the rules to changing circumstances';[7] as a result, social rules were relatively static, established or altered simply on the basis of customary practice. Since neither form of social life could enforce rules except through the exercise of 'diffuse social power',[8] through individuals taking it upon themselves to deliver social sanctions, the maintenance of order was relatively inefficient. To improve their social condition, members require institutions which seek to ascertain the fundamental rules governing them, procedures which facilitate the more rapid formulation or alteration of rules, and mechanisms which allow a more centralised method of administering social pressure. According to Hart, 'the remedy of each of these three main defects in this . . . form of social structure consists in supplementing the *primary* rules of obligations with *secondary* rules',[9] which make it possible that the elementary rules of social life 'may be conclusively ascertained, introduced, eliminated, varied and the fact of their violation conclusively determined'.[10] To improve their social condition, it is necessary that men recognise the utility of establishing a legal system, a public power, over themselves. The achievement of the state is its capacity to manage more complex and developed social relations, relations which are not kinship based in character. The state is expressive of a higher stage of self-consciousness relative to those forms which have preceded it on our analysis, one where members wish to preserve values they care for most: their status as individuals capable of engaging in relations of personal independence and abiding by principles which apply to persons equally, regardless of cultural or ethnic identity. With the move to legal and political society, and with the concomitant development of citizenship, we complete our first set of social stages. We have elaborated a number of progressive stages between a condition in which men have rights in their societies as tribal members and circumstances in which they have rights in a more universalistic association as independent persons or citizens.

The state is the last stage in our present series because it transcends what were originally thought to be fundamental and unalterable cultural differences. The development of freedom has been characterised as an erosion of intersocietal estrangement culminating in the acceptance of a common system of law before which all citizens are equals. It is now law rather than custom which assumes importance in the task of integrating the members of different cultural groups into one cohesive political society. Citizenship replaces kinship bonds as the basis of their association together. The latter no longer embrace the totality of their members' lives, or make the most meaningful claims upon them, but form the primary associations of a more complex and freer form of life. The system of law specifies what it is that kinship members continue to owe to one another, and what they owe to the state, so harmonising family and political obligations and responsibilities. Law is the instrument at man's disposal for the recovery of that harmonious social condition which once existed naturally; and it is so under conditions in which men have developed more individuated and universal lives, and where they have unfolded their capacity to engage in more reasoned and controlled social relations.

10 From Citizenship to Humanity

> Nothing could be more absurd, from the historic point of view, than to regard the conception of an international State of federated humanity . . . as a mere dream, an illusion of sentimental hope. It is a very slight step to take forward compared with that which has substituted the authority of national States for the conflict of isolated clans and local communities: or with that which has substituted a publicly administered justice for the regime of private war and retaliation. (Dewey and Tufts)

Since it recognises the rights of independent persons, its citizens, the state is a higher form of social organisation than those tribal societies which preceded it on our scale of forms. In the state men develop their capacity to exercise reasoned control over the conditions of their existence, and they gain access to a higher level of self-determination than existed before. Relations between citizens, or between citizens and the state, appear as contracts between free and equal parties. But the principles of justice, which the state seeks to enforce within its domain, are not thought to be binding upon human beings themselves; within our account of the state these are regarded as integral to the maintenance of a particular way of life, as internal obligations which are essential to the task of preserving an equal freedom for all members to pursue their separate interests within a given social order. Although founded on an advanced set of social principles the state, as described within the existing scale, remains a particularistic community conscious of its separateness from the world beyond. In the present condition, persons have rights against the state only as its members. While the distinction between morality and self-interest is fundamental to the way in which the latter regard their interaction, it is not yet meaningful in connection with their community's relations with the outside world. These relations remain essentially relations of estrangement. Since the state is a product of man's capacity to construct a more rational social order, ideally it is capable of generating a distinctive set of attitudes and responses to the world outside. We must now consider how the state's relations with other groups can exemplify the development of higher levels of self-consciousness; and we must seek to extend our series of political forms to include the transition from having rights against others as a citizen to having rights against others as a man.

Within the parameters of the present argument, the state can participate in relations with three different types of society: with imperial systems or slave economies which result from one society's conquest or assimilation of another; with relatively unchanged tribal societies; and with similarly constituted political societies, other states. It will be claimed that these three types of external relations form a series with the latter affording a greater opportunity for the construction of more rational and universal relations. Relations between states allow the formation of more complex bases of interaction, and contribute most to the development of freedom in international life. We begin, however, with relations between the state and slave economies.

To the extent that the slave economy displays essentially imperialist designs upon the state, relations between them do not advance significantly beyond original relations of intersocietal estrangement. In accordance with its desire for self-preservation, the state authorises its representatives to conduct its external relations with a concern solely for success. The distinction between private and public morality allows the state's representatives to depart, in the course of ensuring the realisation of its goals, from those principles ordinarily observed within its boundaries. The intensity of these antagonistic relations may be reduced when neither community can realise its optimal goal, the subjugation of the other. Under these conditions, the pacification or stabilisation of relations becomes an important common value requiring the mutual recognition of rights of existence, respective spheres of influence and associated political goals. Here, the emergence of rules of political co-existence and mutual accommodation modify the originally estranged nature of these societies' external relations. These rules are not an expression of a common moral concern, but an example of the ability to define areas of political agreement on the basis of separate pragmatic concerns; international rules, accordingly, need last no longer than the pragmatic considerations which lead to their introduction. To the extent that these social systems remain antagonistic to one another, their external relations are conducted in accordance with self-interested, or pragmatic, calculations.

The state must also determine what its relations will be with those communities which remain, by its criteria, at a lower stage of social development. From the point of view of citizens, the basis of their association together is their equal right to promote their particular interests without impeding one another. Morality exists to constrain what each citizen can do to others. These citizens have not concluded that they are governed by any similarly far-reaching moral constraints with outsiders, with those with whom they are not formally associated. As a result, they adopt an essentially exploitative posture towards lesser developed societies.

A higher conception of international relations appears when the problem of how to conduct relations with lesser developed peoples becomes a principal source of conflict within the state. It involves contesting the morality of an exploitative disposition, advancing the claim that not to conform with some notion of morality in relations with outsiders is to adopt a tribal orientation which denies the humanity of other men, or regards them as if they were natural objects without the capacity to forward claims of their own. Central to it is a protest against the resurrection of the kind of particularism which had typified tribal society. A progressive account of international relations claims that the state's distinctive identity can be displayed not merely in its form of social organisation but in its capacity to extend the boundaries of moral consideration or to enlarge the world of moral claims. As part of their claim to extend human sympathy, or to enlarge the sphere of ethical life, exponents of this perspective begin to detach morality from the social location in which it has functioned hitherto, from its connection with arrangements pertaining only to citizens. By being committed to the idea of a more inclusive morality, the elements of an external concept of obligation, these citizens begin to define the moral principles which should be generated not only within their particular society but also in relations with outsiders. Since members of tribal society take part in relations of personal dependence, rights cannot be recognised in them as individuals, only as participants within a separate, and in this case vulnerable, group. At a higher stage in the development of international society then, it is argued that the state's uniqueness, itself a product of overcoming estrangement between different social groups, should be reflected in its ability to adopt a non-antagonistic or non-exploitative position towards weaker societies. On this basis, some citizens seek to protect simpler societies from the harmful consequences of their fellows by arguing that these communities have rights which should not be infringed with impunity.

The growth of a more rational form of intersocietal life requires that the restatement of a wholly internal point of view should be resisted. It is important that any domestic conflicts about the proper way to treat outsiders should be settled by imputing rights to the latter as independent, human subjects. Such a decision is a progressive development because it represents a significant advance towards the recognition of the rights and duties of all men. However, differences of culture and political capability permit only very elementary examples of this principle to develop in relations between states and tribal societies. For early societies are incapable of pressing very far-reaching claims upon the state; while the state can act upon tribal society with potentially devastating consequences, the latter lacks the resources to make any equivalent impact upon the state in return. At the very least, the state can formulate a principle of not intervening in or interfering with the internal affairs of other societies. Beyond this very minimal constraint, it may attempt to limit or control the effects its presence has upon traditional societies with which it has contact and relations; in addition, it may offer assistance in those areas where other societies lack self-sufficiency.

The importance of these practices is that they advance the understanding that moral principles should be enacted because of their rational content, not because they contribute to the maintenance of an orderly social environment among fellow-citizens. To fulfil obligations towards these groups, without the expectation of receiving an equivalent benefit in return, is to transcend 'plans of geographical morality, parallels not of life but of latitudes'; it is to act on that mode of moral consciousness exemplified in the writings of Kant, on an awareness of the irrationality of action which regards others as means or instruments to one's own purposes, on the desire to act on the basis of principles which are universalisable, which the state could accept were its position and that of the tribal group reversed. As the state comes to regard non-members in this light, it initiates a process whereby it comes to take a more extensive common good into account. It acts on a higher conception of international relations if it is prepared to take action against those of its members who disregard the rights of other communities by exempting themselves from acting in accordance with universalisable principles. Relations between the state and tribal societies provide the first setting in which men identify the outlines of a universalist ethic, in which they perceive, transcending their citizenship, the claims of humanity.

The moral development of the state's external relations can only be more fully advanced when they have to respond to the existence of associations which are capable of formulating relatively similar conceptions of international relations. Let us imagine therefore that the state comes into contact not only with tribal societies and slave economies but with associations which are also based on relations of personal independence and share its social and political structure. We shall assume that when the state confronts other political associations it can be acted upon by outsiders who owe their loyalty to an association responsible first and foremost for the promotion of their private interests. Under these circumstances, a new state of nature comes into existence, and the problem of determining the principles which ought to govern relations between insiders and outsiders once again arises. We shall attempt to argue that more sophisticated types of international practices are produced as states seek to manage and control their interaction. An exploration of modes of interaction between states enables us to set out upon a scale of forms the principal stages of a gradually more humanised international relations. Through defining the basic principles of an international states-system and the elements of an international form of economic life men gradually create the basic preconditions of a universal kingdom of ends. By analysing these forms of interaction, we shall aim to determine what it would mean for reason and freedom to develop in a world of sovereign states. We begin, however, by defining the basic features of the international state of nature.

That state of nature which accompanies man's organisation into states differs considerably from the one described earlier, from one entailed by man's division between several ethnocentric societies. Societies are no longer estranged from, and antagonistic towards, one another as a matter of course given their cultural basis; nor do members derive an enhanced status within their groups from inflicting injury on outsiders. The dissolution of relations of personal dependence has led to the substitution of a different network of social virtues and determinants of status. Political society, moreover, is predicated upon the awareness of the human capacity to amend the conditions of social existence, and it has also produced the idea, practised in its relations with simpler societies and slave economies, that other groups and associations may have rights and duties. There is nothing present in the state's mode of organisation which predisposes it towards permanently hostile and antagonistic relations with outsiders. Indeed, its existing international relations have brought forth the capacity to give these dealings some degree of rational control and direction. And, although it will not be assumed that all states share an equal willingness and ability to impute the same rights and duties to all communities, it will be argued that the state's form of organisation facilitates this end.

To the extent that each state confronts principally particularistic communities able to jeopardise its interests, its experience of international relations will tend to combine a sense of insecurity with an awareness of the loss of freedom. In the present condition, the state is no longer able to determine the general structure of its own social and political institutions; decisions about domestic structures have to be responsive to, and may be swayed by, pressures emanating from the existence of other political systems. Nor is the state assured of being able to exercise a high degree of control over the conditions that define the environment in which it is located. In a world of states, each is to some degree dependent upon the actions of the rest; any single state's security and welfare depends upon circumstances over which it may be unable to exert any powerful influence. Contacts between states subordinate each one to a system of necessitous relations. While the state receives no guarantees from others, it has little choice but to pursue its particularistic interests. Uncertainties in the international state of nature issue from the fact that each state, suspicious of others but unable to escape them, is compelled to act according to its own judgment in order to avert or pre-empt threats to its security and welfare. Hostilities between states are not given in their cultural make-up, as was the case with tribal societies in our scale; they are products of each state's responsibility for a limited common good in an anarchical environment in which states must initially be competitors.

The problem of how to conduct relations with other states can produce differing responses. Some citizens, concerned not only to emphasise the state's role in preserving their freedom, but also its function as a buffer against the dangers of the outside world, may underline the essentially social nature of morality. They will stress considerations encountered before: the fact that the state must promote its interests first and foremost, that its representatives cannot be required or allowed to enact those moral principles which citizens normally respect, and that cooperation with outsiders must satisfy the utilitarian calculations which must always be uppermost in the minds of those with responsibility for foreign affairs. Their perspective emphasises an internal account of moral and political obligation in which the bonds between citizens, and between citizens and the state, are necessarily paramount. They echo Pufendorf's remark that the content of the state's foreign policy must be determined principally by 'the strength of its neighbours'.

However, another position may be adopted, one which is equally responsive to the fact that the state cannot behave as if satisfaction of its interests was assured. Here, rather different elements in the state's understanding of international relations are highlighted. Of particular importance is the fact that members of the state suffer a considerable reduction of the freedom which is unique to their association. The internal social relations of the state open up areas of freedom unknown in earlier societies; government by law is substituted for domination by custom and tradition, and the social environment becomes more consciously a human product. Although this development has not been reversed, it is now the case that government by law operates within, and is conditioned by, that realm of necessity and those impersonal forces which are a manifestation of the unregulated nature of interaction between states. To recover that freedom in society, it is not sufficient to promote merely one-sided interests for this simply evokes a hostile response from others, and further reinforces existing conditions. Although the state's representatives cannot ignore its interests, the circumstances in which the state acts need not be regarded as unalterable; they can be modified by the actions of human subjects. That particularism, to which citizens and their representatives may succumb, neither overcomes the problems of the modern state nor provides an adequate set of criteria with which to measure the legitimacy of political action. Freedom requires not merely the existence and preservation of relations of personal independence within a system of law, but the elimination of that realm of necessity which those who are committed to particularism passively accept or unwittingly sustain. The solution rests with the attempt to secure the freedom of the state's members through gaining and granting a certain kind of recognition: the recognition of the freedom and equality, the sovereignty, of separate political associations whereby states transform their interests into mutually guaranteed rights.

From the present perspective, the state's first ambition is not to secure its one-sided interests but to gain recognition of its responsibility for the enhancement of a particular common good. The state's representatives enact a higher conception of international affairs when they act not on an internal point of view but involve themselves in a claim for a certain kind of recognition from others, a claim for equality which asserts that the basic purposes of their association ought to be taken into account by others prior to their decision to act. Within the international state of nature, if this response from others is not automatically forthcoming, the state will have to devise means of eliciting the status of being regarded as an end by others; recognition will have to be 'sought out and won'.[1] Recourse to the instruments of violence is one method by which the state promotes not simply its interests but declares its intention of being considered a moral equal, whereby it conveys its absolute refusal to be acquiescent towards any policy which neglects its legitimate purposes. Here the state does not use force to advance its one-sided interests; it adopts the position that competition and conflict acquire legitimacy if they are related to the goal of affirming that the state has a dignity which must not go unnoticed by others. Underlying its attitude is an elementary principle of justice, the belief that it wishes to claim no more than it is willing to allow to others.

The instruments which states select in order to elicit the respect of others have implications which transcend their immediate purposes. To proceed without any concern for the interests of other states is to precipitate their hostile and perhaps combined opposition. Certain forms of conduct will be resisted violently because they disregard other societies' conception of themselves as ends. These forms of behaviour, and the responses of others to them, constitute the most primitive kind of international law-making or international government. They are the instruments through which states make determinate what could not be known in advance, namely mutual understandings of what is acceptable and unacceptable in their dealings with one another. At a very elementary stage in the development of international society, the action and reaction of states constitutes a form of dialogue through which they come to ascertain the principles applicable to their relations. Recognition can be extracted from other states as each comes to realise that what it claims can be either claimed by others to its eventual disadvantage or opposed immediately because it jeopardises their vital interests. In this way states come to terms with each other's existence within a system of norms which constitute their common international political framework.

Certain understandings, which emanate from initial contacts between states, mark their movement from an originally anarchic condition to an international system or society of states. The basic principles of this society reduce the level of uncertainty attached to relations between states by determining the fundamental rights and duties which they ought to acknowledge in one another. It is claimed here that a progressive development of international relations necessitates the transference of understandings of social relations from their original domestic setting to the international arena. With the promotion of the idea that states like individuals can have rights and duties it becomes possible for them to acquire the status of membership of a society of free and equal communities. At a higher stage in the development of international relations, states determine the rights and duties which their more unstructured interaction had sought to uncover. In particular, each state is assured the right of exercising sovereign authority within its own territorial jurisdiction, and its citizens are recognised as having the inalienable right of selecting their own system of government. In addition to proscribing intervention in the internal affairs of others, states acquire rights of equal representation upon any diplomatic forum. From their domestic experience they derive the constituents of an international legal system based on the understanding that international law must issue from the consent of sovereign associations. Finally, states commit themselves to the institution of the balance of power in an attempt to maintain their freedom in the face of any threat to their political independence. All states agree then upon a particular conception of international order, or of the right organisation of mankind, which maintains that its normatively preferred structure should comprise free and equal communities. An agreement upon this principle signifies the further extension of the area of the common good within a world of separate societies. It makes determinate a distinct realm of human obligation, an understanding of what each man owes the rest, albeit not as individuals but as citizens of different communities.

The above developments of the international system correspond with a movement from a world of international relations based on the Hobbesian principles assimilated into the thought of Pufendorf to the universalism expressed in the writings of Vattel. States have solved their initial political problems by constructing a framework of political rules which place significant constraints upon their representatives. Important as these constraints are for the gradual humanisation of international relations, they remain radically defective in several respects. For they are simply the laws of a political framework which stem from each state's decision to undertake the primitive step of recognising the other's independence. The agreements which constitute the law of the political framework need to be supplemented by more detailed principles of foreign policy. For example, although states have agreed that violence should not be used in order to destroy a community with equal rights as a member of the society of nations, they have not sought to control the scale of violence which any state might unleash in the pursuit of one of its legitimate goals. Recognising the sacrosanct nature of sovereignty still leaves a considerable degree of discretion in the hands of potentially self-regarding associations. The society of states is capable of further development in the area comprising the means and ends of foreign policy. Without that advancement, the problem of heteronomy remains inherent in a world of states.

If they are to achieve a higher level of control of their interaction, states must take it upon themselves to expand the system of determinate international principles. If the acceptance of an international political framework based upon the principle of sovereignty marked 'the starting-point for the free organisation of international society', the refusal to 'budge from that point' may thwart the possibility of attaining higher levels of international organisation.[2] Insistence upon sovereign rights is rational if states cannot be certain that their existence will be recognised and their purposes considered by others. Beyond this point, however, the principle of sovereignty becomes a barrier to the realisation of the goals which it was originally summoned to protect. To safeguard its own citizens from the dangers of uncontrolled violence, to give only one example, it becomes necessary to establish the laws of war. The emphasis of foreign policy must shift from claims for freedom and equality to cooperative acts aimed at determining a more effective system of social rules. After universal recognition of sovereignty comes a consensus about how it is to be properly exercised.

Earlier, we described the state securing its rights as an independent community through a process of action and reaction, stimulus and response. Now the objectives of their 'conversation' alter as states seek a different kind of recognition: for determinate, and universally applicable, principles of international relations. To this end, the state must articulate the principle upon which it proposes to act, or in Kantian terms publicise the maxim underlying its action. When all states behave in this way, a new and higher dialogue is initiated whereby states enact their roles as members of an international law-making community. By grounding the totality of their relations upon principles of justice, states make a significant move towards regarding the species, albeit still organised into a plurality of sovereign states, as the primary ethical reference group in the area of foreign policy. The enactment of an external point of view prepares the way for a higher kind of association in which all individuals, as self-determining beings, acquire fundamental rights in a universal community of mankind. It is to the final stages in our scale of political forms that we now turn.

International relations become humanised as they become moralised, as ethical life gains a foothold there. What is important in the moral development of international society is the fact that states refrain from asserting that they have non-negotiable rights by virtue of their sheer existence, other than the fundamental right of being recognised as an instrument for the promotion of a local common good. Beyond this elementary right, they refer not to what is inherent in their structure, but to what would be granted to them by the reasoned consent of the whole society of states. With the introduction of an external point of view in the area of foreign policy, international relations adopt the language of moral claims and counter-claims.

At this level, states advance moral claims, which are 'undecided rights'[3] referred to the community of nations for its consideration; the appropriate channel for their communication is diplomacy. States act on the understanding that a valid international right supposes that others have duties, and recognise their responsibility to discharge them. Sovereign states proceed neither by demands nor by pleas, but by claims, and they recognise that the whole society of states alone possesses the competence to transform these into international rights. To proceed on the basis of claims is to respect the equality of other parties. While the demand assumes that others have no right of refusal, and the plea assumes that they have every right of refusal, the claim assumes that others are equals, that they are capable of responding sensitively and fairly to the content of the claim; it supposes that others will issue counter-claims on the basis of their commitment to grounding international relations on principles of justice. The language of international moral claims presupposes and extends relations which already possess some moral content; it is a language which, in the course of promoting international ethical life, not only brings forth and more widely applies man's rational powers but also makes determinate a network of international principles which have elicited the consent of all.

When states engage in the language of claims and counter-claims they transcend the world of immediate self-interest and the pragmatic acceptance of international norms. The representatives of the state do not enact that conception of political life which asserts that its consent is the exclusive source of 'perfect' international obligation. Foreign policy is not regarded as successful because it manoeuvres others into accepting the state's particularistic view of the world, or entrenches its one-sided interests in the structure of the international order, but because it cooperates with others to generate universally acceptable principles of international affairs.

By adopting an external concept of obligation, the state accepts that its rights are negotiated, and must ultimately be subject to renegotiation if necessary, by the whole society of states. These rights cannot be derived from any 'hypothetical state of nature preceding the existence of any community', but from what the world community regards as 'natural', in the sense of being 'that which ought to be in a particular stage in the development of the relations between the community and the states which constitute an essential element of its structure'.[4] They are not 'absolute' or 'self-subsistent', but 'require restatement and modification as historical circumstances change'.[5] The conversation of moral claims leads to the formation of 'community expectations about right action'.[6] A more universalist foreign policy declines to condone any refusal to conform with international principle, on the grounds that it is unacceptable that a state should be unwilling 'to acknowledge the will and welfare of the world community as an important determinant of national policy';[7] a sovereign state's acceptance of the 'obligation to demonstrate the reasonableness of a controverted national claim is a development of legal accountability that extends beyond the classical notion that a sovereign state is entitled to do whatever it is not forbidden from doing'.[8] The growth of a more rational and free form of intersocietal life depends upon the capacity to take the whole of organised humanity, not merely the interests of those who are associated together, as the central ethical reference group. As universalism progresses, the emphasis upon the importance of sovereignty undergoes a corresponding decline.

If earlier stages in the moral development of the state's external relations represented a move from Pufendorf's to Vattel's conception of international relations, the existing stage will appear reminiscent of the Kantian theory of international society. As a riposte to the idea that the Kantian system is purely formal, it is important to defend the claim that the system of international principles, to which we have referred, is not empty or capable of receiving any content.[9] The state cannot act on any principle which it would be prepared to universalise, nor can the will of the international community accept any rule as a principle of international society, if the existing form of intersocietal life is to be regarded as progressive. We shall attempt to defend the proposition that there are clear constraints on what may be selected within the present condition.

The content of these principles of international relations can be derived from the self-knowledge which men have obtained through the medium of their historical development. To be aware that the existing form of intersocietal life is not a natural but an historical product is to require a very particular account of human beings and their necessary ends. In the existing condition, men would be aware that they had unfolded various powers unique to their species in the course of their history. Their historical creations have revealed what could not have been known in advance, namely man's capacity to produce individuated forms of life and to overcome relations of intersocietal estrangement. In short, they would be aware of their capacity as individuals to develop their powers within social arrangements which recognise the equality of men, their existence as non-natural beings capable of creating the conditions favourable to their own development.

Their self-knowledge, and particularly knowledge of their transcendence of the natural world, places definite constraints upon the forms of life which men may reasonably enter. At this level of self-consciousness, it would be necessary to accept the Kantian proposition that not to allow others to promote their self-development is not to recognise their humanity, the capacities which differentiate them from the natural world. To understand the relationship between history and self-knowledge, to adopt an 'expressivist' theory of man, is to require acceptance of the Marxian claim that man should eliminate from his environment those obstacles to the further development of his distinctively human powers. With these understandings, it becomes essential for men to determine what each individual owes the other members of his species by virtue of their common humanity, their equal status as free beings. They must seek satisfaction as self-determining beings, as progressive beings with fundamental obligations to all other members of their species, not as self-interested beings or maximisers who pursue their interests within the self-regarding and utilitarian framework of the separate, sovereign state. With this development we come to the final phase in the scale of forms of international relations, where men identify with, and have rights in, a properly universal society.

This last transition may be regarded as a clarification and further extension of what underlies the superimposition of a web of universal rules upon the international states-system. The very possibility of these rules reflects the existence of a common, rational nature (not a nature which is without a history but one which unfolds as human subjects act and reflect upon their actions) which exists alongside the vertical divisions stemming from man's organisation into separate, sovereign states. The capacity to abide by these rules indicates the transcendence of the moral claims and powerful psychological constraints exerted by citizenship. Universally applicable rules provide the focal point for the evolu[illegible] loyalty which extends beyond the parameters of the sov[illegible] state; a more pronounced sense of obligation to human[illegible] an advanced form of moral consciousness, an intimation [illegible] the prospect of a higher kind of international political life.

The above stages in the development of the international states-system reveal increasingly more adequate accounts of moral and political obligation. But, hitherto, obligations between human beings have not been enacted by the individual members of different political communities directly, but indirectly, through the mediation of their states. In an earlier condition, the state appeared as the most satisfactory kind of association, and the states-system seemed the legitimate form of world political organisation. With the development of the individual's moral relationship with his species, changes in the structure of political life become essential. It is important to replace the sovereign state, with its particular guarantees to those who have been associated together historically, with a global legal and political system which affords protection to all human subjects as moral equals. The expansion of moral community involves the surrender of the sovereignty of those associations which mediate between the individual and the species. In accordance with this ideal, it is necessary that the gradual renunciation of the classical discretionary power of the sovereign state should culminate in the establishment of new principles of international organisation. Ethical universalism is promoted by the dissolution of both the state's right to determine when it will use force and the government of international relations by principles based upon the consent of its constituent sovereign parts; it is advanced further by ensuring that the practice of humanitarian intervention in the previously sovereign affairs of a community is incorporated into the structure of a progressive international order; its development necessitates replacing the balance of power, with its underlying state-centric assumptions, with a more centralised and principled form of international government. The institutional expression of the idea of an international kingdom of ends is a movement beyond the world of state-centred theory and practice.

Finally, an account of the stages in the development of a more free international relations would be defective if it concentrated solely on legal and political practices. In Marx's thought, it will be recalled, an understanding of freedom could not ignore its economic and social conditions, and a critique of political life could not be advanced in abstraction from a critique of productive life or civil society. Following Marx's position on the economic and social preconditions of human freedom, it is necessary to conclude that an account of the deficiencies of the international states-system would be incomplete in isolation from an analysis of the nature of international economic life. With the specification of the principles of an international economic system transformed to satisfy the goal of human freedom, we conclude our scale of political forms.

If freedom refers to that set of circumstances in which individuals collaborate to maintain conditions favourable to their own development, then it ought to include cooperation to ensure individual rights of access to a basic level of economic and social resources. For the freedom of individuals or communities is simply formal in the absence of the capacity to exercise that freedom. Thus, in the form of international society discussed earlier, the sovereign equality of states may reflect legal but not economic and political facts. Sovereign control of national resources, the right of taking economic decisions as an independent, self-regarding entity, and the capacity to extract a disproportionately large share of the world's resources, may render the principle of sovereign equality meaningless. An adequate realisation of this principle involves a redistribution of the world's resources in order to eliminate the substantial gaps between one society and another. A similar concern for social and economic justice is important in connection with that higher form of intersocietal life where men have rights as individuals in a global political system. Their individual freedom will be incomplete in the absence of a security of access to basic economic and social resources. We must measure progress in international relations by the extent to which particularistic economic activity has given way to a universalistic perspective sympathetic to the goal of world distributive justice. Thus, to realise their freedom or humanity, citizens must progress beyond the conception of the state as a repository of absolute rights of ownership of their territorial resources, beyond the view that the state's representatives have economic obligations to insiders which are not similarly due to outsiders, and beyond the notion that international economic cooperation will be perpetuated only insofar as it promotes the state's particularistic goals.[10] By imputing rights to one another within a world political system which exercises control over the totality of their resources, members of the human species complete the move from particularism to universalism.

We have now executed our basic task of connecting a political theory of international relations with a theory of the history of human subjects. A brief but adequate summary of what has been represented in the scale of ascending types of international relations would be that men have deepened or broadened their concepts of rights. We have described a hypothetical extension of rights to other subjects, beginning with tribal members recognising rights in outsiders, and proceeding first to individuals recognising rights in each other as citizens, and to sovereign states acknowledging the rights of adjacent societies, and ending with individual men respecting the rights to which each is entitled as a free being. Our scale of types has also sought to represent a deepening of the content of these rights. Beginning with a condition in which tribal members were guaranteed security, we proceeded to the state with its protection of the interests of its citizens, and ended with the principles of world political organisation which secured freedom first to political associations and then to all individuals. We began our scale with an image of a tribal society for which intersocietal estrangement was the norm, and in which human powers were barely developed. Having outlined various stages representative of the idea of humanity we conclude it by envisaging a form of international political life in which all men have inalienable rights, including the right of access to material resources subject to their control; a type of international community in which they have rights simply as human beings and solely for the purpose of promoting their individual development.

Concluding Remarks

This work began with an analysis of a conflict within our specifically modern experience of political life, of the way in which associated selves comprehend their relations with outsiders. In the course of the argument, we have sought a theoretical basis from which to effect a reconciliation between obligations to other citizens and obligations to other men. It will be recalled that the earliest attempts to engineer a synthesis of an internal and external account of obligation were advanced within the rationalist tradition. If rationalism began with an acquiescent acceptance of life in a world of states, it ended in the writings of Kant with the adoption of a radical or critical theory of international relations. We have argued that under the pressure of a variety of modern criticisms the idea of a morally or politically unified humanity cannot be revived in its classical form. While we have conceded that the principal foundations of the Kantian theory of international relations cannot withstand the historicist critique, it has been claimed that, with suitable modification, the more advanced elements of rationalist thinking can be recovered by re-locating them within a theory of history. A theory of the historical development of human freedom offers good reasons for the belief in the existence of obligations to humanity; it also provides the philosophical resources which enable us to present a vision of a unified moral and political experience, one which can accommodate the fact of obligations to humanity without permitting these to conflict with the roles and responsibilities of other communities.

Within the scale of types of international relations, frequent reference was made to the development of the idea of humanity alongside the realm of civic obligations. Early in the scale, in the discussion of relations between states and simpler societies, it was argued that a progressive conception of international relations involved the specification of what citizens owed outsiders as fellow human beings. In relations between states, we found that obligations to other men could be defined firstly as obligations to recognise the equality and independence of the communities of which they were part; secondly, the idea of humanity involved grounding relations between states upon international principles sensitive to the existence of human freedom; and finally it conveyed the idea of a duty to create the conditions which would enable all men to promote their individual development.

The conclusion to draw is that the conflict between men and citizens has a history or development; it does not possess the same content at each level in our forms of intersocietal life. For example, the sense of obligation to members of simpler societies is not the same as the belief in the need to conform with obligations to other states, or to enact duties to individual persons elsewhere. In the simpler forms of international relations, the dichotomy between men and citizens conveys the belief that the distinction between morality and self-interest should apply not only within but also in relations between separate societies. Here, the belief in a realm of human obligation which transcends citizenship is not necessarily used to criticise the division of humanity into separate, sovereign states. Through their appeal to their humanity, citizens serve notice upon their states that they will refuse to comply with any law or command issued contrary to the state's international moral and legal obligations. In a more advanced experience of international relations, the appeal to a realm of human obligation does not simply challenge the state on those occasions when its representatives contravene their international obligations; beyond this, it challenges the rationale for a state-centred international relations; it articulates the vision of a more humanised international relations, an entirely reconstructed system of economic and political life designed to express acceptance of the idea of a universal kingdom of ends. It is not surprising that the realm of moral obligation transcendent of citizenship should possess varying content; for different understandings of the dichotomy between men and citizens may be identified relative to stages in the development of international society. Like the stages of intersocietal life themselves, these distinct understandings may be placed upon a scale of types which signifies their relative degree of development.

In accordance with this perspective, the present argument has found the claim that we can neither specify the content of duties to humanity nor envisage an international community responsible for their enactment unconvincing. An application of the principles of philosophical history allows us to determine the postulates of a more advanced form of intersocietal life than the modern states-system. In particular, it leads to the criticism of three postulates of modern political life. None of these escapes being contested, nevertheless, together they form the underlying principles of a system of states. These are the idea that the state has certain absolute rights as a separate, political association (in some versions because of the consent of its members); the conviction that the morality appropriate to the enactment of those public roles which are concerned with statecraft differs from the ethics relevant to the circumstances normally encountered by ordinary citizens; and the supposition that cooperation between states rests not upon any fundamental human obligations but upon concerns for interests. We have attempted to show why these cannot be the eternal principles of a rational international society.

The scope of the present argument has not allowed an investigation into the ethics of particular areas of foreign policy. We regard this as a limitation, albeit an inevitable one within the parameters of this work. Nor have we investigated a number of more concrete circumstances in which citizens believe that they cannot honour their obligations to their fellow men without endangering the welfare of their own society. The general remark that we should be concerned to eliminate the conditions which force this choice upon us may be adequate from a theory concerned mainly with the problem of structure; but it is clearly inadequate from the perspective of a theory of action. The above argument has been concerned mainly with the problem of structure. While the arguments encountered there necessarily impinge upon debates about the problem of action, about the problem of foreign policy, the need clearly exists for a theory of the practice of international relations. In addition to the principles discussed above, it is essential to explore the theory of action, a theory of normative constraints in empirical circumstances. What has been developed above provides no more than a starting point in this regard.

In conclusion, the attempt here to find an alternative philosophical foundation for some of the important constituents of rationalist international thought has led to the acceptance of a theory of the historical development of freedom. Freedom has been defined in opposition to both natural constraints and quasi-physical constraints present in social relations and in interaction between different social systems. With this in mind, the scale of forms has sought to represent the advance of freedom in international relations as the supersession of estrangement and necessity in relations between groups, phenomena which are dominant when these groups have not comprehended the nature of their shared humanity. Social and political freedom involves, even if it is not exhausted by, the establishment of a universal society of human beings. We have, accordingly, agreed with the Marxian vision, which closely resembles Kant's, of a universal association in which men have transcended the designations which they have acquired by their incorporation into a specific state, and their corresponding non-integration into other political communites; in which, in other words, they confront one another essentially as human beings.

The final word must be left with Kant and Marx, the two great exponents of moral or political universalism within the tradition of philosophical history. As part of his effort to reconcile man to his history, Kant claimed that the entire range of human powers could not be expressed in a single individual or particular community, but only in the species as a whole in the course of its long historical development. For Marx also the many-sidedness of human powers could be realised only in what Kant described as the bosom of the species as a whole. His principle that the free development of each is the condition for the free development of all recognises the importance of cooperation within the most inclusive human association of all, a form of collaboration whereby men promote one another's development and overcome their own individual one-sidedness. A universal association was not then an end in itself (perpetual peace for Kant was only the highest *political* goal), nor did it simply bring the international state of nature to a close; it was an essential part of the conditions required by human beings when they turned, late in their history, to the task of perfecting themselves. This ideal, as it is understood by Kant and Marx, requires the development from an association of citizens to an association of men. Within their theories, we find the most convincing defence for a properly international community: that only within a structure which aims at maximising the conditions favourable to individual and collective self-determination can men further their historically evolving capacities while recapturing morally integrated lives.

A Postscript on Habermas and Foucault

> ... modern natural-law constructions ... are best suited to the identity of world citizens, not to that of citizens of a particular state that has to maintain itself against other states. (Habermas)

> to erase man like a face drawn in sand at the edge of the sea ... (Foucault)

The argument of *Men and Citizens* began with the observation that a tension between the obligations of citizenship and the obligations of humanity has been a recurrent feature of both the theory and practice of the modern states-system. This formulation acknowledged the force of the realist claim that modern political communities will remain particularistic as long as conflict and competition endure between them. But it also observed that notions of moral obligation have not been exhausted by the demands of citizenship alone. Throughout the development of the modern system of states the case for the primacy of citizenship has come into conflict with various forms of ethical universalism and their attendant visions of a global community which supersedes the sovereign state. The tension between citizenship and humanity has persisted because the notion of the state's answerability to universal principles has also been an ineluctable feature of the modern states-system.

With this in mind, *Men and Citizens* proceeded to consider three distinct philosophical perspectives: the contractarian tradition to which Pufendorf, Vattel and Kant belong; the historicist perspective exemplified by the writings of Meinecke and Treitschke; and the tradition of philosophical history developed in the writings of Kant, Hegel and Marx. A survey of these perspectives was designed to ascertain whether it was possible (at least in principle) to overcome the antinomy between humanity and citizenship.

The main line of argument held that two of the exponents of social contract theory, Pufendorf and Vattel, failed to reconcile the tension between citizenship and humanity – as Kant suggested in his critique of modern natural law theory. In response to this failure, Kant's international thought aimed to solve the problem of the bifurcated moral subject. However, Kant's argument was committed to the problematical assumption that there is an immutable and universal moral test of human conduct. The difficulties with this position were emphasised first by Hegel and, subsequently, by the historicist writers mentioned above. Their critique of Enlightenment universalism – which has affinities with the more recent post-structuralist or anti-foundationalist critique of universalist thinking which we shall consider below – emphasised the incommensurability of rival moral codes. Even so, the historicist critique of universalism generated its own set of problems. Historicism denied ethical universalism while paradoxically proclaiming cultural diversity as a universal ideal.

Proceeding from this point, *Men and Citizens* argued that the German tradition of philosophical history provided the resources which made the resolution of the tension between citizenship and humanity possible. The upshot of this part of the argument was that moral community in the modern world is not exhausted by the claims of citizenship. Nevertheless, the antinomies of moral experience reveal that social and political arrangements which institutionalise duties to humanity have yet to be constructed on a global scale. This being so, *Men and Citizens* defined moral progress as a twofold process: as the demise at the philosophical level of any rigid moral distinction between citizens and outsiders; and the implementation at the practical level of principles which treat citizens and non-citizens as moral equals. These considerations underpinned the attempt to set out 'a scale of forms' of international relations in the final sections of the book. The scale of forms defined moral progress in international relations as the ascent towards ethical universality.

Since the publication of *Men and Citizens* in 1982, two developments in social and political theory have become increasingly important in the study of international relations.

These are the attempt to construct a critical theory of international relations and, more recently, the appearance of a post-structuralist or anti-foundationalist challenge to the major systematic positions in the field.[1] The first development invites the question of how far Habermas's project of incorporating the moral aspects of human development within a reconstructed form of historical materialism can strengthen the position taken in *Men and Citizens*. The second development, which takes issue with critical approaches to international relations (and with conventional approaches as well), raises the question of whether the argument of *Men and Citizens* with its reliance upon notions of moral progress, universality, human subjectivity and autonomy can escape Foucault's claim that all forms of 'discourse (are) a violence which we do to things, or, in any case . . . a practice which we impose upon them'.[2] More specifically, the anti-foundationalist turn in contemporary international relations requires a specific rejoinder to the claim that the critical-theoretical project of extending community in international relations overlooks one crucial point about the modern subject – and that is that 'the man described for us, whom we are invited to free is already in himself the effect of a subjection much more profound than himself.[3]

The postscript begins by considering the significance of Habermas's critical project for the argument developed in *Men and Citizens*. It suggests that critical theory can answer the anti-foundationalist challenge. But in the light of anti-foundationalism it suggests that a critical theory of international relations should clearly embrace the proposition that there are limits to universality just as there ought to be limits to difference. Furthermore, this postscript argues that anti-foundationalism, and Foucault's social thought in particular, can be harnessed to the task of developing a critical theory of international relations. In short, Foucault's genealogical writings can be employed to construct a project which extends certain themes outlined in *Men and Citizens*. This is the project of developing a critical sociology of moral development in international relations.

HABERMAS

Reference to the tension between citizenship and humanity occurs in Habermas's writings. It is linked with Habermas's claim that the critical theorist ought to address 'mankind as such'. And this in turn is connected with the argument that classical Marxism failed 'to penetrate beyond the level of particular historical class interests to disclose the fundamental interests of mankind as such'.[4]

For Habermas, the capacity to adopt a universalistic moral point of view – one that takes account of the welfare of the species as a whole – stems from a complex process of social development which Marx and classical Marxism failed to explain. In the *Grundrisse* Marx did outline an explanation of the evolution of the modern subject. There Marx discussed what is, in Habermas's perspective, the fundamental human capacity for 'universalisation, decentration, autonomisation and becoming reflective'.[5] But the analysis wrongly assumed, in Habermas's view, the primacy of material production. In opposition to the paradigm of production, Habermas argues for a new 'empirical philosophy of history' which accounts for the evolution of moral discourse and the development of 'communicative rationality'. Habermas maintains that a reconstructed historical materialism should add the rationalisation of communication to classical Marxist analyses of the rationalisation of the instruments of production.[6]

Habermas's attempt to reconstruct the Marxist tradition argues that the normative claims of critical theory can be defended by analysing the structure of human communication. In his statement of this argument, Habermas maintains that the possibility of the unification of the human race is contained within the very first speech act. The linguistic turn in Habermas's attempt to rework the foundations of critical theory has been the subject of much controversy. His critics have argued that the enterprise of explicating the formal and universal presuppositions of human communication does little to solve the complex moral problems and dilemmas which human beings face in a range of particular circumstances. Many of his critics have argued that Habermas's belief that there are analogies between the phases of individual moral development and the stages of historical development displays an ethnocentric bias which was already evident in Kohlberg and Piaget's cognitive psychology. There is no agreement that the linguistic and psychological dimensions of his work provide critical theory with more secure ethical foundations.[7]

A more successful though less ambitious means of achieving this objective may well be provided by Habermas's notion of 'the unforced force of the better argument'.[8] Habermas's belief that moral development is illustrated by the universalisation of rights (by the process which extends them to human beings as such) reveals the possibilities of this approach. In defence of Habermas it may be argued that, over time, the force of the better argument has come to favour moral inclusion as against moral exclusion. The merits of the case for inclusion are especially evident in arguments about conducting relations between the sexes, races and classes within societies. But its strengths have become important too in reflections about the principles which should govern relations between nation-states. Across numerous domains, spurious moral distinctions between human beings have been identified and challenged and, as a result, some of the moral boundaries which have stood between 'equals' and 'unequals' have been gradually broken down. This destruction of the moral boundaries which exclude others from enjoying equal rights has been an important part of what is meant by social and political progress.

The contention that moral development involves the progressive universalisation of norms was crucial to the argument of *Men and Citizens*. As a result, the claim that it is important to know far more about the way in which human beings developed their power 'to distinguish themselves from nature by recognising their own historical being; their capacity to undergo individuation and to recognise the universality of human nature; (and) their ability to create and control institutions and conditions which enable them to promote their individual and social development'[9] has affinities with Habermas's argument for a sociology of the evolution of individuation, universalisation and reflectiveness in human history. But whereas Habermas tends to emphasise the way in which these phenomena evolve within specific societies, *Men and Citizens* claimed that relations between societies, states and civilisations form one of the key domains in which the struggle between moral particularism and moral universalism has occurred – one of the main realms in which the case for ethical universality has often been fought out and won. An awareness of the part that relations between states and civilisations have played in moral development is not entirely absent from Habermas's thought.[10] But international relations receive scant attention nonetheless. In this respect, Habermas's writings reflect a more general (though now diminishing) neglect of international relations by most schools of modern social theory.

Men and Citizens made the case for a sociological analysis of moral development in international relations; but the specifics of that enterprise fell outside the scope of its principal area of inquiry. The scale of forms of international relations sought to discuss the meaning of increasing universality in the conduct of external affairs. It endeavoured to substantiate the additional point that an evolutionary approach to international relations is both possible and desirable. The issue of how a sociology of moral development in international relations might be constructed was deferred until another occasion. Some points concerning possible future directions will be discussed in the final sections of this postscript.

FOUCAULT

According to anti-foundationalism, evolutionary sociology lacks secure and objective foundations; it rests upon an arbitrary set of philosophical assumptions. Foucault, for one, argued that there is no progress in history, only movement between different modes of repression: 'Humanity does not gradually progress from combat to combat until it arrives at universal reciprocity, where the rule of law finally replaces warfare; humanity installs each of its violences in a system of rules and thus proceeds from domination to domination'.[11] In a famous passage he argued that all claims to knowledge are intertwined with claims to power: 'power and knowledge imply one another; . . . there is no power relation without the correlative constitution of a field of knowledge, nor any knowledge that does not presuppose and constitute at the same time power relations.'[12] To put it another way, every claim to knowledge creates an 'other' who has to be normalised, marginalised, or controlled. Critical social theory and the politics of emancipation do not form a special case. Despite their purpose, they cannot overcome structures of domination; they can merely reconstitute them.

This being the case, it may seem paradoxical that Foucault did not conclude that all opposition to the reigning power/knowledge configurations is entirely futile. While he took issue with 'global systematic theory' and with projects of universal emancipation, he did endorse local resistance and efforts to find expression for 'subjugated knowledges'.[13] The apparent inconsistency between Foucault's conviction that all perspectives are 'incommensurably bad'[14] and his support for specific struggles concerning prison reform and gay rights prompted Habermas to pose the question 'Why fight?'[15] How could Foucault dismiss the language and politics of human emancipation yet clearly endorse political resistance at the same time?

Several points need to be made in this context. In the first place, Foucault has been interpreted as arguing that knowledge and power are inter-related rather than identical. The point for Foucault was then to explore the connections between knowledge and power rather than to assume that one entailed the other.[16] Without such an assumption, it might be added, Foucault could not have justified the distinction between regimes which are 'indifferent to' and regimes which 'prescribe' the truth.[17] Secondly, although Foucault supported political action to strip arrangements and structures of any false claims to legitimacy, he strongly emphasised the need for caution; and he did this 'not (because) everything is bad, but (because) everything is dangerous'.[18]

This concern that resistance would produce new forms of domination or reconstitute old ones was a fundamental theme in Foucault's thought. It was linked with the observation that the great heir to the Enlightenment, Marxism, with its all-encompassing, totalising view of history and its project of universal liberation, had failed to fulfil the promise of emancipation. In fact, to introduce a third and final point, all projects of enlightenment and emancipation jeopardised the human capacity for cultural diversification and improvisation; all threatened to destroy existing social differences in the name of an entirely spurious universal moral consensus. Foucault's contention that the 'search for a form of morality acceptable by everyone in the sense that everyone would have to submit to it, seems catastrophic to me'[19] is reminiscent of the historicist critique of the dull uniformity promised by

Enlightenment universalism. In each case, the search for universality is strikingly opposed by the defence of difference.

The relationship between universality and difference has become an important theme in contemporary social thought, particularly in discussions about the anti-foundationalist challenge to critical theory. Bernstein notes that Foucault, Derrida and Rorty oppose the universalistic aspirations of critical theory with a plea for a 'plurality' of life-forms. However, as Bernstein argues, the differences between critical theory and anti-foundationalism are not as major as some observers suggest. A 'hidden form of universality' underlies the anti-foundationalist defence of 'an active principle of tolerance'.[20] As for critical theory, Habermas refers to the inevitability of conflicts of interest and values. He further suggests that while human beings live in the expectation of the future resolution of their differences, there is absolutely no guarantee that a complete reconciliation of their moral disagreements will ever come about.[21]

It is important to stress that Habermas's claim that there are limits to universality is not simply resignation to the fact that moral problems often resist solution. These limits are grounded in Habermas's explicit commitment to a plurality of life-forms. They arise out of an argument for the continuation of cultural differences. For critical theory, as Habermas understands it, a 'fully transparent ... homogenized and unified society' is not an ideal at all.[22] What is more, there is no conflict between a willingness to make moral claims answerable to a universal test and the desire for a 'pluralism of life forms and interest(s)'.[23]

The nature of the argument can be further clarified by considering Habermas's reasons for rejecting the speculative philosophy of history present in the writings of Hegel and Marx. In opposition to the teleological assumptions associated with this approach, Habermas argues for an approach to historical evolution which assumes 'neither unilinearity nor necessity, neither continuity nor irreversibility'.[24] Moreover, all accounts of human progress must now be 'stripped' of the notion of 'foreclosure against an open future'.[25] Without attempting to minimise the differences between critical theory and anti-foundationalism, it is important to note that both positions advocate cultural diversity. The importance of social pluralism for critical social theory, however, might have been clearer if Habermas and others had developed the notion of the limits to universality more clearly. A lengthy defence of the case for plurality may seem unnecessary when the belief that 'historical progress will culminate in the dissolution of all social differences within a universal association' has been largely abandoned'.[26] But the case should have been stated more fully nevertheless.

The claim that there are limits to universality needs to be counterbalanced by the claim that there are limits to diversity too. Critical theorists have been far more explicit than anti-foundationalists about the need for placing limits upon the celebration of difference. Nevertheless, Foucault did not appear to embrace the Nietzschean thesis that since 'nothing is true, everything must be permitted'. At some points, Foucault seemed to assume a universalistic philosophical stance which sat uncomfortably with other dimensions of his thought and which seemed more in keeping with the tenor of Habermas's analysis of moral rationalisation. His comments about the plight of the Vietnamese boat people are a striking example: 'there exists an international citizenry, which has its rights, which has its duties, and which promises to raise itself up against every abuse of power, no matter who the author or the victims'. This being so, 'the will of individuals must inscribe itself in a reality over which governments have wanted to reserve a monopoly for themselves – a monopoly which we must uproot little by little every day'.[27] Certain political actions or practices are evidently ruled out. But no philosophical defence of this apparently universalist critique of the denial of human rights was ever presented.

Understandably, Bernstein argues that anti-foundationalists 'obliterate the difference between legitimate and illegitimate claims to universal normative principles'.[28] It might also be noted that in Foucault's case the defence of diversity restates the sceptic's point that a tolerant society is one in which individuals renounce all claims to absolute truth. But the supposition that there is no truth contains the disquieting consequence that the grounds for defending tolerance and diversity are no more secure than the grounds for advocating intolerance and domination. This was the problem inherent in the historicist goal of affirming diversity in the face of the homogenising influence of Enlightenment universalism.[29] In short, a universalistic claim was already implicit within the historicist argument for plurality; and, as already noted, it is also posited by the more recent argument of anti-foundationalism.

With justification, Peter Dews has argued that the case for diversity is best anchored in an explicitly universalistic perspective[30] – in one, it might be suggested, which recognises the need for limits to universality and limits to difference. The possibility of such a perspective would appear to be denied by anti-foundationalism. The latter avoids the issue of deciding what can and what cannot – what ought and what ought not to – be universalised. It has failed to raise the key question of how the defence of universality and the claim for difference might be woven into a single theoretical perspective. It has failed then, as Bernstein notes, to deal with 'the hard question that any serious political theorist has to face today (which) is how to balance legitimate claims to universal ethical and political principles and the recognition of the integrity of otherness, *differance*, and plurality'.[31]

ON THE FORCE OF THE BETTER ARGUMENT

At this point, it may be useful to return to Habermas's idea of the 'unforced force of the better argument'. This notion takes issue with two perspectives in the history of social and political thought. The first, which is exemplified by various forms of ethical absolutism, maintains that universal and immutable moral truths exist independently of human subjects; the second, which is present in numerous formulations of ethical relativism, contends that competing moral codes are unalterably incommensurable. According to the first position, binding and universal moral standards clearly exist; according to the second, there are no grounds for preferring one moral perspective to any of the alternatives. Moral judgments and preferences are simply arbitrary.

The idea of the force of the better argument suggests that ethical relativism and ethical absolutism are equally erroneous positions. Neither conveys the character of moral deliberation and argument. Neither captures the point that the aim of moral discourse is to fasten upon the best arguments of the time in order to develop a rational (but invariably incomplete and even temporary) consensus about the principles which ought to regulate social and political life.

As far as this third perspective is concerned, the groundrules of social and political life change and develop. Through learning-processes in what Habermas calls the 'moral-practical' sphere, moral agents recognise the spurious grounds upon which certain social practices may rest. They proceed to break with principles of social interaction and political legitimacy which were previously taken for granted. Social and political principles which survive philosophical scrutiny then become the operative basis for social and political interaction until such time as their inadequacies and limitations start to appear. The search for a more adequate inter-subjective consensus (as opposed to the arbitrary selection of alternative means of imposing order upon social existence or the creation of norms which are a closer approximation to eternal moral truths) is then renewed. The crucial point is that moral principles are neither immutable and universal nor are they arbitrary and groundless means of organising a meaningless reality. The point, as the German tradition of philosophical history maintained, is that reason has a history – a history in which there is, to repeat Habermas's words, 'neither unilinearity nor necessity, neither continuity nor irreversibility', but progress nevertheless.

Charles Taylor illustrates the argument in this way. In his critique of the anti-progressivist nature of much contemporary social thought, Taylor suggests that the force of the better argument required the extension of the suffrage to women. The expansion of the suffrage occurred because of the necessity of 'lifting ... an indefensible restriction, grounded on a misguided view of the human potentialities of half the race'.[32] Political change eventuated because the force of the better argument made it clear that a specific form of moral exclusion could no longer be legitimated – because an evolving consensus resolved to open one of the 'doors to otherness (that had been) closed'.[33]

On a more general level, the challenge to systems of exclusion based on race, nationality and ethnicity, gender and class has been one of the distinctive features of Western political theory and practice during the last two hundred years. In this period the dominant moral discourse has come to support inclusion; and unsurprisingly, given that moral discourse has its own logic of development, the language of inclusion has been turned against the West itself by Third World societies in their political struggle against the former's practices of exclusion. These practices have included denial of access to political equality and independence as well as resistance to racial, cultural and economic equality. On this score, Habermas is right to criticise Foucault for having neglected 'the development of normative structures in connection with the modern formation of power', and for having analysed 'processes of subjugation' and 'contexts of more or less consciously strategic action' in abstraction from developments in the sphere of 'values, norms and processes of mutual understanding'.[34] In fact, this weakness of Foucault's goes further since 'moral-practical learning processes have to present themselves to him as intensifications of processes of empowerment'.[35]

THE FORCE OF THE BETTER ARGUMENT AND THE NOTION OF THE OTHER

Men and Citizens supported this approach to moral rationality and universality, albeit in different terms. It was concerned with the philosophical problems involved in affirming the duties of citizenship where these conflict with the duties to humanity. It argued that the existence of a conflict between citizenship and humanity revealed that the force of the better argument no longer favoured the primacy of the state. It defended the need for including insiders and outsiders alike as moral equals in political communities which supersede the nation-state.

This formulation left two crucial questions unanswered. The first is the problem which Hegel endeavoured to solve in *The Philosophy of Right*. This is the issue of how difference and universality can be accommodated within the structure of the modern state. Suffice it to note that this has become a crucial question not only for the political theory of the modern state but for the political theory of international relations as well.

Arguably, Hedley Bull's claim that the time may be 'ripe for the enunciation of new concepts of universal political organisation which would show how Wales, the United Kingdom and the European Community could each have some world political status while none laid claim to exclusive sovereignty' reveals one way to proceed.[36]

The second question concerns practice and transition, the complex issue of how a world order which overcomes the tension between citizenship and humanity can be constructed over time. This is not a matter which can be dealt with satisfactorily here. Suffice it to note that the philosophical and empirical analysis of ethical problems in world politics may well provide the best means of solving the problems encountered in this area of inquiry. As many recent discussions of basic human needs and inalienable human rights have demonstrated, the issue here is one of developing the politics of extending community between nation-states.[37]

What the concluding sections of this postscript can do is consider one dimension of the debate between critical theory and anti-foundationalism which has special significance for the task of developing a sociology of moral development in the sphere of international relations. More specifically, two themes which are present in Foucault's social theory coupled with the Habermasian notion of moral-practical learning suggest one direction the analysis might take.

In a critical essay on Foucault's analysis of power, freedom, truth and the subject, Charles Taylor makes the observation that Foucault's studies of the prison, the clinic and the asylum offer the kind of detailed analysis of constraining regimes of power and truth which the tradition of critical social theory has yet to provide.[38] For the most part, critical theorists have failed to develop empirical investigations of the constraining role of micro- and macro-social and political structures. Inquiries into methodology and the philosophy of the social sciences and more recently, in Habermas's work, studies of communicative action and communicative rationality have outpaced empirical analyses of the contexts in which human beings confront (to use the language of the Frankfurt School) unnecessary social constraints and distorted forms of culture and communication. Bearing this criticism in mind, it is arguable that Foucault's genealogical studies are significant for critical social theory in general and for the specific task of developing a critical theory of international relations in two important respects.

First of all, in his analyses of the prison, the clinic and the asylum, Foucault described how societies construct self-constituting dichotomies between the normal and the abnormal, the sane and the insane; how, as the dominant understanding of rationality comes to be established, societies construct the 'other' who does not belong and who becomes the object of strategies of marginalisation, normalisation and control. Through a series of disciplinary practices, through various regimes of truth, Foucault argued, all societies arrive at their 'principles of exclusion'.[39] By such means each society constructs 'the boundaries ... by which (it) reprobates something that lies outside itself'.[40] Through the establishment of moral boundaries between the 'rational' self and the 'irrational' other, each '(specifies) ... a place heterogenous to all others and closed in upon itself'.[41]

A second feature of Foucault's thought which is pertinent to the project outlined above emerges in the history of sexuality. In these writings, Foucault referred to the need for an analysis of 'moral subjectivation' – the means by which the individual constitutes him/herself as a moral subject. Foucault identified four areas of inquiry which are germane to this mode of inquiry: the way in which the moral agent defines that part of the self which is subject to moral obligation; the procedures which the moral subject employs to define binding rights and obligations; the nature of the 'self-forming activity' which human beings believe they must undergo to become competent moral subjects; and the approach taken to the question of the 'telos' or purpose of moral compliance.[42]

One might ask if Foucault's analyses of the other and his subsequent consideration of modes of subjectivation suggest an important area of investigation for the critical theorist of international relations. That is the analysis of the means by which societies construct 'the moral other' in international relations whom they exclude and whom they seek to marginalise, manipulate or control. This area of inquiry would be concerned with the various modes of objectification which accompany the definition of the moral boundaries which separate communities from each other. It would analyse what

Hobhouse called 'the tie which keeps the members of a society together while separating them in a greater or less degree from the rest of the world'.[43] The principles of 'separability'[44] which constitute societies by including some and excluding others then become the object of the inquiry.

What is required is the delineation of the areas of inquiry most germane to a sociology of modes of objectification which analyses the relationship between the constitution of the self and society and the constitution of the other. Todorov's classification of the epistemic, axiological, and praxeological dimensions of the construction of the other – the three main 'axes of alterity' – is useful in this regard.[45] The epistemic axis is concerned with the conceptual framework which each society brings to bear upon its characterisation of the other; the axiological axis refers to the moral assessment which each society makes of other forms of life; while the praxeological axis deals with the relationship each society proposes to have with other societies. These distinctions are useful for typological purposes. They allow the critical theorist to work towards drawing an empirical map of the main modes of objectification which have appeared in the history of international relations; and this in turn paves the way for an historical sociology which endeavours to explain the origins and development of different ways of depicting and interacting with the other.

If anti-foundationalism is correct then this is all that can be attempted. It would be impossible to construct a scale of forms of international relations which assigns each its specific place in the light of its approximation to, or distance from, the optimal point of ethical universality. Anti-foundationalism claims that such a 'totalising' conception of history makes the unwarranted assumption that there is a privileged point, an Archimedean perspective, which enables the observer to assign each society its place in the ascent to rationality. In the first place, then, those who privilege one particular understanding of moral rationality simply impose an arbitrary conceptual framework upon our knowledge of the social world. But, in the second place, there is the additional danger that those who assume the right to judge the level of rationality achieved by others will force the irrational or the less rational to comply with the life-forms which the former happen to favour.

Two points need to be kept separate here. The contention that various methods of conceptualising and acting towards others are commensurable entails no more than this: that there are ground-rules which make the moral assessment of different forms of inclusion and exclusion possible. It is then perfectly legitimate to argue that some orientations towards the other are compelling while others warrant criticism and, perhaps, condemnation. The important issue, which Taylor makes in his comments on the extension of the rights of suffrage, is whether 'indefensible restrictions' on the other's right to equal moral consideration exist and ought to be lifted. The question of whether a society has the right of intervention to change another society's form of life or definition of the other is a different matter. There are circumstances when intervention may be plausible and there are circumstances when it may not. In either event, the issue is, as Lukes' apposite distinction reveals, not ethical self-*development* but ethical *self*-development.[46] There is no logical connection between the moral critique of another form of life and its manner of conducting its external relations, and the advocacy of intervention and forceable conversion.

The upshot of the argument is that it is possible to proceed beyond the construction of typologies of the other to the domain of moral evaluation. There are grounds for explicating and criticising distorted cultural understandings of the other and there is justification, as Habermas's notion of social learning in the moral sphere implies, for arranging different modes of objectification upon a scale of forms. And as Taylor and others have suggested in a different context, any analysis of moral inclusion and exclusion in international relations which does not endeavour to reveal how 'the doors to otherness . . . have (been) closed' is radically incomplete. An inquiry into the constraining effects of power/knowledge configurations should therefore attempt to specify the conditions in which individuals will be able to acquire a level of power, freedom and dignity which they have previously lacked. This is the domain in which the method of 'ideologiekritique' developed by members of the Frankfurt School can be employed to challenge spurious grounds for disallowing the other equal moral consideration. It is the domain in which it is possible to analyse moral systems for evidence of cultural contradictions and in which it is feasible to invoke the method of 'immanent critique' to reveal how these contradictions can be overcome by a more coherent account of the moral relations between the self, society and the other.[47]

These points are mainly concerned with the ethical and philosophical themes that underpin the analysis of different modes of moral objectification and separation. At face value they may not seem to have much significance for historical and sociological inquiries into the forms of otherness. Yet they can also contribute to the development of a critical theory of international relations which examines the origins, reproduction and transformation of the moral boundaries which separate the societies which comprise specific intersocietal systems. To explain this point further, it is worth noting that Taylor's contention that progress entails the deconstruction of 'indefensible restrictions' upon the moral equality of others is more than an interesting move within social and political theory; it also has significance for empirical forms of social and political inquiry.

In short, there is an invitation here to develop empirical accounts of the way in which methods of excluding the other have broken down historically because of the evolution of more sophisticated forms of moral argument. What is more, there is an invitation to analyse the way in which the delegitimation (and, in some cases, the destruction) of the mechanisms of social closure which have prevented women, subordinate castes, social classes, racial groups, national minorities etc. from enjoying the rights and privileges which powerful groups have reserved for themselves has occurred not only within social systems but in relations between societies, states and civilisations too. In the international domain, this process has been manifested by the demise of the modes of objectification which denied slaves the right to freedom and by the delegitimation of the epistemic frameworks which had the practical consequence of denying the 'savage' rights to cultural survival and, on the material level, rights to continued occupation of the land. It has been manifested too by the gradual delegitimation of the forms of moral closure which deny that the members of one society have obligations to assist the poorer and weaker members of other societies; and it has been expressed in the gradual, incomplete yet tangible realisation that the belief that citizens belong to an exclusive community which has no moral obligations to the members of other societies is not a tenable doctrine in our time.

Of course, it is important that a comparative sociology of moral codes in international relations should address the fact that a logic of moral universalisation has developed in some states and civilisations while in others the boundaries of moral community have been sealed more permanently or reaffirmed in the face of a universalistic challenge. But because logics of moral universalism and ethical inclusion have occurred in numerous states and civilisations, there is a case for considering how the force of the better argument prepared the way for the move beyond initially unproblematical forms of moral exclusion.[48] It is important to understand how the systems of justification which underpinned forms of moral exclusion broke down in different states and civilisations. And it is essential to understand exactly how different societies came to draw the line between universal identity and cultural difference in the course of creating new and more inclusive social relationships and arrangements – where, that is, they were concerned with drawing such a boundary at all.

The range of empirical case-studies relevant to this form of comparative sociology is clearly immense. The ideal-types which were organised in *Men and Citizens* in the shape of a scale of forms of international relations suggest some of the areas which can be considered from this perspective.[49] Relations between early societies – pre-literate societies, hunting and gathering societies etc. – form one possible realm of inquiry. Interaction between states or empires and 'peripheral societies' comprises a second area of investigation. A third is the sociology of systems of states; a fourth the study of inter-imperial relations and inter-civilisational relations; a fifth the way in which empires have ordered the relations between the various groups which they have brought within their realms.

There is a case for researching different forms of international relations drawn from each of these five main areas. But there is a stronger case for selecting cases which deal with the way in which states have often simultaneously constructed and sought to contain universalising discourses and universalistic identities.[50] One might therefore focus upon case-studies drawn from the following four areas of inquiry.

The first is designed to highlight the moral questions which arose when European states conquered non-European peoples and their territories. As the Spanish conquest of America so vividly revealed, these questions were initially concerned with whether or not, and on what basis, indigenous peoples had any rights against their conquerors. Subsequent to conquest and settlement the issues concern the duties that dominant groups now have towards the indigenous peoples. A second area concerns the competition between power, order and morality in different states-systems, not only in the modern states-system but also, to follow Martin Wight's lead, in the states-systems of Ancient China and the Hellenic and Hellenistic world. A 'sociology of states-systems'[51] should be principally concerned with the interplay between three 'distinct' yet 'overlapping' societies: the specific state to which human beings belong, the wider society of states and the nascent community of humankind.[52] A third area concerns the moral issues which have arisen in relations between ego-centric and universalising civilisations such as Christendom, Islam and China where the specific problem has been whether, and how, to confer equality upon the other and how to organise external relations in accordance with the principle of reciprocity. The fourth and final area concerns the methods of inclusion and exclusion which the ruling strata of different empires employed in their attempt to construct order between radically different groups.

If, as Hedley Bull once wrote, a general historical analysis of the 'political structure of the world as a whole' is ever written,[53] then these are some of the questions which its author might wish to consider. Just as importantly – to return to the issues with which this postscript began – the debate between critical theory and anti-foundationalism may not only advance international relations theory by underlining the need for a philosophical position which defends the need for limits to universality and limits to diversity. It may also contribute to an empirical understanding of one theme which has become central in recent attempts to consider the tension between the writings of Habermas and Foucault. This theme concerns 'the question of the other'.[54] Within the field of international relations, this theme can underpin an analysis of the way in which various societies have done violence to the other; how some have regarded the other as a subject of rights; how 'conception of the good life and the virtues (has come to be) one that cannot and should not exclude in principle any member of the human species',[55] and how the structure and practices of modern international relations have been changed in the past, and might be changed again in the future, to include those who have been systematically excluded.

Notes and References

PREFACE

1. For examples of this renaissance, see especially the works by Donelan, Gallie and Midgley. The earlier collection of essays edited by Butterfield and Wight was the main instigator of a revival of interest in the political theory of international relations.
2. See Q. Lauer, *Hegel's Idea of Philosophy* (New York, 1974) p. 84.
3. In opposition particularly to Wight's position in his influential essay 'Why is there no International Theory?' in Butterfield and Wight (eds). For further discussion see Ch. 1.
4. The idea of 'a scale of forms' arises in the writings of Collingwood (1950) Part III.
5. This term is explained below, Ch. 6, pp. 102–3.

CHAPTER 1: THE CASE FOR INTERNATIONAL POLITICAL THEORY

1. Butterfield and Wight, pp. 17–18.
2. Butterfield and Wight, p. 21.
3. Butterfield and Wight, p. 20 and p. 22.
4. Butterfield and Wight, p. 33.
5. Butterfield and Wight, p. 26.
6. Butterfield and Wight, p. 33.
7. For more general discussion, see Bull (1976) and his introduction to Wight (1978).
8. Mitrany (1970) p. 74.
9. S. Hoffmann, *Contemporary Theory in International Relations* (New Jersey, 1960) p. 4.
10. Mitrany (1971) p. 543.
11. For further discussion see Keohane and Nye.
12. Cole, p. 311.
13. See K. N. Waltz, 'The Myth of National Interdependence', in C. P. Kindleberger (ed.) *The International Corporation: A Symposium* (Cambridge, Mass., 1970).
14. Haas, p. 33 and p. 49.
15. Haas, p. 34.
16. This argument is considered in more detail below, see Ch. 7, pp. 124–5 and Ch. 8, pp. 151–2.
17. For a very detailed account of natural law theory see Midgley.
18. Butterfield and Wight, p. 20.

19. Hegel (1956) pp. 267–71.
20. Green's observation is important here: 'We only know that the earliest ascertainable history exhibits to us communities, relatively very confined, within any one of which a common good, and in consequence a common duty, is recognised as between the members of the community, while beyond the particular community the range of mutual obligation is not understood to extend. Among ourselves, on the contrary, it is almost an axiom of popular Ethics that there is at least a potential duty of every man to every man – a duty which becomes actual so soon as one comes to have any dealing with the other.' (Green (1906) p. 238.) The ability to conceive of 'the extension of the area of the common good', as Green calls it, is one of the prerequisites of the development of international political theory.
21. Locke, *Second Treatise*, especially Chs 2 and 8.
22. Filmer, p. 285; see the discussion in Plamenatz (Vol. 1) pp. 178–9.

CHAPTER 2: MEN AND CITIZENS IN INTERNATIONAL RELATIONS

1. The principal exponent of this perspective was Hegel; see Hegel (1956) pp. 252–3, and (1952) paragraphs 260–1, especially the additions. A detailed discussion can be found in Plant, Ch. 1, and Taylor, Chs 14–15.
2. O'Malley, pp. xl–lxiii.
3. Taylor, p. 385 and pp. 395–7; also Colletti.
4. Plato, p. 184.
5. Plato, p. 185.
6. Aristotle, p. 334. (I am grateful to Michael Donelan for drawing my attention to this section of the *Politics*.)
7. Phillipson (1911) p. 37.
8. Bozeman, p. 81. There is an interesting twist to this remark in the writings of Isocrates: In his call for concerted Greek action against the Persians, Isocrates pointed to the inconsistency of asserting that within states Greeks had the right to govern barbarians while in their external relations the failure to unite against Persia could only result in the barbarian ruling the Greek. Isocrates writes: For verily it is shameful for us, who in our private life think the barbarians are only to be used as household slaves, to permit by our public policy so many of our allies to be enslaved by them. (See p. 149.)
9. Bozeman, p. 89; see also Aristotle, p. 334: But when it comes to politics most people appear to believe that mastery is the true statesmanship: and men are not ashamed of behaving to others in ways which they would refuse to acknowledge as just, or even expedient, among themselves.
10. Gilbert Murray, quoted by Scott, Vol. 1 (1939) p. 52.
11. Isocrates, p. 149.
12. Sabine, pp. 150–1.
13. This development is analysed by Mazzolani, and also Hammond.
14. Pufendorf (1931) p. 242.
15. Vattel, pp. 5–6.

16. See below, pp. 67–8.
17. Rousseau, *Abstract of the Abbe de Saint-Pierre's Project for Perpetual Peace*, in Forsyth *et al*. (eds.) p. 132.
18. Rousseau, in Forsyth *et al.* (eds) pp. 135–6. Rousseau proceeds to ask 'if this alleged brotherhood of the nations of Europe is anything more than a bitter irony to denote their mutual hatred?'
19. Kant, *Idea for a Universal History from a Cosmo-political Point of View*, in Forsyth *et al.* (eds) p. 183.
20. For a fuller analysis, see Hoffmann.
21. Waltz, to whom we shall return later, remarks that 'war will be perpetually associated with the existence of separate, sovereign states'. Waltz (1965) p. 238. Green maintained that, on the contrary, 'there is no such thing as an inevitable conflict between states. There is nothing in the nature of the state that, given a multiplicity of states, should make the gain of the one the loss of the other'. Green (1966) p. 170. We highlight what is at issue between the doctrines which underlie these propositions later in this chapter.
22. Butterfield and Wight, p. 26.
23. Waltz, p. 233.
24. A concept used by J. H. Herz, *Political Idealism and Political Realism* (Chicago, 1964) p. 14.
25. Rousseau clearly thought that the existence of one state, based on the desire to advance its interests, must provoke the formation of other states: 'It is easy to see how the establishment of one community made that of all the rest necessary, and how, in order to make head against united forces, the rest of mankind had to unite in turn.' *Discourse on the Origin of Inequality*, Cole (ed.), (1968) pp. 205–6.
26. Hedley Bull's argument in *The Anarchical Society* might seem to overcome many of the problems inherent in Waltz's account. Firstly, it recognises that 'the state *qua* state' is a source of war (p. 247); secondly, it notes that the tension between the requirements of international order and the requirements of justice is at the heart of our experience of the states-system (Ch. 4); thirdly, it refers to our 'duty' to promote 'world society or community' (p. 289); and fourthly it claims that 'one reason for the continuing vitality of the states-system is the tyranny of the concepts and normative principles associated with it' (p. 275). Nevertheless, the author's clear preference for the tried over the untried, present international order over alternative forms of world political organisation based, for example, on justice nullifies these points.
27. Waltz, p. 190.
28. Green (1966) p. 171.
29. Green (1906) p. 238.
30. Green (1906) p. 237.
31. Green (1906) pp. 239–40.
32. Green (1966) p. 157.
33. Green (1966) p. 173.
34. Green (1966) p. 179.
35. Rousseau, *The Social Contract*, Cole (1968) p. 114.
36. Hegel (1952) paragraph 209.

37. Rousseau, *A Discourse on Political Economy*, Cole (1968) p. 246.
38. Durkheim (1961) pp. 76–7.
39. See W. H. Walsh, 'Open and Closed Morality', in Parekh and Berki (eds).
40. Hegel (1956) pp. 251–3.
41. For an extended discussion of this theme see Plant.
42. See, for example, Hegel (1956) pp. 317–18.
43. Hoffmann, pp. 78–9.
44. Hegel, quoted by H. Marcuse in *Reason and Revolution* (Oxford, 1941) p. 36

CHAPTER 3: INTERNAL AND EXTERNAL CONCEPTS OF OBLIGATION IN THE THEORY OF INTERNATIONAL RELATIONS

1. The fact that 'international egalitarianism' is made possible by particular forms of domestic social relations, and is excluded by others, suggests larger issues too complex to be explored here. Suffice it to say that connections between social structures and conceptions of international relations, the sociology of conceptions of international relations, is an almost wholly ignored realm. Martin Wight's *System of States* (Leicester, 1977) and Evan Luard's *Types of International Society* (New York, 1976) provide useful starting points.
2. Ullman, pp. 20–4.
3. Ullman, pp. 20–1.
4. Ullman, pp. 20–1.
5. See H. Bull, 'Society and Anarchy in International Relations', Sec II for a fuller discussion; Butterfield and Wight (eds).
6. Bodin, pp. 20–1.
7. Hobbes, Ch. XIV, p. 190.
8. Two points need making here. Firstly, within the contractarian perspective it is clearly undesirable that the individual should refuse to take part in an act of war on the grounds that this involvement jeopardises his interests. But, if interest underlies the decision to enter a state, it is not clear upon what basis this calculation might be denied. The problem arises particularly within Hobbes's thought. Compare, for example, the passage 'a man that is commanded as a souldier to fight against the enemy, though his Soveraign have Right enough to punish his refusall with death, may neverthelesse in many cases refuse, without Injustice; as when he substituteth a sufficient Souldier in his place . . .' (p. 269) and 'every man is bound by Nature, as much as in him lieth, to protect in Warre, the Authority, by which he is himself protected in time of Peace' (pp. 718–19). Further discussion falls outside the scope of the argument here.

   Secondly, internal and external concepts of obligation may be regarded as forming a continuum. A particularistic ethic may respect the pacifist conscience, or any international ideal which may set individuals against the community of which they are part. A society which tolerates these ideals is clearly more liberal than the one discussed above, because it permits the choice of individual ideals. It is arguable that such a society can grant the individual only the privilege and not the right of forming and acting upon these international ideals. Were it to grant the individual the right to disobey the state on account of these higher loyalties, it would move sharply towards a form of ethical universalism. To recognise the individual right to disobey the state is to recognise the existence of certain moral standards which override the obligations of citizens. However, as we have seen, a particularistic ethic can recognise certain forms of internationalism without departing from its more substantial commitment to an internal point of view.

9. Weber, pp. 118–28.
10. Weber, p. 121.
11. Machiavelli, *The Prince*, p. 56.
12. Wolfers, p. 58.
13. Weber, p. 126.
14. Carlyle, pp. 7–11.
15. Walsh, in Parekh and Berki (eds) p. 19.
16. Walsh, in Parekh and Berki (eds) p. 19.
17. Quoted by Bury, p. 287.
18. Of the Enlightenment one recent author has said: Given the view of a common, intuitable human nature, Enlightenment politics can give no satisfactory account for the plurality of states. How can it be that, given this universality of human nature, man has divided himself into all these separated polities? The basic answer is 'irrationalism' – loyalty to dynasties, outmoded religions, foolish customs. In the final end of history, when man realises his universality, there will be a universal state. (See O'Brien, p. 113.)
19. Gentili, p. 55.
20. Gentili, p. 54.
21. *De Potestate Civile*, in Scott (1934) Appendix C, p. xc.
22. *De Potestate Civile*, in Scott (1934) p. lxxxii.
23. Vitoria (1917); see also Hamilton.
24. 'On Charity' in *Selections*, p. 818.
25. *Selections*, p. 376.
26. *Selections*, p. 818.
27. *Selections*, p. 819.
28. Midgley, pp. 92–3.
29. Burke, p. 17.
30. Gentili, p. 68.
31. Kant (1964) p. 140.
32. *Perpetual Peace*, Forsyth *et al.* (eds) p. 216.
33. This concept arises in the writings of George Scelles. See M. S. McDougal, H. D. Lasswell and I. A. Vlasci, *Law and Public Order in Space* (Yale, 1963) p. 97.
34. In a very pertinent statement, Morris Ginsberg wrote of a 'lag in applying to the relations between states many of the criticisms which, in the course of the nineteenth century, were effectively directed against individualism in its bearing upon the internal economy of states'. Ginsberg (1974).
35. Fichte, p. 215. Compare with Pufendorf, below pp. 67–8.

36. Mumford, p. 94.
37. See Bull (1977).

CHAPTER 4: PUFENDORF'S THEORY OF INTERNATIONAL RELATIONS

1. Pufendorf's key works were first published as follows: *Elements of Universal Jurisprudence* (1660); *The Law of Nature and Nations* (1672); *Two Books on the Duty of Man and Citizen* (1673).
2. Phillipson (1968) p. 316. See also the work by Krieger.
3. Pufendorf maintains that 'the very being a man is a state out of which arise certain obligations and certain rights as well'. The institution of slavery 'merits complete disapproval' since 'all men by nature, antecedent to any act of man, are understood to be free'. Pufendorf (1934) pp. 8, 340 and 342; Pufendorf (1931) p. 240.
4. Pufendorf (1934) p. 212.
5. Pufendorf (1934) p. 1330.
6. Pufendorf (1927) p. 48.
7. Pufendorf (1927) p. 48.
8. Grotius, p. 15.
9. Pufendorf (1927) p. 103.
10. Pufendorf (1927) p. 49.
11. Pufendorf (1934) pp. 157–8.
12. Pufendorf (1927) pp. 104–5.
13. Pufendorf (1927) p. 104.
14. Pufendorf (1934) p. 971.
15. Pufendorf (1927) p. 49.
16. Pufendorf (1934) p. 959, and also p. 163.
17. Pufendorf (1927) p. 48.
18. Pufendorf (1931) p. 274, and Pufendorf (1934) p. 169.
19. Pufendorf (1934) p. 949.
20. Pufendorf (1931) p. 242.
21. Pufendorf (1934) p. 958.
22. Pufendorf (1927) p. 106.
23. Pufendorf (1934) p. 968.
24. Pufendorf (1931) p. 237.
25. Pufendorf (1934) pp. 974–5.
26. Pufendorf (1934) p. 1009.
27. Pufendorf (1934) p. 1009.
28. Kant, *Perpetual Peace*, Forsyth *et al.* (eds) p. 211.
29. Hoffmann, pp. 65–7.
30. See above Ch. 2, note 19.
31. Pufendorf (1931) p. 236; Pufendorf (1934) p. 213.
32. '. . . a state of nature never actually existed, except in some altered form, or only in part, as when, indeed, some men gathered with others into a civil state, or some such body, but retained a natural liberty against the rest of mankind; although the more groups there were in this division of the human race, and the smaller their membership, the nearer it must have approached a pure state of nature. So when at the

first mankind divided into different family groups, and now have divided into states such groups live in a mutual state of nature, insofar as no one group obeys another, and all the members have no common master'. Pufendorf (1934) p. 163.

33. Pufendorf (1927) p. 48.
34. Pufendorf (1931) p. 235.
35. Pufendorf (1931) p. 234.
36. Pufendorf (1927) p. 103; Pufendorf (1927) p. 42.
37. Pufendorf (1934) p. 380.
38. Pufendorf (1931) p. 147.
39. Pufendorf (1931) p. 165.
40. For Pufendorf's discussion of the states-system see (1934) pp. 1043–51.
41. Pufendorf (1927) p. 121.
42. Pufendorf (1927) p. 144.
43. Pufendorf (1934) p. 163.
44. Pufendorf (1934) p. 1068.
45. Bull (1977) pp. 152–3.
46. See above, pp. 13–14.
47. Rawls, pp. 378–9.
48. Barry, p. 133.
49. Barry, pp. 128–9.
50. Rawls, p. 378.
51. Barry, p. 133.

CHAPTER 5: VATTEL'S SOCIETY OF STATES

1. Vattel, p. 6.
2. Vattel, pp. 9a–10a.
3. Vattel, pp. 5–6.
4. Pufendorf writes that each man 'should think of himself as being put in the place of the other with whom something is to be done, and the other in turn set in his place'; a further example of what would now be termed the universalisability principle is his remark that 'no one, who has not acquired a peculiar right, [should] arrogate more to himself than the rest have, but permit others to enjoy the same right as himself'. Pufendorf (1931) p. 240; Pufendorf (1927) p. 43.
5. Vattel, p. 7.
6. Vattel, p. 115.
7. Vattel, p. 135.
8. The term, of course, is Hedley Bull's.
9. Vattel, p. 222.
10. Vattel, p. 7.
11. Vattel, p. 116 and p. 119.
12. Vattel, p. 225.
13. Vattel, pp. 6–7.
14. See above, Ch. 3, note 12.
15. Vattel, p. 13.
16. According to one of his commentators, 'Fearing the hegemony of a

pope or of an emperor, he resolutely argues against even the idea, so dear to Wolff, of a maxima civitas, in which all the states would be subject to a single law, as if they had only one common superior'. Introduction to *The Law of Nations* by A. de Lapradelle, pp. xi–xii. Vattel rejects the idea of 'civitas maxima' on p. 9a. In his *Law of Nations*, Christian Wolff advanced the idea of 'a supreme state' consisting of 'all nations in general'. The supreme state was, Wolff argued, 'a certain sort of state, consequently a society, moreover, since every society ought to have its own laws and the right exists in it of promulgating laws with respect to those things which concern it, the supreme state also ought to have its own laws and the right exists in it of promulgating laws with respect to those things which concern it'. Moreover, 'in the supreme state the nations as a whole have a right to coerce the individual nations, if they should be unwilling to perform their obligation, or should show themselves negligent in it'. See pp. 13–14.

17. 'The division of Europe into a number of independent states, connected, however, with each other by the general resemblance of religion, language and manners, is productive of the most beneficial consequences to the liberty of mankind.' Gibbon, *The History of the Decline and Fall of the Roman Empire*, Vol. 1 (revised and edited by H. H. Milman) (London, 1890) p. 58.
18. Vattel, pp. 7–8.
19. Vattel, p. 5.
20. Vattel, p. 248.
21. Vattel, p. 249.
22. Vattel, p. 249.
23. Vattel, p. 248.
24. Vattel, p. 250.
25. Vattel, p. 251.
26. Hinsley, p. 188.
27. Hinsley, p. 187.
28. Vattel, p. 251.
29. Vattel, p. 251.
30. Vattel, pp. 114–15.
31. For a fuller discussion see Bull (1977) Ch. 5.
32. Rousseau, *Discourse on the Origin of Inequality*, p. 194.
33. Bull (1977) Ch. 4.
34. Bull 'The Grotian Conception of International Society', in Butterfield and Wight (eds) p. 69.
35. Butterfield and Wight, p. 52.
36. Butterfield and Wight, p. 73.
37. Grice, p. 152.

CHAPTER 6: KANTIAN ETHICS AND INTERNATIONAL RELATIONS

1. Gallie, p. 33.
2. Kant (1961) p. 82.
3. Paton, p. 163.

4. Kant (1961) p. 88.
5. Kant (1961) p. 91.
6. Kant (1961) pp. 95–6.
7. Kant (1961) p. 96.
8. Kant (1961) p. 98.
9. Kant (1961) pp. 98–9.
10. Kant (1961) p. 100.
11. Kant (1961) p. 100.
12. Kant (1961) p. 106.
13. Rousseau, *The Social Contract*, p. 12.
14. Kant (1961) p. 101.
15. '... we need by no means assume that this contract... based on a coalition of the wills of all private individuals in a nation to form a common, public will for the purposes of rightful legislation, actually exists as a fact, for it cannot possibly be so... It is in fact merely an idea of reason, which nonetheless has undoubted practical reality; for it can oblige every legislator to frame his laws in such a way that they could have been produced by the united will of a whole nation, and to regard each subject, insofar as he can claim citizenship, as if he had consented within the general will. This is the test of the rightfulness of every public law.' See Reiss's introduction to Kant, *Political Writings*, p. 79.
16. For Hegel's statement that Kantian theory is 'an empty formalism', see Hegel (1952) paragraph 135. An interesting discussion of the Kant–Hegel relationship occurs in the writings of Singer.
17. Kant (1961) pp. 92–3.
18. Murphy, pp. 85–6.
19. Kant (1961) p. 107.
20. Murphy, pp. 99–102; see also the interpretation of Kant's material moral philosophy in the writings of Gregor.
21. Kant (1964) p. 116, and Gregor, p. 192.
22. 'To will my own happiness and, at the same time, be indifferent to the happiness of others would be morally wrong because my maxim regarding happiness would lack the universality of a law.' Gregor, p. 193.
23. Kant (1965) p. 76.
24. Kant (1965) p. 76.
25. Kant (1965) pp. 34–5.
26. For analysis of the fact that this is the 'test' but not the 'essence' of moral conduct, see Paton, p. 157.
27. Kant did not accept the distinction as characterised by either Pufendorf or Vattel: 'But by a broad duty is not understood a permission to make exceptions to the maxim of the actions, but only the permission to limit one maxim of duty by another (e.g., the general love of one's neighbour by the love of one's parents).... Imperfect duties are, therefore, merely duties of virtue. The fulfilment of them is merit but their transgression is not forthwith an offence but merely moral unworth, unless the subject made it a principle not to conform to these duties.' Kant (1964) p. 48.
28. Kant (1965) p. 37.

29. Ward, pp. 85–6.
30. Meldin, pp. 56–63.
31. Kant (1964) p. 77. It may also be claimed that 'To say that someone has a duty [or owes it] to himself to do something is an emphatic way of asserting that he has a right to do it – that there are no moral considerations against it – and that it would be foolish or imprudent for him not to.' Singer, pp. 314–15.
32. For further discussion see Singer's consideration of 'state of nature situations', pp. 152–61.
33. This point is put most forcefully by Hume when he writes of the prospect 'that it should be a virtuous man's fate to fall into the society of ruffians, remote from the protection of laws and government; what conduct must he embrace in that melancholy situation? He sees such a desperate rapaciousness prevail; such a disregard to equity, such contempt of order, such stupid blindness to future consequences, as must immediately have the most tragical conclusion, and must terminate in destruction to the greater number, and in a total dissolution of society to the rest. He meanwhile can have no other expedient than to arm himself... To make provision of all means of defence and security: And his particular regard to justice being no longer of use to his own safety or that of others, he must consult the dictates of self-preservation alone, without concern for those who no longer merit his care and attention'. Quoted by Singer, pp. 154–5.
34. We may regard these rules as important in effecting the transition from relations of estrangement to relations of familiarity.
35. Rousseau, *Discourse on the Origin of Inequality*, p. 206.
36. See Ch. 2, note 19.
37. Quoted by Despland, p. 49.
38. Kant, *Perpetual Peace*, in Forsyth *et al.* (eds) p. 229.
39. Kant (1965) pp. 43–4.
40. Kant (1965) p. 116.
41. Kant (1965) p. 81.
42. The separation of states 'is, however better, according to the idea of reason, than the fusion of all the states into a universal monarchy by one power that has outgrown the rest and subjected them to its sway. This is so because the laws lose always something of their definiteness as the range of a government becomes enlarged; and soulless despotism when it has choked the seeds of good, at length lapses into anarchy'. Kant added that 'the differences of their languages and of their religions' prevented 'the peoples from intermingling', although 'as civilisation increases', their sense of membership of a universal moral community expands. *Perpetual Peace*, Forsyth *et al.* (eds) p. 223.
43. *Perpetual Peace*, p. 223.
44. *Perpetual Peace*, pp. 212–13.
45. The goal of rational states is universal agreement on the proposition that 'There shall be no war' since 'this is not the way in which anyone should prosecute his rights'. Kant (1965) p. 128.
46. Kant (1965) p. 125.
47. *Perpetual Peace*, p. 213.

48. As we observe below in Ch. 8, if 'history is the process by which man becomes rational, he cannot be rational at the beginning'. See Reiss's introduction to *Kant's Political Writings*, p. 38.
49. *Idea for a Universal History*, in Forsyth *et al.* (eds) p. 188.
50. *Perpetual Peace*, p. 206.
51. *Perpetual Peace*, p. 208.
52. Kant maintained that the republican constitution was founded not only upon the 'dependence' of 'subjects' and upon the 'equality' of 'citizens', but also upon the 'liberty' of 'men'. *Perpetual Peace*, p. 206.
53. *Idea for a Universal History*, p. 186.
54. Kant (1965) p. 129.
55. *Perpetual Peace*, p. 236.
56. *Perpetual Peace*, pp. 228–9.
57. Kant (1965) p. 123.
58. *Perpetual Peace*, p. 213.
59. *Perpetual Peace*, pp. 238–9.
60. For further discussion see Murphy, pp. 110–12.
61. *Perpetual Peace*, p. 205.
62. Kant (1965) p. 129.
63. *Perpetual Peace*, p. 205.
64. *Perpetual Peace*, pp. 200–5.

CHAPTER 7: THE DISSOLUTION OF RATIONALIST INTERNATIONAL THEORY

1. Donelan, 'The Political Theorists and International Theory', in Donelan (ed.) p. 82.
2. Donelan, pp. 85–6.
3. For a discussion of romanticism see Lovejoy.
4. Bradley, p. 164.
5. Krieger, p. 91.
6. 'Those ancient social organisms of production are, as compared with bourgeois society, extremely simple and transparent. But they are founded either on the immature development of man individually, who has not yet severed the umbilical cord that unites him with his fellowmen in a primitive tribal community, or upon direct relations of subjection.' Marx (1970) p. 79.
7. See below, p. 151.
8. Durkheim (1969) p. 28.
9. Marx (1973) pp. 83–7.
10. Vico, p. 51.
11. Hobhouse, p. 233.
12. See Rousseau's remark: 'The philosophers, who have inquired into the foundations of society, have all felt the necessity of going back to a state of nature; but not one of them has got there. . . . Every one of them, in short, constantly dwelling on wants, avidity, oppression, desires and pride, has transferred to the state of nature ideas which were acquired in society.' *Discourse on the Origin of Inequality*, p. 161.

13. Our principal examples of historicism in international relations thought are Meinecke and Treitschke. By historicism, we mean that approach which sought 'to grasp the individual pattern of historical humanity'. See Meinecke, p. 19. For further discussion see Aron and Sterling.
14. Treitschke, in Aron, p. 586.
15. For Treitschke, 'the rays of the divine light appear limitlessly refracted among the different peoples; each manifests another image and another idea of the divinity'. Aron, p. 587.
16. Treitschke, in Forsyth *et al*. See, for example, his remark that 'in a single state the whole range of culture could never be fully spanned'. p. 326.
17. Treitschke, in Forsyth *et al*., p. 326.
18. Treitschke, in Forsyth *et al*., p. 337.
19. Treitschke, in Forsyth *et al*., p. 327.
20. Meinecke, quoted by Sterling (1965) p. 261.
21. Treitschke, in Forsyth *et al*. (eds) pp. 327–8, and pp. 334–5.
22. See L. Colletti, *From Rousseau to Lenin* (New York, 1972) p. 39.
23. See Fleischer, pp. 17–20; also Engels 'The Part Played by Labour in the Transition from Ape to Man', in Marx and Engels (1968) pp. 358–68.
24. Simon, pp. 161–2.
25. See the essay by O'Connor for further discussion.
26. Taylor, Ch. 1.
27. For a full description see Taylor, pp. 15–24.
28. Hegel (1952) paragraph 4.
29. See Evans, pp. 72–9, and Hobsbawm.
30. Hegel (1952) addition to the Preface; also Hegel (1956) p. 54.
31. Kant, *Idea for a Universal History*, in Forsyth *et al.* (eds) p. 191.
32. This is an extension of Colletti's argument.

CHAPTER 8: FREEDOM AND HISTORY IN THE POLITICAL THEORY OF INTERNATIONAL RELATIONS

1. See, for example, Habermas's claim that: 'Historical materialism aims at achieving an explanation of social evolution which is so comprehensive that it embraces the interrelationships of the theory's own origins and application. The theory specifies the conditions under which reflection on the history of our species by members of this species themselves has become objectively possible'. *Theory and Practice* (Boston, 1973) p. 1.
2. Kant (1957) is a collection of Kant's most important historical writings; for an interpretation, see Despland, especially Part One.
3. For the case that Kant's later historical and political writings represent 'a point of departure', see Raschke, pp. 191–2.
4. Despland, Part One.
5. Kant, *Conjectural Beginnings of Human History*, in Kant (1957) pp. 53–8.
6. See above, pp. 102–3; also Cassirer, Part One.
7. Fackenheim, pp. 389–94.
8. Kant (1957) p. 13.

9. The essays by Fackenheim and Wilkins provide more detailed interpretation.
10. *Conjectural Beginnings of Human History*, Kant (1957) pp. 59–60.
11. *Conjectural Beginnings of Human History*, Kant (1957) p. 59.
12. See Ch. 6, note. 39.
13. Taylor, p. 60.
14. Taylor, Ch. 15.
15. Hegel (1956) pp. 144–5.
16. Hegel (1956) p. 239.
17. Hegel (1956) p. 250.
18. Hegel (1956) p. 253.
19. Colletti refers to the way in which this process was represented in the writings of Rousseau, Hegel and Marx.
20. Hegel (1956) p. 19.
21. Hegel (1952) paragraph 270; Hegel (1956) p. 70: 'As it is not the brute, but only the man that thinks, he only – and only because he is a thinking being – has freedom.'
22. Hegel (1952) paragraph 338.
23. Plamenatz, Vol. 2, pp. 266–7.
24. Hegel (1952) paragraph 340.
25. S. Avineri, *Hegel's Theory of the Modern State* (Cambridge, 1972) p. 207.
26. Hegel (1956) pp. 86–7 where Hegel claims that America 'is the land of the future'.
27. Hegel (1952), addition to paragraph 339.
28. Hegel writes that those theorists who held that man was free in the state of nature took 'no account of the moment of liberation intrinsic to work'. Hegel (1952) paragraph 194.
29. Marx (1967) pp. 174–82.
30. Marx (1970) p. 177.
31. Quoted in B. Ollman, *Alienation: Marx's Concept of Man in Capitalist Society* (Cambridge, 1971) p. 114.
32. Marx and Engels (1965) p. 39.
33. Marx (1973) p. 158.
34. Marx (1970) p. 334.
35. Marx and Engels (1965) p. 42.
36. Marx (1970) p. 358.
37. Marx and Engels (1965) p. 42.
38. *The Communist Manifesto*, in Marx and Engels (1968) p. 38.
39. Marx and Engels (1965) pp. 75–6.
40. Marx (1973) p. 410.
41. Marx (1970) p. 592.
42. Marx and Engels (1965) p. 49.
43. Engels, pp. 324–5.
44. McBride, Ch. 7.
45. Marx and Engels (1965) p. 88.
46. Marx and Engels (1965) p. 88.
47. Marx (1973) p. 490.
48. Marx (1973) p. 491.
49. Marx (1973) p. 474.

50. Marx (1970) p. 87.
51. Marx (1973) pp. 161–2.
52. Marx (1973) p. 161.
53. Marx (1973) p. 162.
54. Marx and Engels (1965) pp. 48–9.
55. Marx and Engels (1965) p. 49.
56. Marx and Engels (1965) p. 84.
57. Suggested by K. Lowith, *Nature, History and Existentialism* (Evanton, 1966) p. 96.
58. Fleischer, pp. 18–19, 32–3, 65–6 and 70.

INTRODUCTION TO PART THREE

1. See above, p. 154 ff.
2. Hegel (1952) addition to paragraph 32.
3. *The Idea for a Universal History*, in Forsyth *et al.* (eds.) p. 191.

CHAPTER 9: FROM TRIBALISM TO POLITICAL SOCIETY

1. Perhaps it ought to be allowed, following a Hegelian theme, that the warrior's willingness to fight to the death is an expression of his intention not to be assimilated into the natural world, or to be treated as if he were a natural object by outsiders. See A. Kojeve, *An Introduction to the Reading of Hegel* (New York, 1969) pp. 6–7.
2. See above, pp. 145–6.
3. For empirical counterparts, we need look no further than the experience of the Persian and Roman Empires which are particularly informative in this regard.
4. See above, p. 156.
5. For further analysis of this conception of the state see Plamenatz, Vol. 1, pp. 351–6.
6. Hart, p. 91.
7. Hart, p. 90.
8. Hart, p. 91.
9. Hart, p. 91.
10. Secondary rules are 'on a different level from the primary rules, for they are all *about* such rules; in the sense that while primary rules are concerned with the actions that individuals must or must not do, these secondary rules are all concerned with the primary rules themselves'; with stating, changing and enforcing them. (Hart, p. 92.)

CHAPTER 10: FROM CITIZENSHIP TO HUMANITY

1. A term used by Hegel in connection with freedom: Hegel (1956) pp. 40–1.
2. Mitrany (1933) p. 53.
3. The idea that a claim is an undecided right is to be found in Hegel, 'The German Constitution', in *Hegel's Political Writings* (Oxford, 1964) p. 211.
4. Jenks, p. 90.

5. Ginsberg (1974) p. 171.
6. Falk (1970) p. 34.
7. Falk (1965) p. 247.
8. Falk (1965) p. 237.
9. The problem with the principle of universalisation, it is often argued, is the fact that a subject may be prepared to universalise almost any maxim. The most powerful objection arises in the writings of R. M. Hare. Hare refers to the example of the fanatical Nazi who is prepared to universalise the maxim that all Jews should be exterminated even if it involves, on the discovery of his own Jewish ancestry, committing his family and himself to the gas-chamber. Clearly, in this case, an appeal to the principle of universalisation does not deter the Nazi from enacting his racialist beliefs. See Hare, Ch. 9, and especially p. 184 where the author remarks that the Nazi 'will remain unshaken by any argument that I have been able to discover'. Hare acknowledges 'a very great debt to Kant' (p. 34) while arguing that the principle of universalisability, the supposed core of the Kantian system, is powerless against the fanatic. It has been claimed, however, that on Kantian principles, 'the Nazi would be obliged to desist in his persecutions'. See Curtler, pp. 295–7 for an argument reliant on Kant's notion of human dignity. In accordance with the argument of Chs 7 and 8 above, we seek to extend this point by locating the idea of human dignity within a theory of the historical development of man's freedom.
10. Constraints on human freedom may emanate from another aspect of the modern nation-state, from a principle which is distinct from nationality or territoriality, namely from the rights of individuals and associations to engage in private, external relations not only within but beyond their national boundaries. Here we take note of Marx's observation that relations of personal independence make possible global economic and social interdependence; and that with this development, the members of different communities experience an increased subjection to forces beyond their control. To overcome this constraint upon human freedom, it would be essential to abolish an autonomous sphere of international economic relations; in the manner which Marx suggested, it would be necessary to secure the freedom of all through exercising control over the totality of social relations within the world-system. Given the focus of the present work, our observations about international economic relations must necessarily be brief. Suffice it to say that a complete theory of international relations would place various forms of economic life upon a scale of ascending types.

A POSTSCRIPT ON HABERMAS AND FOUCAULT

1. For an introduction to these developments, See M. Hoffman, 'Critical Theory and the Inter-Paradigm Debate', *Millennium*, 16 (1987) and N.J. Rengger, 'Going Critical?; Response to Hoffman', *Millennium*, 17 (1988). See also the Summer 1988 issue of *Millennium* entitled 'Philosophical Traditions in International Relations'.

2. Quoted in W. Connolly, 'Taylor, Foucault and Otherness', *Political Theory*, 13 (1985) p. 366.
3. M. Foucault, *Discipline and Punish: The Birth of the Prison* (Harmondsworth, 1979) p. 30.
4. Quoted in T. McCarthy, *The Critical Theory of Jurgen Habermas* (London, 1982) p. 383.
5. J. Habermas, *Communications and the Evolution of Society* (Boston, 1979) p. 117.
6. For a succinct discussion, see R. Roderick, *Habermas and the Foundations of Critical Theory* (London, 1986) and M. Pusey, *Jurgen Habermas* (London, 1987).
7. For futher elaboration, see the essays in J. B. Thompson and D. Held (eds.) *Habermas: Critical Debates* (London, 1982).
8. J. Habermas, *Legitimation Crisis* (Boston, 1975) p. 108.
9. See above, p. 165.
10. See Habermas (1979) pp. 112–16.
11. Quoted in P. Dews, *Logics of Disintegration: Post-Structuralist Thought and the Claims of Critical Theory* (London, 1987) p. 208.
12. Foucault (1979) op. cit., p. 27.
13. See Connolly (1985) op. cit., p. 50; and D. C. Hoy (ed.) *Foucault: A Critical Reader* (Oxford, 1986) p. 119.
14. See Charles Taylor, 'Connolly, Foucault and Truth', *Political Theory*, 13 (1985) p. 379.
15. See T. Keenan, 'The Paradox of Knowledge and Power: Reading Foucault on a Bias', *Political Theory*, 15 (1987) p. 5.
16. Ibid., p. 12.
17. See Dews (1987) op. cit., p. 219.
18. See P. Rabinow, *The Foucault Reader* (Harmondsworth, 1986) p. 343.
19. See Hoy (1986) op. cit., p. 119.
20. R. J. Bernstein, 'Fred Dallmayr's Critique of Habermas', *Political Theory*, 16 (1985) p. 590.
21. See McCarthy (1982) op. cit., pp. 325–33.
22. See J. Habermas, 'A Philosophical-Political Profile', *New Left Review* (1985) pp. 94–6.
23. Ibid.
24. J. Habermas (1979) op. cit. p. 140.
25. J. Habermas, 'Response to the Commentary of Bernstein and Dove', in D. P. Verene (ed.), *Hegel's Social and Political Thought: The Philosophy of Objective Spirit* (New Jersey, 1980) p. 250.
26. See above, p. 48.
27. Keenan (1987) op. cit., pp. 20–4.
28. Bernstein (1985) op. cit., p. 590.
29. See above, pp. 130–1.
30. Dews (1987) op. cit., pp. 217–18.
31. Bernstein (1985) op. cit., p. 590.
32. Taylor (1985) op. cit., p. 382.
33. Ibid., p. 383.
34. J. Habermas, *The Philosophical Discourse of Modernity*, (Cambridge, 1987) pp. 287 and 290.

35. Ibid., p. 289.
36. H. Bull, *The Anarchical Society* (London, 1977) p. 267.
37. See R. J. Vincent, *Human Rights and International Relations* (Cambridge, 1986).
38. C. Taylor, 'Foucault on Freedom and Truth', in Hoy (1986) op. cit., p. 81.
39. Quoted in Habermas (1987) op. cit., p. 240.
40. Ibid.
41. Ibid. p. 141.
42. For a good discussion, see A. I. Davidson, 'Archaeology, Genealogy, Ethics', in Hoy (1986) op. cit., pp. 221–33.
43. L. T. Hobhouse, *Morals in Evolution: A Study in Comparative Ethics* (New York, 1906) p. 48.
44. For further discussion of this term, see J. G. Ruggie, 'Continuity and Transformation in the World Polity: Towards a Neo-Realist Synthesis', *World Politics*, 35, 1983.
45. T. Todorov, *The Conquest of America: The Question of the Other* (New York, 1982).
46. S. Lukes, *Individualism* (Oxford, 1973) p. 130.
47. For a short discussion of the method of critical theory, see A. Linklater, *Beyond Realism and Marxism: Critical Theory and International Relations* (London, 1989) Ch. 1, and Hoffman (1987) op. cit.
48. Let us call this the process of moral rationalisation and further note that it interacts with three additional processes: the rationalisation of the means of production, the rationalisation of the instruments employed to direct and control human beings, and the rationalisation of the means of creating order between different groups including states and civilisations. For some preliminary comments on the significance of rationalisation processes for the sociology of community, see my 'Marxism and International Relations: Antithesis, Reconciliation or Transcendence', in J. Richardson and R. Higgott (eds.) *New Directions in International Relations* (forthcoming).
49. See above, pp. 172 and 185.
50. Michael Mann's *The Sources of Social Power* (Cambridge, 1986) provides numerous illustrations of this theme.
51. This is Martin Wight's term: see *System of States* (Leicester, 1977) p. 33.
52. Mann (1986) op. cit. pp. 223–7 develops this approach in his analysis of the Hellenic states-system.
53. Bull (1977) op. cit., p. 11.
54. Todorov (1982) op. cit.
55. R. Bernstein, *Philosophical Profiles: Essays in a Pragmatic Mode* (Cambridge, 1986) p. 137.

Select Bibliography

Acton, H. B., *Kant's Moral Philosophy* (London, 1970).
Aristotle, *The Politics*, translated by E. Barker (Oxford, 1960).
Aron, R., *Peace and War: A Theory of International Relations* (London, 1966).
Bakunin, M., *The Political Philosophy of Bakunin*, edited by G. P. Maximoff (London, 1964).
Barry, B., *The Liberal Theory of Justice* (Oxford, 1973).
Bodin, J., *Six Books of the Commonwealth*, translated by M. J. Tooley (Oxford, 1955).
Bozeman, A., *Politics and Culture in International History* (Princeton, 1960).
Bradley, F. H., *Ethical Studies* (Oxford, 1962).
Bull, H., 'Martin Wight and the Theory of International Relations', *British Journal of International Studies*, 2 (1976) 101–16.
——, *The Anarchical Society: A Study of Order in World Politics* (London, 1977).
Burke, E., *The Philosophy of Edmund Burke: A Selection from his Speeches and Writings*, edited with an introduction by L. I. Bredvold and R. G. Ross (Michigan, 1960).
Bury, J. B., *The Idea of Progress* (New York, 1955).
Butterfield, H., and Wight, M., *Diplomatic Investigations: Essays in the Theory of International Politics* (London, 1966).
Carlyle, A. J., *A History of Medieval Political Theory*, Vol. 1 (London, 1930).
Cassirer, E., *Rousseau, Kant and Goethe* (New York, 1963).
Cole, G. D. H., 'The Nature of the State in View of its External Relations', *Proceedings of the Aristotelian Society*, 16 (1915–16) 290–315.
Colletti, L., 'The Idea of "Bourgeois–Christian" Society', in *Marxism and Hegel* (London, 1973).
Collingwood, R. G., *An Essay on Philosophical Method* (Oxford, 1950).

——, *The Idea of History* (Oxford, 1961).
Curtler, H. M., 'What Kant Might say to Hare', *Mind*, 80 (1971) 295–7.
Despland, M., *Kant on History and Religion* (Montreal, 1973).
Dewey, J., and Tufts, J. H., *Ethics* (New York, 1908).
Donelan, M. D. (ed.) *The Reason of States: A Study in International Political Theory* (London, 1978).
Durkheim, E., *Moral Education* (New York, 1961).
——, 'Individualism and the Intellectuals', trans. with introduction by S. Lukes, *Political Studies*, 17 (1969) 14–30.
Engels, F., *Anti-Duhring* (Moscow, 1975).
Evans, M., *Karl Marx* (London, 1975).
Fackenheim, E., 'Kant's Concept of History', *Kant–Studien*, 48 (1956–7) 381–98.
Falk, R. A., *The Role of Domestic Courts in the International Legal Order* (Syracuse, 1964).
——, 'World Law and Human Conflict', in E. B. McNeil (ed.) *The Nature of Human Conflict* (New Jersey, 1965).
——, *The Status of Law in International Society* (Princeton, 1970).
Fichte, J. G., *The Science of Rights* (Philadelphia, 1869).
Filmer, Sir R., *Patriarcha and other Political Works*, edited with an introduction by P. Laslett (Oxford, 1949).
Fleischer, H., *Marxism and History* (London, 1973).
Forsyth, M. G., Keens-Soper, H. M. A., and Savigear, P. (eds.), *The Theory of International Relations: Selected Texts from Gentili to Treitschke* (London, 1970).
Frank, T. M., *The Structure of Impartiality: Examining the Riddle of One Law in a Fragmented World* (New York, 1968).
Gallie, W. B., *Philosophers of Peace and War* (Cambridge, 1978).
Gentili, A., *Three Books on the Law of War*, Classics of International Law (Oxford, 1933).
Ginsberg, M., 'The Individualist Basis of International Law and Morals', in *Essays in Sociology and Social Philosophy*, Vol II (London, 1947).
——, 'The Persistence of Individualism in the Theory of International Relations', in R. Fletcher (ed.) *The Science of Society and the Unity of Mankind* (London, 1974).
Green, T. H., *Prolegomena to Ethics* (Oxford, 1906).
——, *Lectures on the Principles of Political Obligation* (London, 1966).
Gregor, M. J., *Laws of Freedom: A Study of Kant's Method of*

Applying the Categorical Imperative in the Metaphysic der Sitten (Oxford, 1963).
Grice, R. G., *The Grounds of Moral Judgment* (Cambridge, 1967).
Grotius, H., *The Law of War and Peace*, Classics of International Law (Oxford, 1925).
Haas, E. B., *Beyond the Nation-State* (Stanford, 1964).
Hamilton, B., *Political Thought in Sixteenth Century Spain* (Oxford, 1963).
Hammond, M., *City-State and World State in Greek and Roman Political Theory until Augustus* (Harvard, 1951).
Hare, R. M., *Freedom and Reason* (Oxford, 1963).
——, *Applications of Moral Philosophy* (Berkeley, 1972).
Hart, H. L. A., *The Concept of Law*, (Oxford, 1961).
Hegel, G. W. F., *The Philosophy of Right*, translated by T. M. Knox (Oxford, 1952).
——, *The Philosophy of History*, translated by J. Sibree (New York, 1956).
Hinsley, F. H., *Power and the Pursuit of Peace* (Cambridge, 1963).
Hobbes, T., *Leviathan*, edited with an introduction by C. B. MacPherson (Harmondsworth, Middlesex, 1968).
Hobhouse, L. T., *Morals in Evolution* (London, 1925).
Hobsbawm, E., 'Introduction' to *Karl Marx's Pre-Capitalist Economic Formations* (London, 1964).
Hoffmann, S., 'Rousseau on War and Peace', in *The State of War: Essays in the Theory and Practice of International Politics* (London, 1965).
Isocrates, *Selections*, Vol. I, translated by G. Norlin (London, 1928).
Jenks, C. W., *Law, Freedom and Welfare* (London, 1963).
Kant, I., *On History*, edited by L. Beck (New York, 1957).
——, *The Moral Law: Kant's Groundwork of the Metaphysic of Morals*, translated by H. J. Paton (London, 1961).
——, *The Metaphysical Principles of Virtue*, translated by J. Ellington (New York, 1964).
——, *The Metaphysical Elements of Justice*, translated by J. Ladd (New York, 1965).
——, *Political Writings*, edited by H. Reiss (Cambridge, 1971).
Keohane, R. O., and Nye, J. S., *Power and Interdependence: World Politics in Transition* (Boston, 1977).

Kreiger, L., *The Politics of Discretion: Pufendorf and the Acceptance of Natural Law* (Chicago, 1965).
Laski, H., *The State in Theory and Practice* (London, 1935).
Lauterpacht, H., 'Spinoza and International Law', *British Yearbook of International Law*, 8 (1927) 89–107.
Locke, J., *Two Treatises of Government*, edited by P. Laslett (Cambridge, 1960).
Lovejoy, A., 'The Meaning of Romanticism for the Historian of Ideas', *Journal of the History of Ideas*, 2 (1941) 260–78.
Machiavelli, N., *The Prince and Discourses*, edited by M. Lerner (New York, 1950).
Marx, K., *Economic and Philosophic Manuscripts*, edited by D. J. Stirk and translated by M. Milligan (London, 1967).
——, *Capital*, vol. I (London, 1970).
——, *Grundrisse*, translated by M. Nicolaus (Harmondsworth, Middlesex, 1973).
Marx and Engels, *The German Ideology* (London, 1965).
——, *Selected Works in One Volume* (London, 1968).
Mazzolani, L. S., *The Idea of the City in Roman Thought: From Walled City to Spiritual Commonwealth* (London, 1970).
McBride, W. L., *The Philosophy of Marx* (London, 1977).
Meinecke, F., *Machiavellism: The Doctrine of Raison d'Etat and its Place in Modern History* (London, 1962).
Meldin, B., 'Ultimate Principles and Ethical Egoism', in D. P. Gauthier (ed.) *Morality and Rational Self-Interest* (New Jersey, 1970) pp. 56–63.
Midgley, E. B. F., *The Natural Law Tradition and the Theory of International Relations* (London, 1975).
Milne, A. J. M., *The Social Philosophy of English Idealism* (London, 1962).
Mitrany, D., *The Progress of International Government* (London, 1933).
——, 'The Functional Approach to World Organisation', in C. A. Cosgrove and K. J. Twitchett (eds) *The New International Actors* (London, 1970).
——, 'The Functional Approach in Historical Perspective', *International Affairs*, 71 (1971) 532–43.
Mumford, L., *The Transformations of Man* (London, 1957).
Murphy, J. G., *Kant: The Philosophy of Right* (London, 1970).
Numelin, R., *The Beginnings of Diplomacy: A Sociological Study of Intertribal and International Relations* (London, 1950).

O'Brien, G. D., *Hegel on Reason and History* (Chicago, 1975).
O'Connor, D. J., 'Aquinas and Natural Law', in W. D. Hudson (ed.) *Modern Moral Philosophy* (London, 1970).
O'Malley, J. 'Introduction' to Marx's *Critique of Hegel's Philosophy of Right* (Cambridge, 1970).
Parekh, B., and Berki, R. N. (eds.) *The Morality of Politics* (London, 1972).
Paton, H. J., *The Categorical Imperative: A Study in Kant's Moral Philosophy* (London, 1953).
Phillipson, C., *The International Law and Custom of Ancient Greece and Rome* (London, 1911).
——, 'Samuel von Pufendorf', in J. McDonnel and E. Manson (eds) *Great Jurists of the World* (New York, 1968).
Plamenatz, J. P., *Man and Society* (London, 1963).
Plant, R., *Hegel* (London, 1973).
Plato, *The Republic*, translated by A. D. Lindsay (London, 1920).
Pufendorf, S. von, *The Two Books on the Duty of Man and Citizen According to the Natural Law*, Classics of International Law (New York, 1927).
——, *Two Books of the Elements of Universal Jurisprudence*, Classics of International Law (Oxford, 1931).
——, *The Law of Nature and Nations: Eight Books*, Classics of International Law (Oxford, 1934).
Raschke, C. A., *Moral Action, God and History in the Thought of Immanuel Kant*, Dissertation Series No. 5 (Montana, 1975).
Rawls, J., *A Theory of Justice* (Harvard, 1971).
Riley, P., 'On Kant as the Most Adequate of the Social Contract Theorists', *Political Theory*, 1 (1973) 450–71.
Rousseau, J. J., *The Social Contract and Discourses*, translated by G. D. H. Cole (London, 1968).
Sabine, G., *A History of Political Theory* (London, 1961).
Schiffer, W., *The Legal Community of Mankind* (Columbia, 1954).
Scott, J. B., *Law, the State and the International Community* (Columbia, 1939).
——, *The Spanish Origin of International Law: Francisco de Vitoria and His Law of Nations* (Oxford, 1934).
Simon, Y., *The Tradition of Natural Law* (New York, 1965).
Singer, M., *Generalisation in Ethics* (London, 1963).

Sterling, R. W., *Ethics in a World of Power: The Political Ideas of Meinecke* (Princeton, 1968).
——, 'Political Necessity and Moral Principle in the Thought of Friedrich Meinecke', in R. Hilsman and R. C. Good (eds) *Foreign Policy in the Sixties: Issues and Instruments* (Baltimore, 1965).
Suarez, F., *Selections from Three Works*, Classics of International Law (Oxford, 1944).
Tarn, W. W., *Hellenistic Civilisation* (London, 1952).
Taylor, C., *Hegel* (Cambridge, 1975).
Ullman, W., *Principles of Government and Politics in the Middle Ages* (London, 1961).
Vattel, E. de, *The Law of Nations or The Principles of Natural Law Applied to the Conduct and to the Affairs of Nations and of Sovereigns*, Classics of International Law (Washington, 1916).
Vico, G., *The New Science*, translated by T. G. Bergin and M. H. Fisch (Cornell, 1970).
Vitoria, F. de, *De Indis et De Jure Belli Reflectiones* (On the Indians Lately Discovered, or On the Law of War made by the Spaniards on the Barbarians). Classics of International Law (Washington, 1917).
Waltz, K. N., *Man, the State and War: A Theoretical Analysis* (Columbia, 1965).
Ward, K., *The Development of Kant's View of Ethics* (Oxford, 1972).
Weber, M., *From Max Weber*, edited by H. H. Gerth and C. W. Mills (London, 1948).
Wight, M., *Power Politics* (Leicester, 1978).
Wilkins, B. T., 'Teleology in Kant's Philosophy of History', *History and Theory*, 5 (1966) 172–85.
Wolfers, A., *Discord and Collaboration: Essays in International Politics* (Baltimore, 1962).
Wolff, C., *The Law of Nations*, Classics of International Law (Oxford, 1934).

Index